Recursive Algorithms

ABLEX SERIES IN COMPUTATIONAL SCIENCE

Derek Partridge, University of Exeter
Series Editor

Artificial Intelligence and Business Management
Derek Partridge and K.M. Hussain

Artificial Intelligence and Software Engineering
Derek Partridge (Editor)

Binding Time—Six Studies in Programming Technology and Milieu
Mark Halpern

A New Guide to Artificial Intelligence
Derek Partridge

Pathfinder Associative Networks: Studies in Knowledge Organization
Roger W. Schvaneveldt (Editor)

Recursive Algorithms
Richard Lorentz

In Preparation

Computer Analysis of English: Lexical Semantics and Preference
Semantics Analysis
Brian Slator

Database in Practice Rather Than in Theory
K.G. Jeffrey

Intelligent Systems
Eric Dietrich and Chris Fields

Machine Tractable Dictionaries: Design and Construction
Cheng-ming Guo

New Generation Architectures and Languages
Stephen J. Turner

Recursive Algorithms

Richard Lorentz

Ablex Publishing Corporation
Norwood, New Jersey

Printed in the United States of America.

Library of Congress Cataloging-in-Publication Data

Lorentz, Richard J.
    Recursive algorithms / Richard J. Lorentz.
      p. cm. — (Computational sciences)
    ISBN 0-89391-913-6. — ISBN 1-56750-037-4
    1. Recursive functions. 2. Algorithms. I. Title. II. Series.
QA9.615.L67 1994
005.13′1 — dc20
                                93-9056
                                CIP

Ablex Publishing Corporation
355 Chestnut Street
Norwood, New Jersey 07648

Contents

List of Figures

Preface*

Recursion is a topic that is ubiquitous in computer science. Most students first encounter it in their first programming course, popularly called CS 1. It is in this course that basic programming techniques are taught, usually via a language like Pascal, and recursion is typically mentioned briefly towards the end of the course as an example of the power of procedures and functions. This is usually followed by a few simple examples, like *factorial,* and *Fibonacci numbers*. At this point students now have some general notion about recursion but are not very comfortable with the idea and are certainly not able to design their own recursive procedures. In fact, many students in these early stages believe that a recursive call is nothing more than a *GOTO* back to the top of the procedure. Perhaps, however, this is to be expected. With so few examples and so little time spent on the subject one can hardly expect recursion to be mastered. It is asking too much to expect students to become experts on recursion in CS 1.

Recursion is then studied in more depth in CS 2, the first course in data structures. Because of the recursive nature of many of the most useful data structures, it is here that students first discover the true power and usefulness of recursion. It is here we expect the student to master recursion. Unfortunately, recursion is often presented too late; after some recursive data types like linked lists have already appeared and even after some recursive algorithms like quicksort have appeared. Also, simply because of the sheer volume of information that needs to be conveyed to students in CS

*I would like to thank Jim Pinter-Lucke for the many comments and suggestions he provided as this book evolved.

2, recursion does not get adequate attention in the classroom and does not get adequate space in the textbook. The result is that too many students leave CS 2 still not fully understanding recursion.

Recursion continues to appear in various guises throughout the rest of the student's undergraduate career. It is seen again when other languages, like Lisp, are studied. Its importance is reaffirmed when advanced courses in data structures and algorithms are taken. It even appears in theoretical courses when studying topics such as recursive functions and denotational semantics.

Despite the obvious importance of recursion and its numerous appearances in the curriculum many students fail to master it. Why? We've already discussed a few of the reasons. Another is that recursion only appears in small doses in a variety of different places preventing the student from seeing the underlying theme that all recursive algorithms possess. A student's first exposure in CS 1 is often a frightening experience. Their next exposure in CS 2 is equally imposing because it is typically not even mentioned until it is needed for some fairly complicated applications like tree traversals. Also, at this point it has been a long time since they've seen anything recursive so it is almost like seeing it for the first time. (In fact, it is the first time in many cases.) Students then conclude that recursive algorithms must be incomprehensible, or at least very difficult, and so they give up on them.

The point of this book is to provide a leisurely and perhaps even entertaining journey through recursion. It begins with the most basic of recursive algorithms and slowly guides the reader to more and more advanced applications. Most importantly, however, it is a unified treatment so that by the end of the book the reader will have learned that a sophisticated recursive algorithm to find the median in linear time has a great deal in common with a simple recursive algorithm to output an array. Once one learns to use the recursive paradigm it is easy to use and is often the correct way to go.

Many people scoff at recursive algorithms claiming that they are too inefficient. Certainly many recursive algorithms can be retooled to an iterative form and be made to run faster by some constant factor that is typically small. But this is usually irrelevant. Who cares if the iterative implementation of an algorithm sorts an array with 1,000 elements ten milliseconds faster than the recursive one? For example, I wrote iterative and recursive functions to find factorials. Since very little is done inside the recursive function, the price we pay for using recursion will stand out. It turned out (at least on my computer and using my compiler) that the iterative version ran only 25 percent faster. I was able to calculate 15! 300 times in 100 seconds using the recursive function while it only took 75 seconds in the iterative case. Not much of a penalty in my mind. And this example was designed to make recursion look bad. In most cases the difference would be much less.

In fact, the important measure of the efficiency of an algorithm is the order of the algorithm, the "big-oh" complexity. If the order of two algorithms is the same, as was the case with the two factorial examples mentioned above, it is really hard to say that one is better than the other. Other factors enter, such as the time to design, write, and debug the program. What good is it having a program that runs twice as fast if it took ten times longer to write and will only be used a couple of times anyway? Readers of this book will discover just how easy it is to write recursive algorithms and how easily they can be converted into Pascal.

I have chosen Pascal as the vehicle for implementing the recursive algorithms because it is still the language most often used in CS 1 and students who only know languages like Modula or Ada are able to easily decipher Pascal code while the reverse is less often true. However, choosing any specific language as an implementation language has its pitfalls. The syntactic idiosyncrasies of a language as well as features unique to that language can confuse unnecessarily. To mitigate this, especially in extreme cases, pseudocode is sometimes used to ease the transition into Pascal code. Pseudocode is used most often when a new topic is introduced and eventually dropped as the reader becomes familiar with that material

There are a couple of situations where the text becomes quite Pascal specific. I consider this a feature. Every language has its own ways of dealing with various built-in data structures and one must often understand how this is done to properly understand the efficiency of algorithms implemented in that language. For example, in Section 5.3 Pascal sets are discussed in some detail because it is important to understand how efficiently a Pascal compiler is likely to implement the various set operations if we are to properly calculate the efficiency of procedures that use Pascal sets. Other languages might have different built in data types, but the process is the same. One must understand how these types are implemented by the compiler to correctly evaluate efficiency. The importance is not so much on the actual analysis we do on the specific Pascal structures but on the realization that sometimes the compiler must also be studied.

This book takes great care to analyze the complexity of all of its algorithms and emphasizes the importance of this. After all, there is a big difference between a linear algorithm and an exponential one and, unfortunately, exponential behavior can creep into recursive algorithms quite unexpectedly. Inefficiency of this kind cannot be ignored. So, not only do we spend a lot of time discussing how to design recursive algorithms, we learn how to analyze them as well.

Owners of this book are likely to carry it around with them to many different classes. It will help them through their first exposure to recursion in CS 1. It will be a big help when the recursive crunch comes in CS 2. But most important, by reading this book they will become comfortable and proficient at recursive programming and this will prove helpful throughout a computer scientist's career, through school, and beyond.

1

The Basics

1. A FIRST LOOK

1.1 Recursion Verses Iteration – Adding Numbers

A recursive algorithm solves a problem in a way that is different from the way most people solve everyday problems. Most algorithms that people normally create are iterative. For example, your algorithm for solving the problem of putting a nail into a board is most likely an iterative one. You will hit the nail with the hammer repeatedly until the nail is pounded all the way into the board. Using pseudocode, it probably looks something like Figure 1.1.

In reality, of course, your algorithm is considerably more complicated. There are surely special conditions to deal with situations like hitting your thumb instead of the nail or hitting the nail off center and having it bend, or worse, break. Nevertheless, the point is that the algorithm is iterative. You are iterating, or looping, on a command or set of commands until your goal is achieved.

Similarly, most computer algorithms you develop are probably iterative. For example, the problem of adding up all the nonnegative integers from 0

```
while (nail is sticking up) do
    hit nail with hammer
```

Figure 1.1. An Iterative Algorithm

1

```
function sumup(n : integer) : integer;
var counter, sum : integer;
begin
     sum := 0;
     for counter := 1 to n do
          sum := sum + counter;
     sumup := sum
end;
```

Figure 1.2.   The Last Iterative Algorithm in This Book

to n is solved by starting with a sum of 0 and then adding 1 to the sum, then 2, then 3, etc., iteratively adding integers until n is finally added to the sum. This algorithm expressed as a Pascal function looks like Figure 1.2.

How do we solve this problem recursively? First let's do it for a specific case. Let us suppose we want to add up all the nonnegative integers from 0 to 1,000. Further, suppose yesterday we solved the problem of adding up the integers from 0 to 999. Can we use this to solve today's problem? Of course! All we have to do is add 1,000 to the number we calculated yesterday and we are done. We are taking advantage of the fact that we have already solved a similar, but easier, problem. That's where most of the work was done. All that remains is to use this information to solve our harder problem. In this case we simply have to add 1,000 to yesterday's sum and we are done. Notice that this idea works for any sum we wish to compute, almost. (We will see why "almost" in a moment.) For example, if we want the sum of all the nonnegative integers from 0 to 67,843, and if we were lucky enough to have already calculated the sum up to 67,842 some time in the past, then all we have to do is take this result and add 67,843 to it.

The following diagram (Figure 1.3) for the case $n = 5$ might help you visualize the algorithm. Why doesn't this idea always work? I suggest you stop reading and try to think of a nonnegative integer to sum up to where yesterday's work can't be used to solve today's problem. Did you figure it out? If you decided the number is 1, you were on the right track. Suppose you needed to add all the numbers from 0 to 1. Of course, you really have

$$1 + 2 + 3 + 4 + 5 = \underbrace{1 + 2 + 3 + 4}_{10} + 5 = 15$$

Figure 1.3.   Graphical Representation of a Recursive Algorithm to Sum

to do no adding at all, so there is no need to hope you got lucky and did something helpful yesterday. On the other hand, if yesterday you had calculated the sum up to 0, which is trivially 0, you can still use it to solve today's problem. You can add yesterday's 0 to today's 1 and get the correct answer. So, summing the integers up to 1 still falls into our pattern of using yesterday's work on an easier problem to solve today's harder one.

So, which nonnegative integer doesn't allow us to use yesterday's work? It is 0. The reason is that adding up all the numbers from 0 to 0 is the easiest possible problem of this type. There are no smaller nonnegative integers. There is nothing you could have done yesterday to help you solve today's problem. The answer is 0 by definition and there is nothing else to be done.

We can use these ideas to specify our recursive algorithm for summing the integers from 0 to n completely. First, we observe that to add the integers from 0 to n, if we know the sum of the integers from 0 to $n - 1$, then just add n to this sum to get the desired result. Second, we note that the easiest problem of this type is to find the sum of the nonnegative integers up to 0. More generally, we take a hard problem (summing to n) and use the solution of an easier problem of the same type (the sum up to $n - 1$) to solve the hard problem. Then we describe the easiest problem of the given type (the sum from 0 to 0 is 0). These two pieces completely describe the recursive algorithm.

Even though this is the way most recursive algorithms are developed, most programming languages require you to specify the easiest case first. When we discuss how recursion works in chapter 3, you will learn why this is so. Let's look at a final Pascal version (Figure 1.4) of the recursive algorithm for summing the nonnegative integers.

Through this example we have demonstrated the two main rules for developing recursive algorithms. First, find a way to turn the hard problem into an easier problem of the same type and then find the easiest problem of the given type. As simple as this may sound, there are many pitfalls that must be avoided. You must be sure you have indeed made the problem

```
function sumup(n : integer) : integer;
begin
    if n = 0 then { specify the easiest case }
        sumup := 0
    else           { add n to the sum of the 1st n − 1 ints }
        sumup := sumup(n − 1) + n
end;
```

Figure 1.4. Pascal Function to Add Integers From one to n

$$1 \times 2 \times 3 \times \bullet\bullet\bullet \times (n - 1) \times n = \underbrace{\frac{1 \times 2 \times 3 \times \bullet\bullet\bullet \times (n - 1)}{\text{This product, the easier case}}} \times n$$

Figure 1.5.   Graphical Representation of a Recursive Factorial Algorithm

easier. This is not always as simple as it sounds. Similarly, it can sometimes be difficult to correctly determine the easiest case. Let's look at some more examples.

1.2. Another Similar Example—Factorial

A problem very similar to the one we just solved is the problem of finding the product of all the positive integers from 1 to n. This number is usually denoted $n!$ and is called *n-factorial*. To solve this problem recursively, we must first ask how we can use a simpler version of the same problem to solve this one. In this case it should be obvious. If we can calculate $(n - 1)!$, then all we have to do is multiply this result by n and we will have $n!$. Pictorially, Figure 1.5 shows the graphical representation of this recursive factorial algorithm.

As always, the second question we must ask is, what is the easiest case? Again, the answer is easy. $1!$ is simply 1. There is no simpler value. With these two ideas in mind, we can now write the algorithm (Figure 1.6).

You may notice a subtle difference between the algorithms of Figures 1.4 and 1.6. In the first the easiest case was when $n = 0$ and in the second the easiest case was when $n = 1$. Why the difference? The reason is simply that in each case it was the most natural way to express the easiest case. In the first case we could have made the easiest case correspond to $n = 1$, but then the problem would have to change accordingly. The problem would then be to add up the integers from 1 to n rather than from 0 to n. Why start at 0? There is no overwhelming reason. It just seemed a bit more natural to me.

```
function factorial(n : integer) : integer;
begin
    if n = 1 then {specify the easiest case}
        factorial := 1
    else             {n! = (n − 1)! * n}
        factorial := factorial(n − 1) * n
end;
```

Figure 1.6.   A Pascal Factorial Function

In the case of factorial, I claim it is much more natural to make the easiest case $n = 1$. If we choose to make $n = 0$ the easiest case, then we must be very careful about what we decide 0! should equal.At first blush, we might jump to the conclusion that 0! should equal 0. But what will this mean? Recall that the algorithm tells us that 1! $= 0! * 1$. But if we say that 0! $= 0$ this means that 1! $= 0 * 1 = 0$, which is not what we want. Do you see what we have to do to make things work if we want $n = 0$ to be the easiest case? We will have to define 0! to equal 1, so then 1! will also equal 1 and all the other factorials will be correct as well. It should be pointed out that because of this (and some other reasons) it is common practice to define 0! $= 1$. We have seen our first example where finding the easiest case is not as easy as it looks.

1.3. One More Example—Even or Odd?

This problem is of a completely different kind. Simply stated, given an arbitrary nonnegative integer, is it even or not? You are probably saying to yourself, "what's the big deal?" Indeed, that is a good question. After all, it has a simple solution using the *mod* function. (I hope you can think of it!) But just for the fun of it, let's pretend you are not allowed to use the *mod* function. Well, it's still no big deal. Deciding if n is even or not is equivalent to deciding if (n *div* 2) $\times$ 2 is still n or not. (You might want to verify this for yourself.) So, just for the fun of it let's also assume that we are not allowed to use *div*. In other words, for the sake of having an interesting problem, we want to find a way to determine if some nonnegative integer is even without using the *mod* function and without using the *div* function.

We must find a way to take the hard problem of determining if n is even and turn it into an easier problem of the same type. The secret is to look at $n - 2$. If n is even then so is $n - 2$. If n is odd, again, $n - 2$ will also be. So the hard problem of determining if the big number n is even or not can be turned into an easier problem of the same type by simply determining if the smaller number $n - 2$ is even or not.

We need to be a bit careful in determining the easiest case. Certainly $n = 0$ is the smallest, and, therefore, easiest nonnegative integer, and we all know that 0 is even. So if we write the Pascal function that easily falls out from these ideas we end up with the following (Figure 1.7), a function that you might *think* is correct.

I've hinted heavily that this function is not correct. Look at it and decide why this is so before you read on. If you don't see it right away, try working a few examples and see what happens. Avoid looking ahead until you've figured it out.

The first thing you may have noticed is that nowhere in the function is a *false* value ever assigned to the function. This should have been your first

```
function even(n : integer) : boolean;
begin
     if n = 0 then
          even := true
     else
          even := even(n - 2)
end;
```

Figure 1.7. An Attempt at a Pascal Function to Determine if an Integer is Even

clue as to what is wrong. If the function is never assigned *false*, then just
what happens when the function is presented with an odd number like 3?
According to the algorithm, since 3 is so big we must look at a smaller
integer, 3 − 2 = 1, and decide if that smaller number, 1, is even. The
algorithm does not deal with this case specifically, so we must again apply
the recursive step and so to decide if 1 is even we must see if 1 − 2 = −1
is even. (Uh-oh, −1 is not a nonnegative integer.) Again, the algorithm
doesn't deal with this case specifically either so applying the recursive step
again we must now decide if −1 − 2 = −3 is even. As you can see, this will
never stop. Also, the problem was to determine if some *nonnegative*
number was even. Neither −1 nor −3 are nonnegative so we have turned
a problem not into an easier case of the same type, but into a different kind
of problem. This, of course, is bad. Since 1 is the smallest nonnegative odd
number, we must recognize this fact. In other words, this problem requires
two easiest cases, not just one. The correct Pascal function looks like Figure
1.8.
     You might find these last two examples disturbing. In one the easiest case
wasn't as easy as we thought and in the other there were actually two easiest
cases. What are the rules for determining just how many easiest cases there
are? How do we know when we've found the correct easiest case? There are

```
function even1(n : integer) : boolean;
begin
     if n = 0 then
          even1 := true
     else if n = 1 then
          even1 := false
     else
          even1 := even1(n - 2)
end;
```

Figure 1.8. A Correct Pascal Function to Determine if an Integer is Even

no cut and dried answers to these questions, unfortunately. However, as we look at more examples and as you start writing more recursive algorithms you will develop a feel for it. In practice, it is usually more difficult (and more fun) finding the easier case. The easiest case usually comes pretty naturally.

2. RECURSIVE ALGORITHMS ON ARRAYS

2.1. Summing Up

Now let's turn to some simple array problems and find recursive algorithms for them. The first problem is similar to the first two in the last section. Given an array of integers with n elements, what is the sum of all the elements in the array? As always, we try to solve the problem by using the solution to a easier problem of the same type. In this case it should come as no surprise that the easier problem is one where the array has $n - 1$ elements. So, if we know the sum of the first $n - 1$ elements of an array, can we use this to find the sum of all n elements? Certainly. We need only add the nth element of the array to this sum.

What is the easiest case? A one-element array certainly seems easy enough. In this case the sum of all the elements is simply the value of that one element. If we assume that we have a data type called *array_type,* which is simply an array of integers indexed from 1 to 100, say, then the algorithm looks like Figure 1.9.

Notice that the function requires two arguments. One argument is the array that is being summed. The second argument corresponds to the number of elements in the array that are currently being used. Be careful not to confuse the n being passed to the function with the size of the array that is defined in the declaration, which in this case is 100. In the declaration we determine how big the array actually is. The n that is passed into the

```
function array_sum(values : array_type;
            n : integer {the size of the array}) : integer;
begin
    if n = 1 then {the easiest array—a one element array}
        array_sum := values[1]
    else
        array_sum := array_sum(values, n − 1) + values[n]
end;
```

Figure 1.9. A Pascal Function to Sum the Elements of an Array

function corresponds to how much of the entire array available is actually being used. Of course, *n* will have to be less than 100. If we want to work with larger arrays we must change the declaration.

Before we move on, let's think a little more about the easiest case. It is hard to argue the point that a one-element array is a pretty easy array to work with. But is there an easier array still? Does it make sense to talk about an array with no elements in it? There is no definitive answer here. However, in many cases it does make sense to talk about a zero-element array, and that includes this case. What, then, is the sum of all the elements in an array that doesn't have any elements? If there are no elements to add up, then zero seems to be the natural answer. No other choice could possibly make sense if no numbers are to be added. Also, what value for *n* should be passed to the function to denote an array with no elements? Again, the obvious choice is zero. If 1 is not going to be our easiest case then the algorithm better do something for the next integer smaller than 1 namely zero. So, another recursive algorithm for summing an *n* element array is the following (Figure 1.10).

Both of the above algorithms (Figures 1.9 and 1.10) solve the problem, so we can't say either is wrong. In fact it is hard to say one is better than the other. It is simply a matter of taste as to which one we feel more clearly and concisely solves the problem. It also depends on just what exactly the problem is. Does the problem statement allow or not allow zero-element arrays? Personally, I am always in favor of getting the simplest possible easiest case (the *easiest* easiest case?) so I prefer the second one. This means we are, in effect, choosing the most general form of the problem. So, whenever it makes sense, I will choose an array with no elements to be the easiest case.

2.2. Output

This next problem may seem so trivial that it is hardly worth talking about, but it will show us other ways of dealing with the easiest case, it will show

```
function array_sum1(values : array_type;
            n : integer {the size of the array}) : integer;
begin
    if n = 0 then {the easiest array—a ZERO element array}
        array_sum1 := 0
else
    array_sum1 := array_sum1(values, n − 1) + values[n]
end;
```

Figure 1.10.   Another Pascal Function to Sum the Elements of an Array

us different ways of making a problem easier, and it will prepare us for a similar but much less trivial problem. The problem is to output an array.

2.2.1. Direct approaches. In our previous examples we found it convenient to first recursively find the solution to an easier problem and then use that solution to solve the original harder problem. In this case we will find it better to first do some work then finish up by recursively solving the easier problem.

What are we doing when we output an array? The first thing we do is output the first element of the array, then we output the rest of the array. As you can see, this wording suggests a recursive algorithm. The idea is to output the leftmost element of the array and then recursively output the smaller array that remains. Notice that we now have to be careful about how we actually specify the array we will be passing to the procedure. The array is getting smaller from the left side rather than from the right as in our previous examples. This means in addition to passing the array to the procedure, we have to pass the left boundary of the array and the right boundary (which we were calling *n* previously).

What is the easiest case? As I mentioned previously, I prefer an easiest case where the array has no elements in it. This would mean that the left boundary of the array has not just reached the right boundary (when the left boundary *equals* the right boundary the array has exactly one element) but has actually passed it. In other words the left boundary is greater than the right boundary and so there are no elements in the array. What should we do in this case? Since there are no elements to output we decide that there is absolutely nothing to do. Figure 1.11 looks at this algorithm.

Why do we have to pass three arguments in the above procedure? It is because we need to know both how big the array is (*right*) and how much remains to output, (starting at *left*), as well as the array itself, of course. In our other array examples, since the array was getting smaller from the right

```
procedure out_array( nums : array_type; left, right : integer);
begin
    if left > right then {there are no elements in the array}
        { so there is nothing to do                          }
    else begin
        write(nums[left]);        {output the first element}
        out_array(nums, left + 1, right) {output the rest}
    end                              {  of the array  }
end;
```

Figure 1.11. A Pascal Procedure to Output an Array

and since we assumed all of our arrays begin with an index of 1 it was enough to keep track of the right boundary. Of course if we don't know that our arrays start at 1 then we would have to change the easiest cases in our other examples. This issue is dealt with further in the exercises.

Let us try to develop another recursive algorithm for outputting an array where the array gets smaller from the right and so we will be able to pass one less argument to the procedure. Remember how we came up with the other algorithm? We said that first we output the first element and then the rest of the array. This meant that we did the easier problem of the same type second. Our goal now is to try to do something easier first. It would be good for you to try to figure out how to do this before you read on. The easier problem in this case would have to be to output all but the last element. Then output the last element. Try to visualize the difference between these two algorithms. We have a big array and in the first case we pluck off the first element and in the second case we pluck off the last element. In both cases the recursion is applied to the remaining array. Figure 1.12 shows what the second algorithm looks like.

2.2.2. Complicated approaches. Are there any other recursive algorithms out there for outputting an array that we haven't thought of yet? Let's summarize the two we have so far. The first algorithm outputs the first element and then outputs the rest of the array. The second algorithm outputs all but the last element then outputs the last element. In both cases the recursive call is made on an array that is one smaller than the original array. Perhaps there is a way to break up the problem so that the recursive call is on a much smaller array, not just an array that is one smaller. For example, we might first output the first half of the array and then recursively output the second half. But how will the first half get output? Recursively, of course!

A new algorithm is beginning to evolve. Recursively output the first half

```
procedure out_array1(nums : array_type; n : integer);
begin
    if n = 0 then {there are no elements in the array}
        { so there is nothing to do                    }
    else begin
        out_array1(nums, n − 1); {output all but the last}
        write(nums[n])                {output the last element}
        end
end;
```

Figure 1.12. Another Pascal Procedure to Output an Array

of the array and then recursively output the second half of the array. As always, if there is nothing in the array, there is nothing to output. Figure 1.13 displays the algorithm just described.

Careful study of this algorithm reveals a number of things. First, notice we were careful to include a "+ 1" in the second recursive call. This was done to be sure there was no overlap between the two arrays that are being output recursively. Without the "+ 1," both recursive calls would want to output the element *nums*[(*left* + *right*) *div2*] which is clearly undesirable. You might want to try to figure out what would happen if the "+ 1" were left out.

A more interesting property of the algorithm is the absence of any *write* statements. You should find this a little disturbing. How can this algorithm do any outputting if there are no output statements? Somewhere, sometime, the algorithm must output an array element. We must conclude that the above "algorithm" is incorrect. It does not do what we intended.

Unfortunately, this is not the only problem with this algorithm. There is another, much more subtle error. Remember that every time we make a recursive call we must make sure it is done on an easier problem. At first glance both recursive calls in the above algorithm seem to be on smaller arrays. But look again. Suppose we enter the procedure where both *left* and *right* have the same value, say 7. This means that we are outputting a one element array. A one-element array is not an empty array so we must make two recursive calls. Since the values of both *left* and *right* are 7, the two recursive calls will amount to calls that look like *out_array2*(*num*, 7, 7) and *out_array2*(*num*, 8, 7). Look at that first recursive call. It has the same arguments that were passed into the procedure. The problem has not gotten smaller. Notice this problem only comes up whenever *left* and *right* have the same values coming into the procedure. For any other values both new problems (recursive calls) will be smaller. But, of course, that is not good

```
procedure out_array2(nums : array_type; left, right : integer);
begin
    if left > right then
        { empty array — nothing to output }
    else begin
        out_array2(nums, left, (left + right) div 2);
            { output the left half of the array }
        out_array2(nums, ((left + right) div 2) + 1, right)
            { output the right half of the array }
        end
end;
```

Figure 1.13. An Attempt at Yet Another Pascal Procedure to Output an Array

enough. If there is any situation where we are not taking a hard problem and making it easier then we do not have a recursive algorithm.

We can solve both of our difficulties simultaneously. Since we seemed to have trouble turning a one element array into two smaller arrays, let's just make the one-element array our easiest case. This will solve our other difficulty also because we will simply output the one-element array. Figure 1.14 shows our improved, and correct, algorithm.

Before we lay this problem to rest, let's discuss one final algorithm. The last algorithm we looked at can be summarized as: one-element arrays are output while larger arrays are output by first outputting the first half, then the second half. The basic idea is to cut the array in half and recursively work on each half. Another variation of this theme is: output the first half of the array, output the middle element, output the last half of the array. Notice that a one-element array does not have to be the easiest case now. Performing the algorithm on a one-element array: first output the first "half" of the array (which has no elements), then output the middle element (which is the only element), then output the last "half" (which again is an array with no elements). The more natural easiest case is the array with no elements.

With this algorithm it is clear that the problem always gets easier because we are always removing an element from the array and then making two recursive calls on what is left of the array, which has one less element than the original array had. Figure 1.15 is the algorithm.

2.2.3. Output with newline. You will notice that all of the algorithms considered so far simply output the array on one line. Another, similar problem is to output the array on one line and go on to the next line. With the above algorithms you would have to first call the procedure to do the output and then you would have to get to the next line with an additional

---

```
procedure out_array3(nums : array_type; left, right : integer);
begin
    if left = right then      {easiest case — a one element array}
        write(nums[left])     {output the one element array}
    else begin
        out_array3(nums, left, (left + right) div 2);
            { output the left half of the array }
        out_array3(nums, ((left + right) div 2) + 1, right)
            { output the right half of the array }
        end
end;
```

Figure 1.14.   Yet Another Pascal Procedure to Output an Array

```
procedure out_array4(nums : array_type; left, right : integer);
var mid : integer;
begin
    if left > right then          {easiest case — an empty array}
                                  {nothing to do                }
    else begin
        mid := (left + right) div 2; {find the middle of the array}
        out_array4(nums, left, mid − 1);
            { output the left half of the array }
        write(nums[mid]);
            { output the middle element }
        out_array4(nums, mid + 1, right)
            { output the right half of the array }
        end
end;
```

Figure 1.15. A Final Pascal Procedure to Output an Array

writeln statement. Let us try to solve the new problem of incorporating a new line at then end of the output.

Only one of the algorithms developed above suggests a solution to the new problem. Let us restate the problem so that it might be easier for us to discover the algorithm. The problem is to output an array followed by a carriage return. Do you see which of the algorithms we have already developed can be easily modified to solve this problem?

First let's look at one that doesn't work. Suppose we first try to output all but the last element and then output the last element followed by a carriage return. This does not solve our problem because the easier problem is not of the same type. The smaller array we want to output should not have a carriage return at the end of its output. We only want the carriage return the first time. So in this case we have taken a hard problem and turned it into an easier problem of a different type. This does not fit our rule for a recursive solution so we must give up on this approach.

The correct algorithm is one that plucks off the first element and recursively solves the easier problem on the right. Think about what this is saying. To output a big array with a carriage return at the end we output the first element of the array and then output the smaller remaining array *with a carriage return at the end*. This, of course, is a solution to the problem. What is the easiest array? An empty array makes the most sense. In this case we output all of the elements of the array, of which there are none, and then we output the carriage return, which is the only thing we output. Notice how similar this algorithm (Figure 1.16) is to one of our previous ones (Figure 1.11).

```
procedure out_array( nums : array_type; left, right : integer);
begin
    if left > right then {there are no elements in the array}
        writeln          {so just output the carriage return }
    else begin
        write(nums[left]); {output the first element}
        out_array(nums, left + 1, right) {output the rest of the}
    end                              {array and a car. ret. }
end;
```

Figure 1.16. A Pascal Procedure to Output an Array Followed by a Newline

2.3. Reverse Output

Now let us try something that appears to be much harder but in fact follows immediately from the above ideas. We would like to develop a recursive algorithm to output an array backwards. If you look back at the previous examples on outputting an array you might guess that there are many algorithms for this problem. This is, in fact, true. One algorithm will pluck off the first element, another will pluck off the last element, and we will have a couple of algorithms that will cut the array in half. Let's look at the algorithm that plucks off the first element.

You must now ask yourself what you will do with the first element of the array and the smaller remaining array to get the array output backwards. How can you put those two pieces together so that we will get the array backwards? If the array is to be output backwards then the first element of the array should be output last. So, what should be output before we output the first element? The answer is: the rest of the array, backwards. Think about what is being said here. If we output all but the first element of an array backwards and then we output the first element, we will have output the entire array backwards.

A small example might help. Suppose the array is an array of characters. For the sake of example, assume the array has as elements *s, t, o,* and *p*. The first element of the array is *s* and the rest of the array is *top*. The rest of the array backwards is, of course, *pot*. If we follow that with the first element, *s*, we get *pots*, which is the original array backwards. The following diagram (Figure 1.17) summarizes this.

The following figure (1.18) shows how we can generalize this idea into an algorithm that works for any sized array.

We are now ready to implement this algorithm in Pascal. For the sake of being explicit, and since Pascal insists we fully declare our arrays, we can assume that *array_type* is an array of characters. Of course, this is not

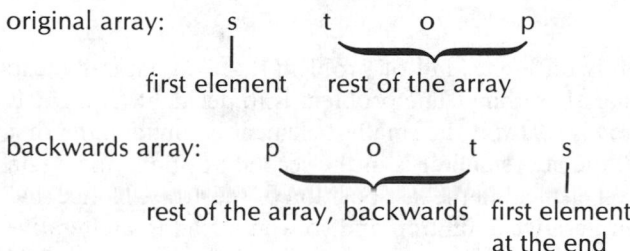

original array: s   t   o   p

                            |
                       first element   rest of the array

backwards array: p   o   t   s

                                                            |
                       rest of the array, backwards   first element
                                                       at the end

Figure 1.17.   Graphical Representation of Outputting an Array Backwards

if the array is empty then
    there is nothing to output
else
    output the first element AFTER the rest of the array is output backwards

Figure 1.18.   Pseudo-code for Outputting an Array Backwards

```
procedure out_backwards( lets : array_type; left, right : integer);
begin
    if left > right then {there are no elements in the array}
    { so there is nothing to do        }
    else begin
        out_backwards(lets, left + 1, right); {output the rest of the}
                                              { array, backwards    }
        write(lets[left]) {output the first element}
        end
end;
```

Figure 1.19.   A Pascal Procedure for Outputting an Array Backwards

crucial to the algorithm, just to the Pascal implementation. The rest of the implementation (Figure 1.19) follows immediately from Figure 1.18.

We said that there are many algorithms for outputting an array backwards, and indeed there are. For each of the algorithms we had for outputting an array forwards, there is a corresponding algorithm for outputting an array backwards. You should now be able to go back to those algorithms and transform them into algorithms that output an array backwards. You will be asked to do this in the exercises.

2.4. Sorted?

Now let us try a slightly different kind of problem that will naturally lead us to some nice sorting algorithms. The problem is to decide if an array is *sorted* or not. An array is *sorted* if the smallest element is found in the first position of the array, the next smallest is in the second position, and so on until we find the largest element in the last position of the array. Notice that this was essentially an iterative definition and so would lead to an iterative algorithm for deciding if an array is sorted. By now I bet you have already thought of a recursive way of deciding if an array is sorted. See if the first element is the smallest element in the array and then check if the rest of the array is sorted. What is the easiest case? As usual, I prefer an easiest case which is the empty array, so what is true if the array is empty? Since there are no elements at all in the array it would be hard to say that the array is not sorted, so we will make the other choice and say that it is sorted.

We now have completely specified the algorithm, but we still need to discuss the Pascal implementation a little. Since the problem is to decide if an array does or doesn't have a certain property (the property of being sorted) our result should be a "yes" or a "no": *yes* it does have the property or *no* it does not. Another, better way to say this is that the result should be "true" or "false." It is either *true* that the array is sorted or it is *false*. This means that our algorithm should be a function and further that our function should return either a "true" or a "false." In other words, we need a *boolean* function. Figure 1.20 is the boolean function that determines whether or not an array is sorted.

This function is a little more complicated than most we have done so far. The while loop determines if *a[left]* is indeed the smallest element in the array. It does this by assuming it is the smallest (setting *smallest* equal to *true*) and going through the array trying to find a smaller element. If it never finds a smaller element, that is, *a[left]* is always less than *a[pt]*, then the loop will be exited because *pt* finally becomes greater than *right* and *smallest* will still be *true*. On the other hand, if there is an element in the array that is smaller than *a[left]* then *smallest* will get set to *false* when *pt* points to that element and the loop will be exited immediately. In either case, *smallest* is set according to whether or not *a[left]* is the smallest element in the array.

The final assignment statement says that the function should return *true* if *smallest* is *true* (*a[left]* is the smallest element in the array) and the recursive call returns *true* (the rest of the array is sorted). This corresponds exactly to our English description of the algorithm.

You might notice an inefficiency in this algorithm. If *a[left]* is not the smallest element in the array there is no reason to make the recursive call because we already know that the array is not sorted. In general, it is usually

```
function sorted(a : array_type; left, right : integer) : boolean;
var smallest : boolean;
    pt : integer;
begin
    if left > right then          { empty array,    }
       sorted := true            { so it is sorted }
    else begin
       smallest := true; {assume a[left] is the smallest}
       pt := left;
       while ((pt <= right) and smallest) do begin {check a[left]}
          smallest := a[left] <= a[pt];        {against others to }
          pt := pt + 1            { see if it really is the smallest}
       end;
       sorted := smallest and sorted(a, left + 1, right)
          { the array is sorted if the first element really is }
          { the smallest and the rest of the array is sorted }
    end
end;
```

Figure 1.20. A Pascal Procedure to Determine if an Array is Sorted

a good idea to avoid making unnecessary recursive calls. However, in this case it turns out not to have a significant effect on the running speed (we will discuss this in much more detail in Chapter 2), but it still is instructive to see the more efficient version (Figure 1.21).

If you are thinking that this last algorithm still seems unnecessarily inefficient, you are correct. After all, if the second part of the array is sorted then we can tell if the first element is the smallest element simply by seeing if it is smaller than its neighbor to the right. On the other hand, if the second part of the array is not sorted then we already know that the whole array is not sorted and it doesn't matter if the first element is the smallest or not. Notice that this idea is similar to the idea that gave us *sorted1* of Figure 1.21. In that case we first checked to see if the first element was the smallest and then used that information to decide whether or not to make a recursive call on the smaller array. In this case we first make the recursive call on the smaller array and then use that result to see if we have to check if the first element is the smallest element. Further, if we do have to make that check we notice it is now much easier to do knowing already that the rest of the array is sorted. Simply compare the first element in the array with the first element in the remaining array. If the remaining array is sorted then its smallest element is in the first position and so if the first element in the array is smaller than that first element in the remaining (sorted) array it must be

```
function sorted1(a : array_type; left, right : integer) : boolean;
var smallest : boolean;
   pt : integer;
begin
   if left > right then    { empty array,    }
       sorted1 := true   { so it is sorted }
   else begin
       smallest := true; {assume a[left] is the smallest}
       pt := left;
       while ((pt < = right) and smallest) do begin {check a[left]}
           smallest := a[left] < = a[pt];    {against others to }
           pt := pt + 1      { see if it really is the smallest}
           end;
       if smallest then {first element is smallest}
           sorted1 := sorted1(a, left+1, right)
               {see if the rest of the array is sorted}
       else      {first element is not the smallest}
           sorted1 := false {so the array in not sorted}
       end
end;
```

Figure 1.21. A Slightly More Efficient Pascal Procedure to Determine if an Array is Sorted

the smallest element in the entire array. This algorithm is much easier to express (Figure 1.22).

There is, however, one small flaw with this new algorithm. It doesn't work! Study it and try to find out what is wrong with it. I'll give you a big hint. Look at how this algorithm works on a one element array.

```
function sorted2(a : array_type; left, right : integer) : boolean;
var smallest : boolean;
       pt : integer;
begin
       if left > right then    { empty array,    }
           sorted2 := true   { so it is sorted }
       else
           sorted2 := sorted2(a, left + 1, right) {rest is sorted}
                   and (a[left] < a[left + 1])    {1st el. smallest}
end;
```

Figure 1.22. An Attempt at a Much More Efficient Pascal Procedure to Determine if an Array is Sorted

The recursive part of this algorithm, the part where the hard problem is made easier, assumes the array has at least two elements. It assumes there's an element at the left end and it further assumes that the remaining array has at least one element that the first element can be compared against. If this function gets a one element array passed to it, it will attempt to access an element that does not necessarily exist, an element to the right. So, we must modify this algorithm so it properly handles one element arrays. Certainly there are many ways to do this, but the simplest is based on the observation that a one-element array is sorted. A one-element array is sorted because the smallest element (which is the only element) is in the first position (which is the only position). So, we need only make one small change to the above algorithm to fix it. Simply change it so that a one-element array is included as an easiest case. Amusingly, this is done by just adding a single character to the above program, producing Figure 1.23.

2.5. Sorting

Now that we can tell if an array is sorted, let's try a much more interesting problem. We want to develop recursive algorithms that will sort an array. We will develop algorithms that rearrange an array so that the values are arranged from smallest to largest. As always, there are many possible recursive algorithms to solve this problem. First let's look at some where the easier problem is an array that has one less element in it than does the original array.

2.5.1. Selection sort. One way to sort an array with n elements is to find the largest element in the array, put it in the last (n^{th}) position and then sort the remaining smaller array that has $n - 1$ elements. For example, suppose we have an array called a with these seven elements, ($n = 7$): 6, 12, 4, 5, 3, 10, 9. The largest element is $a[2]$ with a value of 12. The first step of our

```
function sorted3(a : array_type; left, right : integer) : boolean;
var smallest : boolean;
    pt : integer;
begin
    if left > = right then { empty array or one element }
        sorted3 := true   { array, so it is sorted        }
    else
        sorted3 := sorted3(a, left + 1, right) {rest is sorted }
                and (a[left] < a[left + 1])   {1st el. smallest}
end;
```

Figure 1.23. A Much More Efficient Pascal Procedure to Determine if an Array is Sorted.

algorithm says to put the largest element into the last position of the array. This means that we have to put a 12 into $a[7]$. Unfortunately, we cannot simply assign it over with a statement like $a[n] := a[2]$ because then we would lose the value that is currently there, in this case a 9. We need to be sure we don't lose that 9.

Two ideas leap to mind. The first is to shift all the values over to make room for the 12. This means that the 4, $a[3]$, would shift to the left one position and land in $a[2]$. Next the 5 would shift over to the third position in the array, $a[3]$. Similarly, the 3, 10, and 9 would all shift over to the left, clearing the way for the 12 to be placed into $a[7]$. This will certainly work, but it is wasteful. A lot of data is being moved about just to make room for the 12. Is there a way to put the 12 into the last position without doing all that shifting? A *yes* answer to this question means that you see the second idea.

The second and best way to put the 12 into the last position is to simply exchange it with what is currently in the last position, a 9 in this case. This will put the 9 into the second spot of the array. Upon doing this, we would have the largest element in the last position and the first $n - 1$ elements of the array would contain the remaining elements of the original array. Our example array now looks like: 6, 9, 4, 5, 3, 10, 12. Now if we recursively sort the remaining, smaller array (6, 9, 4, 5, 3, 10), we will end up with a sorted array (3, 4, 5, 6, 9, 10, 12). We can summarize this example as follows:

original array:	6	12	4	5	3	10	9
find largest element:	6	12↑	4	5	3	10	9
exchange with last element:	6	9	4	5	3	10	12
ignore last element:	6	9	4	5	3	10	12
sort smaller array:	3	4	5	6	9	10	12
done:	3	4	5	6	9	10	12

What is the easiest array to sort? An array with no elements is extremely easy to sort. As was pointed out in our discussion on algorithms to test if an array is sorted, such an array is already sorted. This completely describes the algorithm.

This algorithm is usually called *selection sort* because we first *select* the largest element and then sort the rest of the array. Figure 1.24 contains a pseudo-code description of selection sort.

It is clear how we will implement the swap required in Figure 1.24. It is probably slightly less clear exactly how to find *where*, the index of the largest element. It should be implemented as a function that returns the location of the largest element in the array and I will call this function *find_largest*. It is not enough to know what the largest element is. Looking

if the array is empty, the easiest case, then
        the array is already sorted
else
        let "where" be the index of the largest element of the n-element array
        swap a[where] and a[n]
        selection sort the (n − 1)-element array (ignore the last element)

Figure 1.24. Pseudo-code Description of Selection Sort

back at our example we can see that it would not do us any good to know that the largest element in the array is 12. If this is all we knew, how would we know where to put the 9 that is in the last position of the array? We must know where the largest element is so we can then put the element that is currently in the nth position back where the largest element came from.

Just for fun, why don't we write *find_largest* as a function and nest it in the sort procedure. Of course, as long as we're doing it as a function, we might as well do it recursively. We must first take the hard problem of finding the largest element in an array of n elements and turn it into an easier problem of the same type. This should be getting easy by now. We find the largest element of the first $n - 1$ elements and then see if the nth element is any larger. For this function, the easiest case should probably be a one-element array. It is hard to talk about the largest element in an array with no elements. All of these ideas are now collected in the following procedure (Figure 1.25).

You may be thinking that we got unnecessarily cute with that last program. After all, we could have just as easily found the largest element with a simple loop. Of course, you are right but then you would have missed out on another neat recursive algorithm—the one that finds the largest element in an array. However, for the sake of completeness, Figure 1.26 shows another version of the recursive sorting algorithm where the largest element is found in a loop.

Looking back at the high-level description of our sorting algorithm seen in Figure 1.24 we observe that the basic battle plan was to somehow prepare the array in a way that would allow us to make a recursive call so that after the recursive call is made the array is sorted. In this case we prepared the array by finding the largest element and sticking it in the last position in the array. Once the array was so prepared a single recursive call on the rest of the array finished off the work. Our next sorting algorithm just turns this idea around. First, we sort the smaller array, then, we tidy the array up so that the whole array is sorted.

2.5.2. Insertion sort. Let us look at the same example as we did before. We have an array called a with seven elements (6, 12, 4, 5, 3, 10, 9). First,

```
procedure selection_sort(var a : array_type; n : integer);
var smallest : boolean;
  where, temp : integer;

  function find_largest(a : array_type; n : integer) : integer;
  var big_one : integer;
  begin
      if n = 1 then {the largest element in a one }
          find_largest := 1 {element array is that element}
      else begin
          big_one := find_largest(a, n - 1);
                                          {largest of smaller array}
          if a[n] > a[big_one] then     { see if the last     }
              find_largest := n          { element is larger   }
          else                           { than the other      }
              find_largest := big_one { elements in the     }
          end                            { array               }
  end;

begin
  if n < 1 then { empty array, so it }
                    { is already sorted  }
  else begin
      where := find_largest(a, n);
      temp := a[where];  { exchange the largest }
      a[where] := a[n];   { element and the last }
      a[n] := temp;       { element in the array }
      selection_sort(a, n - 1)
      end
end;
```

FIgure 1.25.   A Pascal Procedure for Selection Sort

we recursively sort the smaller array that does not include the last element. This means that the first 6 elements of the array will be rearranged, leaving the last element alone. After doing this the array looks like this: 3, 4, 5, 6, 10, 12, 9. The first 6 elements were sorted by the recursive call while the last element, the 9, was left alone. We now have to decide what to do with that last element to end up with a sorted array.

To finish sorting the array we must *insert* the last element into the array by sliding to the right the values that are larger than 9 and then by placing the 9 next to the first element that is less than 9. In other words, the 12 shifts

```
procedure selection_sort1(var a : array_type; n : integer);
var smallest : boolean;
    where, temp, ct : integer;
begin
    if n < 1 then { empty array, so it }
                  { is already sorted  }
    else begin
        where := 1;    { assume the first element is largest }
        for ct := 2 to n do  { look at the rest of the array }
            if a[ct] > a[where] then    { for larger elements }
                where := ct;
        temp := a[where];       { exchange the largest }
        a[where] := a[n];       { element and the last }
        a[n] := temp;           { element in the array }
        selection_sort1(a, n − 1)
        end
end;
```

Figure 1.26. Another Pascal Implementation of Selection Sort

one spot to the right and ends up where the 9 currently is. Then the 10 shifts over to where the 12 used to be. Now since 6 is less than the value we are inserting, 9, we stop shifting and place the 9 where the 10 used to be. We now have a sorted array. Let us look at this example pictorially.

original array:	6	12	4	5	3	10	9
ignore last element:	6	12	4	5	3	10	9
sort smaller array:	3	4	5	6	10	12	9
insert last element:	3	4	5	6	10	12	9
	3	4	5	6	9	10	12

Since the last element is inserted into the correct position (by sliding larger elements over) this algorithm is usually called *insertion sort*. Let us look at a pseudo-code description of insertion sort (Figure 1.27). You should compare it to the high-level description of selection sort of Figure 1.24.

We have already discussed a little about how the procedure to insert the last element into the sorted array should work iteratively. We will return to it shortly in more detail, but why don't we first do it recursively?

To understand the recursive algorithm we must form the correct mental picture of our array and the element we are inserting. Think of the *n*

if the array is empty, the easiest case, then
    the array is already sorted
else
    insertion sort the first (n − 1) elements of the array
                                   (ignore the last element)
    insert a[n] into its proper location in the array

Figure 1.27. Pseudo-code Description of Insertion Sort

element array as an array with $n − 1$ "real" elements that are sorted and a "gap" in the nth position where there is no real element. If we wish to insert an element into such an array, there are two possibilities. The first is that the element being inserted is larger than $a[n − 1]$. If this is true then the element being inserted is the largest element in the array (remember the algorithm for testing if an array is sorted) and so we insert the element by assigning it to $a[n]$, where the gap is provided. The other possibility is the element being inserted is smaller than $a[n − 1]$. In this case we should shift $a[n − 1]$ to the right, thus, filling the gap that exists in position n and creating a new gap in position $n − 1$. The gap is at position $n − 1$ because we no longer care what value is there since we have copied it to $a[n]$. Of course the old value is still there, we just don't need it anymore because it is also in $a[n]$, where it belongs. We now recursively insert the element into the smaller array with $n − 1$ elements and a gap in position $n − 1$.

What is the easiest case? Unfortunately, a zero-element array cannot be our easiest case this time. It does not make sense to insert an element into an array that has no elements. Also, there is no room in a zero-element array for the gap that must be in all of our arrays that we are inserting into. A one-element array, on the other hand, makes a perfect easiest case. The only element in the one-element array is the gap so we simply put the element we are inserting into that gap.

Remember that what is actually needed for insertion sort is to insert $a[n]$ into the array. In order to get this to fit the picture described in the last two paragraphs, imagine that we get the needed gap in position n by making a copy of $a[n]$ by assigning it to another variable. We then insert this copied value into the array as was described above. Of course if $a[n]$ is the largest value the algorithm will put the copy right back into the gap that was just created. This may seem like an inefficiency, but it is minor and any attempt to remove the inefficiency will just make the algorithm that much more complicated.

All of this is put together in Figure 1.28.

Again, you might be thinking that this is all very cute but it sure would be nice to have this all in one procedure, without the nested recursive procedure. In order to do this we must first discuss an iterative approach to

```
procedure insertion_sort(var a : array_type; n : integer);

    procedure insert(var a : arraytype; n : integer;
                                        x : element_type);
    begin
        if n −1 then            { easiest case          }
            a[1] := x          { put x into the gap }
        else
            if x > a[n − 1] then    { x is the largest element }
                a[n] := x               { put it into the gap      }
            else begin
                a[n] := a[n − 1];         { shift }
                insert(a, n − 1, x)       { insert }
                end
    end;

begin
    if n < 1 then                    { empty array, so it }
                                     { is already sorted  }
    else begin
        insertion_sort(a, n − 1)
        insert(a, n, a[n])           { insert the n-th element }
        end
end;
```

Figure 1.28. A Pascal Procedure for Insertion Sort

inserting an element into an array. It turns out that this is a bit more complicated than you would first think. One straightforward approach is to keep shifting elements to the right until you find an element that is less than (or equal to) the element you are inserting, something like Figure 1.29.

Do you see why we had to save $a[n]$ in x in the first line? If we don't, when we start shifting elements to the right in the loop $a[n - 1]$ would get shifted

```
x := a[n]; { a[n] will be inserted }
i := n − 1;
while a[i] > x do begin
    a[i + 1] := a[i];
    i := i − 1
    end;
a[i + 1] := x
```

Figure 1.29. An Attempt at Inserting Iteratively

to position n, so $a[n]$ would be lost. Also notice that the last line contains "$a[i + 1]$", not "$a[i]$." Be sure it is clear to you why this is so.

If you worked hard to try to understand why the above code is supposed to work perhaps you also discovered why it doesn't work. In other words, you must try to think of a small array where the first $n - 1$ elements are sorted and when the above algorithm is applied to insert the last element something will go wrong. I'll give you a hint. The array will go out of bounds, that is, the algorithm will try to access an array element that is not defined.

The problem arises when the element being inserted is the smallest element in the array. In this case the inserted element will never bump into a smaller element so i will go all the way down to 0 and there is no element $a[0]$ to compare x against.

One way to try to fix this problem is to add another condition in the loop so that i will never go all the way down to 0 (as shown in Figure 1.30).

Unfortunately, with most Pascal compilers this does not help. The idea, of course, is that when i becomes 0 we will exit the loop and so we will not try to shift a bogus $a[0]$ element into position 1. The problem is there are two conditions in the *while* loop. Every time through the loop both conditions will always be checked. In particular, when i is zero the condition $a[i] > x$ will also be checked, but there still is no $a[0]$ element so this is still an error.

One of the best ways to fix this without getting bogged down with a bunch of nested *ifs* is to declare the array a so that there really is an element in position 0. Now we have to find something to put into $a[0]$ so that the loop will exit when i gets down to 0. We need something called a *sentinel* in $a[0]$, that will not want to get shifted, no matter what value we are inserting. In this case the best choice of sentinel is the value we are inserting. Since we only shift if the value in the array is less than the element being inserted, and since a number is never less that itself, the value being inserted is a marvelous choice. Insertion into an array now looks like Figure 1.31.

Notice that the variable x is no longer needed. As long as we are putting the value we are inserting into $a[0]$ we might as well use that variable instead

```
x := a[n];    { a[n] will be inserted }
i := n - 1;
while (a[i] > x) and (i > 0) do begin
      a[i + 1] := a[i];
      i := i - 1
      end;
a[i + 1] := x
```

Figure 1.30. Another Attempt at Inserting Iteratively

```
a[0] := a[n];        { a[n] will be inserted; a[0] is the sentinel }
i := n − 1;
while a[i] > a[0] do begin
    a[i + 1] := a[i];
    i := i − 1
    end;
a[i + 1] := a[0]
```

Figure 1.31. The Correct Way to Insert Iteratively

of x. We can now use this piece of code to finish another algorithm (Figure 1.32) for insertion sort.

3. SUMMARY

In this chapter we have learned the basic method for developing recursive algorithms. First, we turn a hard problem into an easier problem of the same type. Next, we find the easiest case. Looking at the many examples done in this chapter it should be clear that the heart of a recursive algorithm is the first step. To make a hard problem easier we must have a good understanding of the problem so that we can find the easier problem within the harder one. As we saw in the section on outputting arrays, there are

```
procedure inserion_sort1(var a : array_type; n : integer);
var i : integer;
begin
    if n < 1 then     { empty array, so it }
                      { is already sorted  }
    else begin
        insertion_sort1(a, n − 1);
        a[0] := a[n]; { a[n] will be inserted; a[0] is the sentinel }
        i := n − 1;
        while a[i] > a[0] do begin
            a[i + 1] := a[i];
            i := i − 1
            end;
        a[i + 1] := a[0]
        end
end;
```

Figure 1.32. A Pascal Procedure for Insertion Sort Using an Iterative Insertion

often many different ways to make a problem easier. Sometimes we turn the hard problem into more than one easier problems. We saw a few examples of this in this chapter, but we will see many more later. The ability to see smaller problems in larger ones will enable you to write good recursive algorithms.

There are pitfalls, however. The trap you have to be most careful of is thinking you've made the problem easier when, in fact, you haven't. This usually happens not because the whole algorithm is faulty but because you've forgotten some special cases. For example, the problem may get easier for all cases except for the one that is just bigger than the easiest case. This is what happened in *out_array2*. We tried to output a one-element array by outputting a zero-element array and a one-element array. But a one-element array is not smaller than a one-element array so the algorithm failed on one-element arrays. But that is enough to stop it from working for larger arrays since larger arrays will turn their problems into problems using smaller arrays and some of these smaller arrays might be of size one, the size that doesn't work.

Another time you may think you've made the problem easier when you really haven't corresponds to the situation when there is more than one easiest case. Looking back on the example for deciding if an integer is even or not, *even1* failed because we did not have an easiest case for odd numbers. This meant that when the algorithm checked 1, since 1 was not an easiest case it needed to make the problem easier and so it then checked $1 - 2 = -1$ a number which is not valid according to the problem statement. In this case, then, the problem was not made easier but was turned into a different kind of problem for which we had no algorithm. So, making easier problems and finding the easiest one(s) are not quite so separate as you might have first thought.

Finding the easiest case is usually, but not always, easy. As we just discussed, there is overlap in the process of finding easier problems and finding the easiest one so while doing the first you've usually already done the second as well. The biggest pitfall here to be careful of is, again, being sure you found *all* of the easiest cases.

The final thing to remember is that even though recursive algorithms are developed by first finding ways to make the problem easier and then finding the easiest case, Pascal wants it written the other way around. This makes sense intuitively since if we don't check for the easiest case first Pascal will keep trying to make hard problems easier and will never get around to detecting an easiest case.

We've already mentioned a couple of times that there are often many ways to write recursive algorithms to solve problems. When given a choice, which should you choose? There are many factors. A clear, easy to understand algorithm is important. A short, concise algorithm is often desirable. An algorithm that is easy to code may be the best one. The one that is most efficient might be the one you want. How do you determine the efficiency of recursive algorithms? That is the topic of the next chapter.

4. EXERCISES

1. An array need not be indexed from 1 to n. In general, an array may be indexed from an arbitrary integer lower bound to any upper bound. Look at the algorithms in this chapter that assumed the array started at 1, for example, Figures 1.9, 1.11 and 1.19, and modify them so they can work on an array with arbitrary upper and lower bounds. The only changes you should have to make are to introduce another parameter to these algorithms (corresponding to the value of the lower bound of the array) and to tidy up the easiest cases.

2. Create recursive algorithms for outputting an array backwards that corresponds to each of the algorithms for outputting an array forwards. So far, only one of the four possibilities has been presented.

3. Which of the four algorithms from problem 2 is easy to transform into an algorithm for a problem of the form: output an array backwards and go on to a new line? Explain what properties this algorithm has that makes it easy to make the desired transformation. Of course, you should finally write the program in Pascal and test it on some sample arrays.

4. The *greatest common divisor* or the *GCD* of two integers is the largest integer that divides both without leaving a remainder. For example, the greatest common divisor of 90 and 78 is 6, the greatest common divisor of 15 and 28 is 1, and the greatest common divisor of 15 and 45 is 15. A clever algorithm discovered by Euclid for finding the GCD of two integers is based on the following recursive idea: Given two integers x and y with $x > y$, the GCD of x and y is the GCD of y and $x \bmod y$. (a) Use this idea to write a recursive Pascal function that returns the GCD of two integers. (Be especially careful about formulating the easiest case), (b) Why does this algorithm work?

5. You are about to go on a trip and you need to pack some shirts. Let's start by supposing you will be gone for three days. This means you will have to pack three shirts. Let's further suppose your closet has exactly ten shirts in it. As you start packing you become curious as to how many different ways you can choose three shirts from the ten you have. Being recursively minded, you look at the first shirt in the closet and say, "I have two choices. If I take this shirt on my trip then I only have to count how many ways I can choose two shirts from the remaining nine. On the other hand, if I decide not to take the first shirt then I have to count how many ways there are to choose three shirts from the remaining nine. Since I only have these two choices, either

I take the first shirt or I don't, if I add these two (easier) counts together I will know how many ways I can choose three shirts from my ten in the closet." At this point you rush to your computer and write a nice recursive function that solves the general form of this problem, namely, if you have a total of n shirts in your closet, how many ways are there to choose k of them. Use the idea suggested to make two easier problems from the original problem. Be aware that there are two easiest cases for this problem.

6. You need to be able to multiply two nonnegative integers but multiplication on your computer is "broken." You decide to write a function called *mult* that will multiply two nonnegative integers by just using addition. Of course you immediately leap upon this recursive idea: $mult(a,b) = mult(a,b-1) + a$. It then occurs to you that multiplication is commutative, that is, $a \times b = b \times a$. This gives you another idea for a recursive algorithm: $mult(a,b) = mult(b-1,a) + a$. Does this second idea provide a working algorithm? Try programming both of them.

7. Today you discover that *mod* and *div* are broken on your computer so you have to write both of these functions yourself just using addition and subtraction. The following hints should make it easy: $a \bmod b = (a-b) \bmod b$, $a \operatorname{div} b = 1 + (a-b) \operatorname{div} b$. All you have to do is make sure you deal with the easiest case properly.

8. The first two *Fibonacci numbers* are 0 and 1. The nth Fibonacci number is the sum of the two previous ones. For example, the first 8 Fibonacci numbers are 0, 1, 1, 2, 3, 5, 8 and 13. Write a recursive function that returns the nth Fibonacci number. Using your function find the tenth, twentieth, and thirtieth Fibonacci numbers. Now write an iterative function to find the nth Fibonacci number and again find the tenth, twentieth, and thirtieth ones. Notice any difference? You will understand why there is such a big difference after you read Chapter 2.

9. Write a recursive procedure that will reverse all the elements in an array. As a hint, I will restate the problem a little. Write a recursive procedure that will take three arguments, *left, right,* and *a,* and will reverse the elements in *a* between *left* and *right*. The easiest case is when $left > = right$. This actually takes care of two different easiest cases: (a) the array has no elements, and (b) the array is a one-element array.

10. Suppose you have two sorted arrays, *a* which has *m* elements and *b* which has *n* elements. Your task is to *merge* these two arrays into a single array, *c,* so that all the elements from *a* and *b* are in the array *c* and *c* is sorted. Here is one approach: find the larger of $a[m]$ and $b[n]$, put it into $c[m+n]$ and then merge what remains of *a* and *b* (there is one less element in one of them) into *c*. Since the largest of all the elements in *a* and *b* gets put into $c[m+n]$ and since recursion takes care of all the remaining elements the algorithm does work. As is often the case, you will have to be a little careful in identifying and dealing with the easiest case(s).

11. Write a boolean recursive function that decides if an array has any duplicates. One approach is to see if the last element in the array appears earlier in the array and if not see if the smaller array without the last element has any duplicates.

12. Write a recursive function that will decide where in an array of integers a certain value appears, if it appears at all. For this problem, use the idea of cutting the array in half rather than just plucking an element off the front or rear. For example, see if the element we are searching for is the middle element in the array. If it is, we are done. If not, we must search the smaller arrays to the left and to the right of the middle element. Be sure not to include the middle element when the recursive call is made. We have already looked at that element and besides, if you do include the middle element in your recursive call you will discover that on certain arrays the recursive call will be made on an array that is no smaller than the original array.

13. Write a recursive function that will decide where in a *sorted* array of integers a certain value appears, if it appears at all. Do this problem just like you did Exercise 12 only you should notice that in this case at the expense of one extra *if* you can arrange things so that you never have to make two recursive calls. Run this function on some very large arrays and compare how much faster it runs than does the function you wrote for Exercise 12.

14. A children's puzzle called *"The Towers of Hanoi"* is played on a board with three posts and with *n* disks. Each disk has a hole in the middle that allows it to be placed on the board with the post running through it. Each disk has a different diameter. The game is initialized by placing all of the disks on a single post in the shape of a tower, that is, with the largest disk on the bottom and the smallest on top. The idea of the game is to move the tower from the starting post to another post by moving individual disks between posts. Only the top disk on any post may be moved and a disk must always be placed on either an empty post or on top of a larger disk. Hence, if a post is not empty the disks on that post must be arranged in decreasing order from bottom to top. Write a program that will solve this puzzle. You should label the three posts *A, B,* and *C* and you should number the disks 1 through *n*, where Disk 1 is the smallest disk. Think of a *move* as legally moving a disk from one post onto another. Your program should output the sequence of moves that solves the problem. Here is a suggested recursive algorithm. Assume the tower starts on Post *A* . Recursively move the top *n* − 1 disks on to Post *B*. Notice that this will not be a problem, that is, all three posts will continue to be available since the largest disk, Disk *n* , stays on the bottom of Post *A* and any other disk is allowed to be placed on the largest disk. Now move Disk *n* to Post *C* and output a statement to that effect. Finally, recursively move the tower with *n* − 1 disks from Post *B* over to Post *C*. The easiest case is easy to deal with.

2

Efficiency

1. OVERVIEW

1.1. What Do We Mean By Efficiency?

Now that we are getting better at writing recursive algorithms it is important that we get in the habit of analyzing the efficiency of the algorithms that we are writing. The problem is that different people mean different things when they use the word *efficiency* when referring to algorithms. How do we measure the efficiency of algorithms? For example, are we more interested in having algorithms that run fast, or is using less memory more important?

If we are interested in fast algorithms, what do we mean by speed? Do we mean the number of nanoseconds some Pascal implementation takes to run? Which Pascal implementation are we talking about? Do we mean the number of clock cycles used by the computer in executing the implementation? If one Pascal program always takes ten microseconds less to run than another is this significant? If one program takes twice as long to run than another is this significant? If one algorithm usually performs better than another, but not always, which algorithm is better? What do we mean by *usually* in the previous sentence?

Let's try to answer some of these questions. First of all, for the purposes of this book when we discuss the efficiency of an algorithm we will be interested only in the *time* it takes for the algorithm to do its work. The amount of *space* an algorithm requires is also an important consideration but most of the algorithms we have discussed and will discuss do not use significant amounts of memory so we will not concern ourselves with it. In the few cases where memory becomes an important consideration we will briefly examine the implications. Our major concern when analyzing the efficiency of an algorithm will be the time required by the algorithm. This is usually referred to as the *time complexity*.

But how do we measure the time complexity? Notice that this is supposed to be a property of the algorithm, not the implementation. This means that we cannot measure the time complexity in terms of the time a Pascal program for the algorithm takes to run on some particular machine using your favorite compiler. This is because two different machines running the same Pascal program can take dramatically different amounts of time to run. For example, if we write a Pascal program to implement some algorithm on a personal computer and time how long it takes to run with some data and then run that same program with the same data on a supercomputer you will notice a dramatic time savings. Does this mean the algorithm suddenly got better when we moved it over to the supercomputer? Of course not. The implementation is better because it is on a superior machine but the algorithm has not changed.

We could, I suppose, choose one particular machine and one particular compiler for that machine as the standard by which all algorithms would be measured. But this seems silly. After all, not everyone will have access to this machine. And more important, knowing how an algorithm behaves as implemented on one machine will not necessarily tell us much about how it will behave on another machine. We want to know how efficient the algorithm is when implemented on the machine on which it will be used.

You should be noticing that the desire to calculate the time complexity of algorithms is tugging us in two opposite directions. In one direction we are encouraged to base the time complexity solely on properties of the algorithm so that we can reasonably compare the efficiency of two different algorithms. Tugging the other way is the desire to be able to deduce from the time complexity of the algorithm the actual running time on a particular implementation. We must strike a balance so that the time complexity of an algorithm will be able to give us both kinds of information. We want specific enough information so that we can get some idea of how long the Pascal program running on a particular machine will take to run on various data but we also want the information to be general enough so that it is easy to compare two different algorithms. I will begin by explaining the basic idea of how the time complexity is calculated and as we progress into more detail you will see how this approach does indeed strike a satisfactory compromise.

1.2. Time Complexity

Before we can go on we still need to think a bit more about what we mean by the time complexity of an algorithm. The time complexity should give us an idea as to how much work an algorithm has to do to solve a problem. What do we mean by *work*? We simply mean the number of pseudocode or Pascal statements the algorithm must execute to solve a problem. This may seem like a terribly crude number since some statements take much longer to execute than do others but if we define a *statement* to be a primitive operation that has the property that it never takes more than some fixed amount of time to execute we will see that counting the number of statements executed is a good way to define the time complexity. In fact, it is so good we will often say "amount of time" when we really mean "number of statements executed."

But aren't we asking too much of our time complexity to be able to determine how many statements an algorithm will execute for *every* possible problem? It would be much better if we could simply specify how big the problem is and then have the time complexity report how many statements are executed. But there's still a problem here. Many different problems can have the same size yet take enormously different amounts of time to execute. So should the time complexity report the average amount of time taken? Or should it report the least amount of time possible for that particular size? Or should it report the largest amount of time necessary for a problem of a given size?

For various reasons the most common way to describe the time complexity is to report the most number of statements an algorithm will have to execute to solve a problem of a particular size. One advantage of defining the time complexity this way is that even though on certain problems the algorithm may do much better we know it will never do worse than what the complexity tells us. For this reason we usually refer to this as the *worst case time complexity*.

To fully understand what the time complexity of an algorithm is we need to make a bit more clear what we mean by the size of a problem. Since the worst case time complexity tells how many statements need to be executed by the algorithm to solve the worst (or hardest) case among the problems of a given *size*, we must know what the size is. In general, this is usually obvious. If the algorithm works on an array, the size is the number of elements in the array. If the algorithm works on a dynamic structure like a graph or a tree, then the size is the number of nodes in the graph or tree. As we go over examples all of this will become clear.

Let's review what we have decided about the time complexity so far. For any given size, say *n*, it will report the number of statements the algorithm will have to execute to solve the hardest possible problem of size *n*. In other words, it is a function which takes a positive integer and returns another positive integer. We usually name this function $T(n)$, standing for the *time* required by the algorithm for input of size *n*.

2. EARLY EFFORTS

2.1. An Example – The Complexity of Summing

Let us try to dig in now and calculate the time complexity, $T(n)$, of some of our recursive algorithms from the last chapter. We will begin with the first algorithm we considered, *sumup*, which was an algorithm for summing the integers from 0 to n. First of all, we must ask what the size of the problem is. The obvious answer is n. Technically, this is not quite right since the number n is actually stored more compactly in memory and so requires much less space, but we need not concern ourselves with this here. For our purposes it is sufficient to say that if a problem deals with some integer n, then n is the size of the problem.

Next we have to determine what the worst case is for any n. For this problem it is trivial since for any given n there is only one problem, namely, add up the integers from 0 to that number n. So, if there is only one problem of size n it must be the worst problem of that size.

How do we calculate $T(n)$? Since our algorithm is recursive, we would expect to be able to express $T(n)$ in smaller terms, like $T(n - 1)$. This is indeed true. Looking at the algorithm we see that to calculate *sumup(n)* we must do one *if* statement, one addition $(+n)$, one assignment statement, and one recursive call of size $n - 1$. So, the number of statements needed to calculate *sumup(n)* equals 3 plus the number of statements needed to calculate *sumup(n - 1)*. In other words, $T(n) = 3 + T(n - 1)$. Also, when $n = 0$ the number of statements needed to do *sumup* is 2, 1 for the *if* statement plus 1 for the assignment statement. That is, $T(0) = 2$. When we have a function expressed in terms of itself this way we have what is called a *recurrence relation*. We now need to see how to go about solving such recurrence relations.

The trick we will always use is to try to find a pattern by substituting into the right-hand side of the recurrence relation. For example, if we substitute into the original recurrence relation an $n - 1$ everyplace we see an n we get: $T(n - 1) = 3 + T(n - 2)$. We can then substitute this into the right hand side of the original recurrence relation and get $T(n) = 3 + (3 + T(n - 2)) = 2 \times 3 + T(n - 2)$. Similarly, if we substitute into the original recurrence relation an $n - 2$ everyplace we see an n we get: $T(n - 2) = 3 + T(n - 3)$. We can then substitute this into the right hand side of the previous recurrence relation and get $T(n) = 3 \times 3 + T(n - 3)$. We should now see the pattern. If we make similar substitutions $i - 1$ times we will get the equation $T(n) = i \times 3 + T(n - i)$.

But now we can explicitly solve for $T(n)$. Since we know what $T(0)$ is, if we choose $i = n$ in the last equation we get:

$$T(n) = n \times 3 + T(n - n) = 3 \times n + T(0) = 3 \times n + 2.$$

We've done it! We now know that to calculate $sumup(n)$ it will require exactly $3 \times n + 2$ statements.

2.2. A Similar Example—Complexity of Output

Let's try another similar one. What is the time complexity of out_array from the first chapter? The size of the problem is certainly the number of elements in the array we are going to output, which in this case is $right - left + 1$. Every case is a worst case since we must always output every element in the array. This can also be easily seen by looking at the procedure itself and noticing that no matter what the array is there are never any decisions to be made; the same thing will always happen. The only *if* in the algorithm is present to detect the easiest case. There are no other choices to be made.

So, to output an n element array we have one *if* statement, one *write* statement, and one recursive call on an array with $n - 1$ elements. To output a 0 element array requires one statement be executed, the *if* statement that detects the easiest case. Hence the recurrence relation is: $T(n) = 2 + T(n - 1)$ and $T(0) = 1$. Substituting repeatedly as we did before we find that $T(n) = 2 \times i + T(n - i)$. Finally, choosing $i = n$ gives us $T(n) = 2 \times n + T(0) = 2 \times n + 1$.

2.3. "Big Oh"

2.3.1. Why do we need it? A careful examination of the two complexity functions figured out so far might make you wonder if there is not some unnecessary or even misleading information provided by these functions. For example, how important is the "$+1$" in the last complexity function? Actually, not very. In general, we are more interested in the behavior of the algorithm for large values of n. For small values the algorithm is going to run relatively quickly regardless, so it's the *asymptotic* behavior of the algorithm we are interested in. This means that for large values of n the "$+1$" (or "$+2$", or "$+50$" for that matter) is unimportant. To avoid being misled by unimportant details, we will always discard such low-order terms in our complexity functions. With the two cases we've looked at so far we are left with $3n$ and $2n$.

But how accurate are the 3 and the 2? In the case of *sumup* the 3 corresponds to an *if*, an addition, and an assignment, while in the case *out_array* the 2 corresponds to an *if* and a *write*. In essence, we are saying one *write* is equivalent to either an addition or an assignment, and these are also equivalent. Is this true? Probably not. A *write* is actually likely to take longer than the addition and the assignment combined. Therefore, the 2 and the 3 are a bit misleading. When we start analyzing algorithms in pseudo-code this discrepancy can be even greater. A pseudocode statement like *output the absolute value rounded to 2 decimal places* will take much more time than will a statement like *result := sum*. Hence, what we do is simply throw the leading constant away and say that both algorithms have complexity $O(n)$, which is read "big-oh of en," or sometimes "order en."

There are other reasons that justify our calling both of the previous algorithms $O(n)$. Notice that both of these algorithms have the following property: if the size of the problem doubles (from n to $2n$) the time it takes to solve the problem also doubles. This, in fact, is true of any $O(n)$ algorithm. For example, suppose the complexity of some algorithm comes out to be $6n + 5$. How much longer does it take a problem twice as big to run for this algorithm? Another way to ask this same question is: what is the ratio of $6(2n) + 5$ to $6n + 5$? It should be clear that as n gets large $\frac{12n + 5}{6n + 5}$ gets close to 2. This means that for large enough n the running time doubles when the size of the problem doubles. This is what we meant earlier when we said that we were interested in the asymptotic behavior. We want to know what happens when the size of the problem gets large. Also, notice that for this particular problem, n does not have to get too large to exhibit the behavior we are describing. Of course, for very small values of n, like 1, the ratio is 1.56 which is not terribly close to 2. This means that solving a problem of size 2 will take 1.56 times longer than solving a problem of size 1. But, as soon as n gets as large as, say, 10 we see that the ratio is 1.92, which is already pretty close to 2. Hence, a problem of size 20 will take 1.92 (nearly 2) times longer to solve than a problem of size 10. In fact, for most algorithms you are likely to run into you will find that n need not get very large at all to display asymptotic behavior. There are examples where the asymptotic behavior is not exhibited until n is huge; greater than the number of atoms in the known universe, for example. In such cases "big-oh" is not the best way to describe the complexity of the algorithm. Fortunately, however, we will not encounter any such algorithms in this book.

Reviewing the two points made so far concerning $O(n)$: (a) any algorithm with a complexity of the form $kn + c$, where k and c are constants, has complexity $O(n)$; (b) any algorithm that has the property that if the size of the problem doubles, the running time also doubles is a $O(n)$ algorithm. These two intuitive approaches to $O(n)$ prepare us for the formal definition. A (complexity) function $T(n)$ is $O(n)$ if there exist two constants, a and n_0, such that for all $n \geq n_0$, $T(n) \leq an$. In other words, for big enough n, $T(n)$ is always no bigger than an. For example, the function $6n + 5$ is $O(n)$, because if we choose $a = 7$ and $n_0 = 5$ it is easy to verify that $6n + 5 \leq 7n$ for all $n \geq 5$.

Armed with a formal definition of $O(n)$, let's consider one more time the two intuitive approaches. Looking at the first, for any function $T(n) = kn + c$, if we choose $a = k + 1$ and $n_0 = c$, then $T(n) \leq an$ for all $n \geq n_0 = c$. This means we have formally shown that any function $T(n)$ of the form $kn + c$ is $O(n)$. Similarly, if a complexity function for some algorithm is $O(n)$, then it can grow no faster than kn for some k, so doubling the size of the problem can no more than double the running time. This, then justifies the second intuitive argument for $O(n)$.

2.3.2. Making it clear. Before we proceed to analyze other algorithms, let's pursue these points a bit further for more complicated functions. Suppose a complexity analysis of some algorithm reveals a complexity of $6n^2 + 3n + 8$. Again, using a similar intuitive argument to the one used above, we will say that this algorithm has complexity $O(n^2)$. We have thrown away the low-order part, $3n + 8$, and we have disposed of the leading constant, 6. Given a $O(n^2)$ algorithm, if the size of the problem doubles, how much longer does it take for the algorithm to execute? To answer this question we must do the same kind of thing we did before. For the example we are looking at now, we must look at the ratio of $6(2n)^2 + 3(2n) + 8$ to $6n^2 + 3n + 8$. As n gets large we see that the most significant terms are the ones that are squared and $\frac{(2n)^2}{n^2} = 4$, so when the problem size of a $O(n^2)$ algorithm doubles the running time is about four times longer. Again, n will have to get big enough for this behavior to manifest itself, but for this example, when $n = 10$, the ratio is already 3.96 so n doesn't have to get all that big.

It should come as no surprise to you that, formally, a (complexity) function $T(n)$ is $O(n^2)$ if there exist two constants, a and n_0, such that for all $n \geq n_0$, $T(n) \leq an^2$. I will leave it to you to find an a and a n_0 for the example above. Certainly, a $O(n^2)$ function grows much faster than does a $O(n)$ function, so, $O(n^2)$ algorithms are less efficient than $O(n)$ algorithms.

Let's look at this with some numbers. Suppose we have two algorithms to solve the same problem, one is $O(n)$ and the other is $O(n^2)$. Further suppose we have implemented them and we run them both on a worst case problem of size 100 and they both take 1 second to run. How long will they take to run on a problem of size 20,000? Since the problem is 200 times bigger this means that the $O(n)$ algorithm will take about 200 times longer or about 3 minutes. However, the $O(n^2)$ algorithm will take 200^2 or 40,000 times longer or over 11 hours. Hence, for large values of n the $O(n^2)$ algorithm is significantly worse. You will find it instructive to do the same sort of calculations for $O(n^3)$ and even $O(n^4)$ to see how much worse things get for these cases. This will convince you of the importance of developing algorithms with small time complexities.

We are now ready to look at the formal definition of big-oh in its most general sense. We say that a (complexity) function $T(n)$ is $O(f(n))$ if there exist two constants, a and n_0, such that for all $n \geq n_0$, $T(n) \leq af(n)$. In other words, $T(n)$ grows no faster than some constant times $f(n)$. We will study the implications of this definition a bit more in the exercises. Also, as we continue looking at more algorithms, you will be surprised at the number and variety of functions, $f(n)$, that appear as big-oh complexities for these algorithms.

From now on when we calculate the complexity of an algorithm we will be interested in the big-oh complexity. From the previous examples and from the formal definition you can see that this gives a good yardstick for the efficiency of the algorithm without requiring us to get mired down in details. This also means we will not be interested in "speeding up" algorithms by, for example, replacing a multiplication by an addition. This kind of speed up will indeed make the program run faster but it will not affect the big-oh complexity and is clearly not a fundamental improvement in the algorithm; it is simply an implementation-oriented improvement.

3. COMPLETE EXAMPLES

As you may have already guessed, complexities are not always as easy to calculate as they were for the last two examples. To see this, let's calculate the complexity of *out_array4*. This is the algorithm where we output the first half of the array, then the middle element, and then the last half. Looking at this procedure you are likely to suspect that it is also $O(n)$ like our other *out_array* procedure. This is because each element of the array is output exactly once and nothing else is really done. We must confirm this intuition by solving the recurrence relation corresponding to this procedure.

Repeating the description of this algorithm with added emphasis we note that first we output the first *half* of the array, then we output the middle *element*, then we output the last *half* of the array. The algorithm will always do these three things regardless of what is in the array so again every case is the worst case. This means that $T(n) = T(\frac{n}{2}) + 1 + T(\frac{n}{2}) = 2T(\frac{n}{2}) + 1$.

Also, when the array is empty there is one *if* statement to detect this fact so $T(0) = 1$. We must now expand this equation as we have in the past. After we expand it a couple of times a pattern should present itself. Let's see.

Note by the above definition of $T(n)$, we get that $T(\frac{n}{2}) = 2T(\frac{n}{2^2}) + 1$. Substituting this into the original equation we get:

$$T(n) = 2\left[2T(\frac{n}{2^2}) + 1\right] + 1 = 2^2 T(\frac{n}{2^2}) + 2 + 1.$$

We can do this again by noting that $T(\frac{n}{2^2}) = 2T(\frac{n}{2^3}) + 1$ and then by substituting this into the last equation we get:

$$T(n) = 2^3 T(\frac{n}{2^3}) + 2^2 + 2 + 1.$$

The pattern is becoming apparent. We multiply an additional 2 for each 2 we divide from inside the T-term. What about the numbers that are getting added together at the right? Starting from the right, the first number being added is 1 which can also be written as 2^0. The second number being added is just 2^1. The third number is 2^2. Hence, after each substitution we are adding the next power of 2. Armed with all this information we can now write the general form of $T(n)$ after i substitutions:

$$T(n) = 2^i \, T(\frac{n}{2^i}) + \sum_{k=0}^{i-1} 2^k.$$

To figure out what $T(n)$ is, two things remain to be done. First, we need to figure out how to calculate the sum on the right side of the equation. It turns out there is a simple formula, namely, $\sum_{k=0}^{i-1} 2^k = 2^i - 1$. You should test this formula out on a few values of i to see how it works. It's really kind of neat! In any case we now have that $T(n) = 2^i \, T(\frac{n}{2^i}) + 2^i - 1$. The second and final thing that must be done is to select the value of i that will allow us to solve $T(n)$.

We need to select a value for i so that $T(\frac{n}{2^i})$ corresponds to either the easiest case or a case that is near the easiest. Even though our easiest case corresponds to $T(0)$, in this case it is much easier to find a value for i so that $\frac{n}{2^i} = 1$. We know that $T(1) = 3$ from our recurrence relation so as you will soon see this will do just fine.

To find a value of i so that $\frac{n}{2^i} = 1$ is the same as finding a value of i so that $2^i = n$. Do you remember that $i = log_2 n$ does the trick? In other words, $2^{log_2 n} = n$, so using this value for i we get:

$$T(n) = nT(\frac{n}{n}) + n - 1 = nT(1) + n - 1 = 3n + n - 1 = 4n - 1.$$

In other words, $T(n) = O(n)$, so this algorithm is a $O(n)$ algorithm, just like the other output procedures.

This may have seemed like a long around just to find out something you already knew must be true, but you gained a couple of things along the way.

First of all, we did it formally, so not only do we intuitively believe that this is a $O(n)$ algorithm, but we have proved it. Second, the techniques used for this fairly simple algorithm will carry over to some of the more complicated algorithms we will analyze later. If you can understand what we did in this simple case, you will find it easier to understand the analyses we do for the more complicated algorithms later. Finally, we have bumped into $log_2 n$. It turns out that $log_2 n$ turns up frequently in complexity analysis. Again, if you understand how it came up here and how we used it to solve $T(n)$, then you will be fully prepared for the more complicated algorithms coming soon. In fact, $log_2 n$ comes up so often we will almost always simply refer to it as $log\ n$.

3.1. Sorted?

3.1.1. Sorted 1.   In the last chapter we had two fundamentally different algorithms to test if an array is sorted. We said that *sorted1* seemed inefficient so we developed the improved *sorted2*, thinking that we had made it more efficient. Let's see if *sorted2* really is better, that is, let's see if its time complexity is smaller.

The first algorithm, *sorted1*, checked to see if the leftmost element was the smallest element in the array and if it was it recursively checked to see if the remaining array (without the leftmost element) was sorted. For the first time we have a nontrivial worst case to consider. Since the algorithm only makes a recursive call if the first element is the smallest element in the array the worst case will correspond to data such that every possible recursive call is made. Clearly, then, if the first element is not the smallest no more recursive calls will be made and so the algorithm will be much quicker in this case. Since we measure the complexity for the worst case we will write our recurrence relation assuming every possible recursive call is made.

To write the recurrence relation we must first figure out how much time is spent deciding if the first element is the smallest. Looking at the *while* loop we see that in the worst case we will go through the loop once for each element of the array, that is, *pt* will take all possible values from *left* to *right*. Using the notation we are now familiar with, this means that we go though the loop n times, where n, as always, is the size of the array. In this case $n = right - left + 1$. Since there are 2 statements in the loop and the loop itself is a kind of statement, we conclude that the total time needed to determine if the first element is indeed the smallest element is $3n$. At this point you might be thinking, "do we really need that 3?" The answer to this question is a resounding "no." By now we are used to the idea that constant factors and constant terms are not important. The 3 in the $3n$ corresponds to 3 completely different kinds of statements. One is an addition and assignment, one is a comparison and assignment, and one is a loop test. As we said in the past, calling this 3 statements can be misleading. So what should we call it? As you will see in the exercises we can leave the 3 there, we can change the 3 to a 5, in fact, we can put any constant we like there and the complexity will still come out the same. You might already suspect this since you know that a constant factor like this is going to disappear anyway once we determine the big-oh complexity. We might as well make life as simple as possible for ourselves, so the simplest way to go is to choose 1 as the constant and say that it takes n steps to decide if the first element is the smallest.

Summarizing, we see that the number of statements needed to decide if an array is sorted using this algorithm, in the worst case, is n (for deciding that the first element is the smallest) plus the number of statements required to test if array with $n - 1$ elements is sorted (corresponding to the recursive call). In other words, $T(n) = n + T(n - 1)$. Also, trivially, $T(0) = 1$.

You may have noticed that our recurrence relation has ignored a few statements in our algorithm. For example a couple of *if* statements do not seem accounted for. If we worry about every statement we will get a recurrence relation like $T(n) = 3 + n + T(n - 1)$. However, we might suspect that the 3 will not be significant since we already have an n in the equation. This indeed is true. You will be asked in the exercises to solve this recurrence relation so that you can see that it does not affect the big-oh complexity we ultimately derive.

To solve $T(n) = n + T(n - 1)$ we proceed as usual. First, we note that if we substitute $n - 1$ everywhere we see an n in the recurrence relation we get $T(n - 1) = (n - 1) + T(n - 2)$. We then substitute this into the right side of the original recurrence relation and obtain $T(n) = n + (n - 1) + T(n - 2)$. Making this substitution one more time we get $T(n) = n + (n - 1) + (n - 2) + T(n - 3)$. The pattern is now clear. Every time we make a substitution we subtract 1 from inside the T-term and we add the next smaller integer. In general, after making i substitutions we get:

$$T(n) = n + (n - 1) + \cdots + (n - i) + T(n - i - 1)$$

$$= \sum_{k=n-i}^{n} k + T(n - i - 1).$$

As always, we want to eliminate the T on the right hand side of the equation so we must find the appropriate i. In this case if we pick $i = n - 1$ we get:

$$T(n) = \left(\sum_{k=n-(n-1)}^{n} k \right) + T(n - (n - 1) - 1) = \left(\sum_{k=1}^{n} k \right) + T(0)$$

$$= \left(\sum_{k=1}^{n} k \right) + 1.$$

You probably do not know what that summation adds up to off the top of your head. However, it will show up many, many times in our complexity analyses. So please memorize this fact:

$$\sum_{k=1}^{n} k = \frac{n(n+1)}{2}.$$

Knowing this fact, it is now clear that the complexity of this algorithm is $O(n^2)$.

3.1.2. An important aside. In general, the last step in solving a recurrence relation is to pick a value for i so that T on the right side of the equation reduces to a simple case, usually $T(0)$ or $T(1)$. Also, we have usually been careful when defining our recurrence relations to define *exactly* what $T(0)$ is, that is, exactly how many statements are needed by the algorithm for the easiest case. But we now know that constants are not important when doing big-oh complexity analyses. This means that it is irrelevant whether $T(0) = 1$ or $T(0) = 3$. The big-oh complexity will still come out the same. In fact for any given algorithm there is only one worst case of size 0 so $T(0)$ will always be a constant. Hence, in the future, no matter how many statements are executed by the easiest case we will simply say that the easiest case requires a *constant* amount of time and we will be able to write $T(0) = 1$ without any fear of losing relevant information. Also, since this is always true we won't even bother writing down what $T(0)$ is anymore for every algorithm.

In fact, we can take this a step further. By exactly the same argument, for any algorithm, and for any fixed value (say 10, for example) there is only one worst case for that fixed value and this worst case will require the algorithm to execute a certain number of statements to solve it. This number will never change because the worst case cannot change once you have defined the algorithm. What this means is that $T(10)$ is just some fixed constant, so for the purposes of big-oh complexity we might as well call it 1. In general, then, if we find in a recurrence relation $T(k)$ where k is some constant, like 1, or 0, or 10 we can simply replace that $T(k)$ with a 1 because for the purposes of big-oh complexity one constant is as good as any other. Hence, when solving recurrence relations our goal is to turn all Ts on the right-hand side with variables in them (like $n - 1$ or $n/2$) into Ts with constants in them, (like 0, or 1, or 10) for we can then replace these Ts with a 1. Actually, we have been doing this all along. The only difference now is that we won't require the right-hand side of a recurrence relation to be in terms of the easiest case. This means that the constant doesn't have to be 0 or 1 anymore. Any constant will do, or to put it another way, any easy case will do.

Now let's look at the second algorithm for testing to see if an array is sorted, *sorted2*. In this algorithm we tested if the first element is less than the second and we recursively tested the smaller array without the first element. We always did these two things regardless of the data so every case is the worst case. So we immediately see that the recurrence relation for this algorithm is: $T(n) = 1 + T(n - 1)$. We've seen a recurrence relation very similar to this one earlier, so we should be able to solve this one quickly. If we substitute for $T(n - 1)$ we get $T(n) = 2 + T(n - 2)$ and so in general we get: $T(n) = i + T(n - i)$. Choosing $i = n$, $T(n) = n + T(0)$, and since 0 is a constant we get $T(n) = n + 1 = O(n)$. Remember, the exact value of $T(0)$ is not important. $T(0)$ must be a constant, like 1, or 3, or 67 so the big-oh complexity is still $O(n)$ because $n + 1$, $n + 3$, and $n + 67$ are all $O(n)$. We can conclude that the second algorithm is indeed a faster algorithm since the first algorithm is a $O(n^2)$ algorithm.

3.2. A surprising example

3.2.1. Finding the largest element. We will now look at two similar recursive algorithms that have radically different complexities. One of our algorithms for selection sort used a recursive function to find the location of the largest element in an array. That function looked like Figure 2.1.

Doesn't it appear that the variable *big_one* is unnecessary? After all, couldn't we simply substitute the recursive call to *find_largest* in the two places that *big_one* is used? This is, in fact, true, but we may find that there is a good reason for having it anyway. Let's find out by going ahead and

```
function find_largest(a : array_type; n : integer) : integer;
var big_one : integer;
begin
    if n = 1 then             {the largest element in a one }
        find_largest := 1    {element array is that element}
    else begin
        big_one := find_largest(a, n - 1); {largest of smaller array}
        if a[n] > a[big_one] then    { see if the last    }
            find_largest := n        { element is larger }
        else                         { than the other    }
            find_largest := big_one  { elements in the   }
        end                          { array             }
end;
```

Figure 2.1. A Pascal Function to Find the Largest Element in an Array

eliminating *big_one* and renaming the function. We get something like Figure 2.2.

As you may have guessed by now, the reason for looking at these two algorithms is so that we can compare their complexities and see if either is preferable to the other. Looking at the first function, Figure 2.1, first, we see that one recursive call is made to an array that is one smaller than was the original array and one *if* statement is executed along with an assignment statement. This happens no matter what the data is so we can say that any case is the worst case and so $T(n) = 2 + T(n - 1)$. This recurrence relation should look quite familiar, so you should immediately recognize that after substituting i times we get $T(n) = 2 \times i + T(n - i)$, and so picking $i = n - 1$ we have $T(n) = 2 \times (n - 1) + 1 = O(n)$.

3.2.2. Another important aside.   As we continue getting more and more comfortable calculating complexities we begin to notice more shortcuts. In this last example we took a certain amount of effort to come up with the 2 in the original recurrence relation. However, the 2 quickly disappeared when we wrote the big-oh complexity. The reason we wrote 2 was because we said there were two statements executed in addition to the recursive call, however, the crucial observation is that there is a constant amount of work done each time the function is called in addition to the recursive call. The particular constant was not important because it is lost when we write the big-oh complexity. Hence, when solving the complexity for that problem we could have just as easily said that there is one recursive call and a constant amount of additional work for each call to the function. For simplicity, we

```
function find_largest1(a : array_type; n : integer) : integer;
begin
   if n = 1 then              {the largest element in a one }
       find_largest1 := 1 {element array is that element}
   else begin
       if a[n] > a[ find_largest1(a, n − 1) ]
                                      { return the larger    }
                              then    { of the last element}
           find_largest1 := n        { and the largest of }
       else                          { the first n − 1    }
           find_largest1 :=          { elements           }
               find_largest1(a, n − 1)
   end
end;
```

Figure 2.2.   A Slightly Different Pascal Function to Find the Largest Element in an Array

choose the constant to be 1, and we conclude that $T(n) = 1 + T(n - 1)$. The solution to this recurrence relation we know is $O(n)$ and so we are done. This is essentially the same argument we used when we decided to write $T(0)$ $= 1$ whenever the easiest case required a constant amount of work. The moral is we don't have to be terribly careful about our counting. It suffices to notice when a constant amount of work is being done and to simply record this as a 1 in the recurrence relation.

3.2.3. A slower way to find the largest element. Now that we have found that the *find_largest* algorithm of Figure 2.1 requires $O(n)$ time, would you care to guess the complexity of *find_largest1* of Figure 2.2 before we sit down and tackle it. You might be tempted to guess that it too will be $O(n)$ since it is essentially the same algorithm. On the other hand, you may feel that the extra recursive call in *find_largest1* may exact some sort of penalty. Let's see.

For this algorithm we notice that sometimes only the recursive call in the *if* statement is made but should the result of the *if* be true then a second recursive call is made. Since we are interested in the worst case, it is certainly possible for the *if* statement to be *true* every time, so we must calculate our complexity assuming that two recursive calls are made each time. In addition to the recursive calls there is a constant amount of additional work being done, so the recurrence relation is: $T(n) = 2 \times T(n - 1) + 1$. Here is how we solve this recurrence relation:

$$
\begin{aligned}
T(n) &= 2 \times T(n - 1) + 1 && \text{the definition above} \\
&= 2 \times [2 \times T(n - 2) + 1] + 1 && \text{expanding } T(n - 1) \\
&= 4 \times T(n - 2) + 2 + 1 && \text{distributing the 2} \\
&= 4 \times [2 \times T(n - 3) + 1] + 2 + 1 && \text{expanding } T(n - 2) \\
&= 8 \times T(n - 3) + 4 + 2 + 1 && \text{distributing the 4} \\
&= 2^i \times T(n - i) + 2^{i-1} + 2^{i-2} + \cdots + 2 + 1 && \\
&&& \text{recognizing the pattern} \\
&= 2^i \times T(n - i) + \sum_{k=0}^{i-1} 2^k && \\
&= 2^n \times T(0) + \sum_{k=0}^{n-1} 2^k && \text{choosing } i = n \\
&= 2^n + (2^n - 1) && \\
&= O(2^n) &&
\end{aligned}
$$

It may not be totally clear where the two summands in the second to the last line came from. The first summand apparently used the fact that $T(0) = 1$. Even though this algorithm has no problems of size 0, 0 is a constant so we are free to say $T(0) = 1$ just as we might say $T(1) = 1$ or $T(15) = 1$. The second summand comes from a formula we discussed earlier in the chapter, namely, $\sum_{k=0}^{i-1} 2^k = 2^i - 1$, where 1 has been subtracted from each side of this equation. Finally, it is clear that $2^n + 2^n - 2 = O(2^n)$

How bad is this? Certainly $O(2^n)$ is worse than $O(n)$. In fact, it is worse than $O(n^2)$, $O(n^3)$, or $O(n^8)$. Actually, $O(2^n)$ is worse than $O(n^k)$, where k is any number. Let's study $O(2^n)$ more closely to see just how bad this last algorithm is. Remember that a $O(n)$ algorithm takes twice as long to run whenever the problem size doubles and a $O(n^3)$ algorithm takes eight times longer to run whenever the problem size doubles. A $O(2^n)$ algorithm has the frightening property that it takes twice as long to run every time the problem size increases by 1. This is easy to verify by looking at the ratio of 2^{n+1} to 2^n. Intuitively, this is very bad but let's look at some numbers to see just how bad this really is. Suppose you have an algorithm that takes 1 minute to run on a problem of size 20 and the complexity of this algorithm is $O(2^n)$. It will take about 1,000 minutes or over 16 hours to run on a problem of size 30. For a problem of size 40 the algorithm will need to run for almost two years! Comparing this to the 2 minutes required by a $O(n)$ algorithm, 8 minutes required by a $O(n^3)$ algorithm, and the half hour required by a $O(n^5)$ algorithm, you begin to realize just how bad a $O(2^n)$ algorithm really is.

Suffice it to say, then, that this is an extremely bad algorithm and we will try very hard, whenever possible, to avoid $O(2^n)$ algorithms. Also, pay particular attention to how similar these last two algorithms are. In fact, one might be likely to prefer the second algorithm because it doesn't require the use of a local variable. Beware! Remember to always do a complexity analysis on any algorithm you create so you won't be embarrassed later when someone asks you why your program is running so slowly. I would hate to have to return to my boss after he complained about my program and have to calmly explain to him that he needs to be more patient; the program will stop in two years.

4. DON'T OVERDO RECURSION

It is important to try to develop intuition towards algorithms so that you will sense when your algorithm might be bad before you even sit down to do the complexity analysis. The tip-off in the last algorithm is that you are making two recursive calls of size $n - 1$. Making one recursive call of size $n - 1$ isn't so bad. Making two recursive calls of size $n/2$ isn't so bad. We've analyzed both of these kinds of algorithms already. But two recursive calls, neither of which is much smaller than the original problem is trouble. A good rule of thumb is to try to avoid unnecessary recursive calls whenever possible.

4.1. A Slow Find Function

Another good example where this rule of thumb holds true can be seen by solving Problems 12 and 13 of Chapter 1. First let's try to solve Problem 12. We are to write a recursive function that will announce if a certain integer exists in an array of integers. However, we are to do it by first checking to see if the element being searched for is the middle element in the array and if it's not we must then recursively check the first half and the second half of the array. If this function is to be useful it is probably best if it returns where in the array the element is found, if it is found. We will assume the array has positive indices so that if the element is not found the function can announce this by returning a −1. (For example, see Figure 2.3.)

If you suspect this is not the most efficient way to write this function, you are right. There seems to be unnecessary recursive calls here. For example, if we find the element in the left half of the array, we make a second recursive call to find out exactly where it is. Had we saved that value in a local value when we made the first recursive call, we would not have to make the second one. Also the last *else* is actually unnecessary. If we don't find the element in the left half of the array, then the result of the recursive

---

```
function slow_find(nums : array_type; left, right : integer;
                                      val : integer) : integer;
var mid : integer;
begin
    if left > right then      { empty array— the element }
        slow_find := −1    { is not in this array        }
    else begin
        mid := (left + right) div 2; {find the middle of the array}
        if val = nums[mid] then {the element is found here}
            slow_find := mid
        else if slow_find(nums, left, mid − 1) <> −1 then
                                {check the left half   }
            slow_find := slow_find(nums, left, mid − 1)
        else if slow_find(nums, mid + 1, right) <> −1 then
                                {check the right half }
            slow_find := slow_find(nums, mid + 1, right)
        else                            {not in the array      }
            slow_find := −1
    end
end;
```

Figure 2.3. A Pascal Function to Find an Element in an Unsorted Array

call on the right half of the array determines whether or not we will find it at all. We will incorporate these changes into a new function shortly, but first let's see what the complexity of this one is, so that we will be able to see if the new function really turns out better.

We must study this function for a minute to discover the worst case. Certainly we want to make as many recursive calls as possible, so how many can be made by this function? Suppose *val* is found on the left side of the array. In this case there will be two recursive calls made. One where the left side is checked and a second where the assignment to *slow_find* is made. But suppose the *val* is instead found on the right side of the array. There will be one recursive call made to search the left side of the array, a second made to search the right side of the array, and a third made to assign the location of that found element into *slow_find*. For this to happen in every recursive call *val* must be the rightmost element in the array.

Summarizing, in the worst case three recursive calls are made each time, where each recursive call is to an array half the size of the original array and there is a constant amount of additional work done checking for the easiest case, etc. Hence, we get the following:

$$T(n) = 3T(\tfrac{n}{2}) + 1 \qquad\qquad \text{as described above}$$

$$= 3[3T(\tfrac{n}{4}) + 1] + 1 \qquad\qquad \text{expanding } T(\tfrac{n}{2})$$

$$= 3^2\, T(\tfrac{n}{2^2}) + 3 + 1 \qquad\qquad \text{distributing the 3}$$

$$= 3^i\, T(\tfrac{n}{2^i}) + \sum_{k=0}^{i-1} 3^k \qquad\qquad \text{recognizing the pattern}$$

$$= 3^{log_2 n}\, T(1) + \sum_{k=0}^{log_2 n} 3^k \qquad\qquad \text{choosing } i = log_2 n$$

Now we need to make four observations to finish solving this. First, remember the neat formula we had earlier, namely, $\sum_{k=0}^{i-1} 2^k = 2^i - 1$? Well there is a similar, and equally neat one for summing powers of 3. It looks like this: $\sum_{k=0}^{i-1} 3^k = \dfrac{3^i - 1}{2}$. The second observation is one that you should remember from your algebra days, namely, $3^{log_2 n} = n^{log_2 3}$. Next, $log_2 3$ is approximately 1.59. Finally, $T(1)$ is a constant since 1 is a constant. Using these observations we can finish solving for $T(n)$:

$$T(n) = 3^{log_2 n} + \frac{3^{log_2 n + 1} - 2}{2}$$

$$= \frac{2}{2} 3^{log_2 n} + \frac{3}{2} 3^{log_2 n} - 1$$

$$= \frac{5}{2} 3^{log_2 n} - 1$$

$$= \frac{5}{2} n^{log_2 3} - 1$$

$$= O(n^{1.59})$$

4.2. A Faster Find Function

The previous function *slow_find* doesn't have a bad complexity but you probably suspect that there is a $O(n)$ algorithm since, intuitively, you should just have to visit each element once to find the largest one. Let's make the improvements we suggested earlier and see if we are able to improve upon the complexity. Using an extra local variable and eliminating the last *else*, the function looks like Figure 2.4.

As before, since there are no loops in this function the worst case will be when the most recursive calls are made. Since there are only two recursive calls written in the function it will not be possible to get more than two recursive calls, no matter how bad the case is. Also, it is easy to find cases where both recursive calls are made, for example, when the element being searched for is not in the array. In this case the function must check both the left and the right halves of the array before it will know that the element is not present. As before, each recursive call is to an array that is half the size of the original array. Also, there is a constant amount of additional work being done besides the recursive calls so we can now calculate the complexity.

$$T(n) = 2T(\tfrac{n}{2}) + 1 \qquad \text{as described above}$$

$$= 2[2T(\tfrac{n}{4}) + 1] + 1 \qquad \text{expanding } T(\tfrac{n}{2})$$

$$= 2^2 T(\tfrac{n}{2^2}) + 2 + 1 \qquad \text{distributing the 2}$$

$$= 2^i T(\tfrac{n}{2^i}) + \sum_{k=0}^{i-1} 2^k \qquad \text{recognizing the pattern}$$

```
function find(nums : array_type; left, right : integer;
                                     val : integer) : integer;
var mid, location : integer;
begin
    if left > right then        { empty array— the element }
        find := − 1             { is not in this array        }
    else begin
        mid := (left + right) div 2; {find the middle of the array}
        if val = nums[mid] then    {the element is found here}
            find := mid
        else begin
            location := find(nums, left, mid − 1);
                                     {check the left half}
            if location <> − 1 then
                find := location
            else                            {check the right half}
                find := find(nums, mid + 1, right)
        end
end;
```

Figure 2.4. A Faster Pascal Function to Find an Element in an Unsorted Array

$$
\begin{aligned}
&= 2^{log_2 n}\, T(1) + \sum_{k=0}^{log_2 n - 1} 2^k &&\text{choosing } i = log_2 n \\
&= n + 2^{log_2 n} - 1 &&\text{simple algebra} \\
&= n + 2n - 1 &&\text{ditto} \\
&= O(n)
\end{aligned}
$$

So we see that by eliminating one recursive call we are able to reduce the complexity from $O(n^{1.59})$ to $O(n)$.

4.3. The Fastest Find

Now let's look at Problem 13 from Chapter 1. The solution to this problem will be similar to the two above except there will be even one less recursive call. You might want to try to guess what the complexity will turn out to be in such a case.

The problem is the same as the one we've just been looking at, to find an element in an array, only now we assume the array is sorted. This makes a big difference in our algorithm because now if we discover the middle element is not the element that is being searched for, we don't have to check both the left and right sides of the array. We only have to check the side corresponding to whether *val,* the element being searched for, is less than or greater than the middle element of the array. The function will look like Figure 2.5.

Because of the nesting of the *ifs* in this function at most one recursive call can be made and it will be to an array half the size. In fact, because of this property where each recursive call is made to an array half the size of the previous call, this function is usually called *binary search.* The recurrence relation for this algorithm should be self evident so we proceed to solve it.

$$T(n) = T(\frac{n}{2}) + 1 \qquad\qquad \text{obvious}$$

$$= [T(\frac{n}{4}) + 1] + 1 \qquad\qquad \text{expanding } T(\frac{n}{2})$$

$$= T(\frac{n}{2^i}) + i \qquad\qquad \text{recognizing the pattern}$$

$$= T(1) + \log_2 n \qquad\qquad \text{choosing } i = log_2 n$$

$$= O(log_2 n)$$

```
function find(nums : array_type; left, right : integer;
                                    val : integer) : integer;
var mid, location : integer;
begin
    if left > right then      { empty array— the element }
        find := −1            { is not in this array        }
    else begin
        mid := (left + right) div 2; {find the middle of the array}
        if val = nums[mid] then    {the element is found here}
            find := mid
        else if val < nums[mid] then
                                    {the element can only be in }
                                    { the left half of the array   }
            find := find(nums, left, mid − 1)
        else                                  {it can only be in}
            find := find(nums, mid + 1, right) {the right half}
end;
```

Figure 2.5. A Pascal Function to Find an Element in a Sorted Array

This, of course, is a substantial improvement over the previous two algorithms but it is based on the assumption that the data are sorted. More important, however, is to notice the extra cost each additional recursive call places on the algorithm. Avoid unnecessary recursive calls in your algorithms.

5. INSERTION AND SELECTION SORT

The subject of sorting seems to come up over and over again whenever we are discussing algorithms. One reason is that sorting is a important problem that is done frequently on computers. As a result many clever algorithms have been developed to sort. We will look at some of these later, but for now in order to develop a sound perspective on what to expect from sorting algorithms let's find the complexity of the two not so clever sorting algorithms we developed in the last chapter.

The first algorithm we developed was selection sort. In this algorithm we put the largest element in the first position of the array and then recursively sorted the rest of the array. In every case, including the worst case, finding the largest element involved n steps (look at the *for* loop) and the recursive call was to an array of size $n - 1$. So, the recurrence relation is $T(n) = n + T(n - 1)$. However, we already solved this recurrence relation earlier in the chapter so we conclude that selection sort is a $O(n^2)$ algorithm.

Insertion sort was done by first recursively sorting the initial $n - 1$ elements and then inserting the nth element into its proper position. In the worst case the element being inserted would be the smallest element and so all the other elements in the array would have to be shifted over one position (look at the *while* loop) which requires n steps. Thus, the recurrence relation for insertion sort is $T(n) = T(n - 1) + n$. This is the same recurrence relation we got for selection sort so insertion sort is also a $O(n^2)$ algorithm.

6. I CAN'T SOLVE IT

So far we have been very successful in determining the complexities of our algorithms without much difficulty. Indeed, they are usually not that hard to calculate. However, the time will come when you create an algorithm and the recurrence relation will not be easy to solve. We will, in fact, see a few of these in the exercises. Then what do you do? The answer is: try to compute the complexity empirically. This means you should run your program on a bunch of test data and by looking at the time required to solve the problems for the different data try to determine the complexity.

By way of example, let's look at how I did this for insertion sort. Even though we already know that insertion sort has complexity $O(n^2)$, I pretended I didn't know this. First, I wrote a Pascal program that implemented insertion sort. Next, I made an educated guess that the worst case corresponded to the situation where the program must sort an array in backwards order. Of course we know that this guess is in fact right, but let's keep pretending that we are just making good guesses.

To actually figure out the complexity of the program I had to determine how many statements are executed by the program for various worst case arrays of different sizes. I could put a counter in my program and after every statement added a line like *counter* := *counter* + 1 which would increment the counter after every statement. I could then output the value of *counter* at the end of the program and know exactly how many statements were executed. But the exact number of statements executed is not important. We are only interested in the big-oh complexity. So, I incremented the counter inside the *while* loop to take into account the statements inside that loop and I incremented the counter right before I made the recursive call to take into account all of the statements that are not inside the loop. I then output the value of the counter at the end of the program so I would know, to within a multiplicative constant, the number of statements executed.

The next step was to run the program with worst case data of various sizes. I chose a number of different values, being careful to choose some that were large enough to give a good indication of how the program was behaving for large arrays. For each different n, the size of the array, I recorded the number of statements executed and called that value *ct*. I then did some other calculations which are summarized in Table 2.1.

What I did was guess that the complexity was either $O(n)$, $O(n^2)$, or $O(n^3)$. The last three columns in the table show the ratio of these three functions to *ct*. If we look at the column labeled $\frac{n}{ct}$ we see that as n increases the ratio gets smaller and smaller, closer and closer to zero. This means that *ct* is increasing at a much faster rate than is n so the complexity must be greater than $O(n)$. Of course, this fact is also easily seen by just looking at the first two columns of the table.

Looking at the column labeled $\frac{n^3}{ct}$ we see that this ratio is steadily increasing. This means that *ct* is growing slower than is n^3 so n^3 is too large, that is, the complexity must be less than $O(n^3)$. This, of course, is harder to see by just looking at the first two columns and so explains why I created the last three columns. We are trying to find a function of n that grows at the same rate, to within a constant, as does *ct*. Since we are not interested in constants when calculating the big-oh complexity this means that we will have found the complexity.

n	ct	n/ct	n^2/ct	n^3/ct
5	15	0.333	1.667	8.333
10	55	0.182	1.818	18.182
15	120	0.125	1.875	28.125
20	210	0.095	1.905	38.095
25	325	0.077	1.923	48.077
50	1275	0.039	1.961	98.039
100	5050	0.020	1.980	198.020
150	11325	0.013	1.987	298.013
200	20100	0.010	1.990	398.010
300	45150	0.007	1.993	598.007
400	80200	0.005	1.995	798.005
500	125250	0.004	1.996	998.004
600	180300	0.003	1.997	1198.003
700	245350	0.003	1.997	1398.003
800	320400	0.002	1.998	1598.002

Table 2.1. Empirical Data for Insertion Sort

So, looking at the column labeled $\dfrac{n^2}{ct}$ we see that even though the values are increasing, they are increasing very slowly compared to the third column. In fact, they are stabilizing right around the value 2. This means that ct is growing about half as fast as is n^2. We can conclude that the complexity is around $2n^2$, but since we are not interested in constants, we decide that the complexity is $O(n^2)$.

Looking at the middle column you might be tempted to jump to the conclusion that the complexity is $O(n)$ because the ratio is stabilizing around a constant, namely, 0. However, using the logic of the last paragraph, we conclude that the complexity would be around $0n = 0$, which is nonsense. When calculating big-oh complexities we ignore constants like 2 and 15.3 because we are interested in how the complexity function grows, not in particular values of the function. That is why we treat $2n^2$ and $15.3n^2$ the same. They are both $O(n^2)$. They both get four times larger when n doubles. On the other hand, $0n^2$ is quite a different story. This function never changes. It is always 0, and so we must treat the constant 0 differently. If a column starts homing in on 0, like the third column of our table, this does not mean that the numerator and the denominator are growing at roughly the same rates. What it means is that the numerator is growing much slower than the denominator.

In general, then, the strategy for empirically finding the complexity of an algorithm is to first program it in Pascal, introducing a counter to determine the number of statements being executed. The next step is to run the program on a number of different worst cases, increasing the size of n to a point where the program doesn't take too long to run. The last step is to find the complexity by guessing. You do this by guessing what you think the complexity is and then creating columns in a table like we did above. If a column gets closer and closer to 0 then your guess is too small and you must try a "larger" function, that is, one that grows faster. Conversely, if the column is increasing then you have guessed too big and you must try a smaller function. When your guess gives you a column that stabilizes around some constant that is not zero, then you have found the complexity.

Of course you cannot be sure you have the true complexity this way. For example, by building tables as described above, it would probably be quite difficult to distinguish between complexities like $O(n^{1.1})$, $O(nlogn)$, and $O(nlog^2n)$. But this method will give you a good idea of the basic behavior of the algorithm.

7. SUMMARY

We now have learned the major techniques we will need to calculate the complexity of recursive algorithms. As you have seen, the principle method is a straightforward three step process. The first step is to find the recurrence relation. This is almost always easy to do. All you need to do is to see how much work is done ignoring the recursive calls and then look at each recursive call and determine the size of the problem for each of them. All of this produces an equation in terms of n, the size of the problem.

The second step is to repeatedly substitute the right side of the recurrence relation back into the individual occurences on the right side and look for a pattern. Once the pattern is found the recurrence can be rewritten in a more general form, as we did in this chapter. Finding the pattern that allows the rewriting to take place is often the hardest step. In fact, we will see an example in the exercises where this approach appears to be hopeless. The exercise will suggest a possible way around the problem but the ultimate solution will not appear in this book. Complicated recurrence relations can prove quite challenging to solve and sometimes require techniques that are very sophisticated. You will learn how to solve these more complicated ones in an advanced algorithms class. For most of the examples and problems in this book you should be able to find the pattern and do the rewriting without too much difficulty.

The final step is to take the general form of the recurrence that was produced in the second step and remove all occurrences of the function on the right side of the equation. This step is usually trivial and all that usually remains at this point is a summation to evaluate. These summations can sometimes be challenging, but the ones we have already done in this chapter are the most frequently occurring ones. In later chapters, we will get a few more summations and learn a couple of tricks for evaluating them.

Let's step back and see what we now know. Chapter 1 has given us a feel for how to write recursive algorithms and this chapter has taught us how to determine the efficiency of those algorithms. Meanwhile you've probably been asking yourself, ". . . but how on earth can any programming language be smart enough to allow recursive procedures?" It turns out not to be as hard as you might think, as you will learn in the next chapter.

8. EXERCISES

1. Solve the recurrence relation $T(n) = 3 + n + T(n - 1)$. You should get a different answer than we got when we solved $T(n) = n + T(n - 1)$ but you should end up with the same big-oh complexity. Now, solve the recurrence relation $T(n) = 3 + 5n + T(n - 1)$. Again, the answer should be different but the big-oh complexity should be the same. Finally, solve the recurrence relation $T(n) = a + bn + T(n - 1)$, where a and b are arbitrary constants. Explain the significance of your result.

2. Using the formal definition of big-oh, find five different pairs of constants a and n_0 that prove that $6n^2 + 3n + 8$ is $O(n^2)$. Be sure that a is different in all five answers.

3. Using the formal definition of big-oh, find a couple of different pairs of constants a and n_0 that prove that $6n^2 + 3n + 8$ is $O(n^3)$. This suggests that a complexity function that looks like $an^2 + bn + c$, for any constants a, b, and c is both $O(n^2)$ and $O(n^3)$. If an algorithm has this kind of complexity function, should we call it a $O(n^2)$ algorithm or a $O(n^3)$ algorithm? You might want to look at the next problem before you answer this last question.

4. Using the formal definition of big-oh, prove that $6n^2 + 3n + 8$ is not $O(n)$.

5. In this chapter we explicitly solved the recurrence relations $T(n) = k \times T(\frac{n}{2}) + 1$ for k having the values 1, 2, and 3. The case where $k = 2$ turned out much worse than the case $k = 1$, but $k = 3$ was not so much worse that $k = 2$. Solve this recurrence relation for $k = 4$ and $k = 5$. Find a general solution to this recurrence relation in terms of the variable k. You may still want to treat $k = 1$ as a special case.

6. In Problem 1.14 we discussed the "Towers of Hanoi." What is the complexity of the algorithm suggested in the problem? You should end up with a recurrence relation that has already appeared in this chapter. Now pretend that you are a toy manufacturer and you would like to market some of these toys. By using slips of paper for the disks and circles on a piece of paper to represent the posts, determine how long it will take to solve the problem for small numbers of disks. From this information, determine how long it will take to solve a puzzle with 25 disks. Would this make for a good

puzzle? Assuming the average attention span of potential buyers of this puzzle is about 15 minutes, how many disks should be used in the version that will be sold in the toy stores?

7. Table 2.2 shows the data that have been collected from five different algorithms. These five algorithms have been coded into Pascal and a *count* variable has been introduced in appropriate places to give a good approximation of the number of statements executed whenever the program is run. The programs were then run on various worst case data. Not every spot in the table has an entry because of the way the data were chosen. Based on the counts shown in the table, determine the complexity of the five algorithms.

8. Problem 1.8 suggests an algorithm for finding the nth Fibonacci number. In trying to determine the complexity of this algorithm we see that the recurrence relation is $T(n) = T(n-1) + T(n-2) + 1$. Try solving this recurrence relation. You probably discover that as you start expanding no clear pattern develops. You would like to get the right side of the recurrence relation expressed in terms of just one T, but at least two always seem to want to stick around. Since this recurrence relation is indeed difficult to solve, let's try to get a good approximation of its solution. It is easy to see that if we solve the easier recurrence relation $T_1(n) = T_1(n-1) + T_1(n-1) + 1$, the solution will be larger than the solution for T. Similarly, the solution to $T_2(n) = T_2(n-2) + T_2(n-2) + 1$ will be easier to obtain and will be less than the solution to T. From this conclude that the complexity, T, is worse than $O(1.4^n)$ but better than $O(2^n)$. Notice that $O(1.4^n)$ is still very bad. It means that increasing the size of the problem by 1 increases the running time by a factor of 1.4. Algorithms with complexities of the form $O(k^n)$ all have this terrible property that increasing the problem size by one increases the running time by a factor of k. Algorithms

n	alg 1	alg 2	alg 3	alg 4	alg 5
3	44		30		
4		15	80		
5	76		250	10	25
6			730		
7			2200		
8		20			
9		30			
10	191	35	59000	31	30
15	356		14000000		
20	571	60		89	33
30	1151	100		165	35
50		160		355	
100	10811	300		990	40
200				2821	41
500	254011			11200	47

Table 2.2. Data Collected from Five different Algorithms

of this form are said to have *exponential* time complexity and should be avoided like the plague. Since we have concluded that this algorithm has exponential complexity with a value of k between 1.4 and 2, it should be easy to get a more accurate value by running the program with some fairly large values of n and determining which k fits the data the best. As was suggested in Problem 1.8, it might now be a good time to try to write an iterative program to generate the Fibonacci numbers and compare its complexity.

9. Is 2^n $O(3^n)$? Is 3^n $O(2^n)$? Going back to the definition of big-oh, try to determine what is meant by $2^{O(n)}$. Is 2^n $3^{O(n)}$? Is 3^n $2^{O(n)}$? Try to describe the difference between $O(2^n)$ and $2^{O(n)}$. In particular, which seems to be more useful? When would you use one over the other?

10. Problem 1.6 suggests two slightly different algorithms for multiplying two integers by just doing additions. Since these functions take two independent arguments it is best to express the complexity in terms of both of the arguments. Similarly, the recurrence relations will also have two arguments. For example, the recurrence relation for the first algorithm will look something like $T(a,b) = T(a, b - 1) + 1$. Notice that the solution to this recurrence relation ends up not involving a at all. Write the recurrence relation for the second algorithm and solve it. In expressing your answer you might find it useful to use the function *min*, where $min(x,y)$ is defined to be the smaller of x and y.

3

How It Works

1. THE BATTLE PLAN

By now you are probably impressed by the power of recursive algorithms. Complicated problems can be solved by simple recursive algorithms. But how does it work? How is it possible to use a Pascal procedure inside the same procedure? When a procedure calls itself in two different places, how does Pascal keep track of everything during execution? Why don't things get hopelessly confused when a procedure calls itself in one place and then this procedure calls itself someplace else? These are the questions that we will be answering in this chapter.

In order to understand how recursion works in Pascal we will pretend that Pascal does not allow recursive programs to be written (in fact, there are still programming languages being used that do not allow recursion) and so we will be forced to implement our recursive algorithms in Pascal using the techniques that Pascal itself uses. Did you get that? Let's say it another way. When you execute a recursive procedure or function in Pascal, Pascal must do a lot of bookkeeping so it does not lose track of which recursive procedure it is currently executing, where it was in a previous procedure before the recursive call was made (so it can find its way back), what the values of the variables were before the recursive call was made, etc. Pascal does indeed keep track of all this information, you just never get to see how it is done. You just cheerfully write recursive procedures knowing that Pascal is up to the task. Now let's pretend Pascal suddenly got stupid. Pascal is no longer able to keep track of all the information that must be kept track of to allow for recursion. You are no longer allowed to make a recursive call in Pascal. But you still want to implement recursive algorithms using this terribly handicapped Pascal. We must use the features of Pascal that remain to implement our recursive algorithms. The way we will do this will be similar to what Pascal actually does when running recursive Pascal procedures and functions you have written.

2. STACKS

The first and most important step in learning how recursion is implemented is to understand the data structure known as the *stack*. As with all data structures you can't fully understand what a stack is until you know the operations that can be performed on a stack. The operations are *push, pop, top, empty,* and *init.* These operations do things like look at the current status of a stack or add or remove elements from a stack. These elements can be simple data types like integers or characters, or more complicated structures like records, sets, or even other stacks. A stack can only be comprised of one type of element. You may have a stack of integers or a stack of some other type but you cannot have a stack with some integers and some sets. For this reason, to make it clear exactly what sort of elements comprise the stack we often say things like "a stack of integers" or "a stack of records."

More specifically, the different stack operations work as follows. Push is a procedure which modifies a stack. It takes an element and adds it to the "top" of the stack. Conversely, pop is a procedure that modifies a stack by removing the last element that was pushed onto the stack. You now begin to see why the data structure is called a stack. Conceptually, push piles things up on a stack and pop takes things off a stack. For example, a stack of magazines on the floor is a good model for the computer science stack I'm describing. Push places another magazine on the stack. The more magazines you push on the stack, the taller the stack becomes. Pop, on the other hand, removes the magazine from the top. Clearly, the last magazine that was placed (pushed) on the stack is the first one removed (popped).

The top operation does not affect the stack at all. It is a function which simply returns the top value of the stack. Continuing with our magazine analogy, performing the top function is like telling your friend which magazine is currently on top of your pile of magazines. The empty operation is also a function which does not affect the stack. This is a boolean function which simply determines if there is anything on the stack or not. Its main function is to prevent you from accidentally trying to do something that should not be done to an empty stack, though we will see other uses for it shortly. For example, taking the top of an empty stack is certainly a mistake so unless you are sure the stack is not empty it is often wise to use the empty function before trying to find the top of the stack.

The last operation that can be performed on stacks is called init, which is short for initialize. Typically, it is used only one time for a stack. Its purpose is to prepare a stack for use. It modifies the stack so that it is empty. It is like finding a clear spot on the floor to start piling magazines; a spot that isn't already cluttered with magazines. Once you've staked out the spot for the stack of magazines there should never be a need to do it again. Even if the stack becomes empty the space is still there. So it is with our stacks. One call to init at the beginning of the program should suffice.

2.1. Balanced Parentheses

Before we see why stacks are so useful for implementing recursive algorithms let's look at a simple problem that has an elegant solution using stacks. A string composed of the six characters (, [, {,),], and } is said to be balanced if every left-sided parenthesis has a corresponding right parenthesis appearing later in the string, no right parenthesis appears before a corresponding left one, and the parenthesis are properly nested. For example, the following strings are balanced: {()}, [{()}}[]], (); while none of the following is balanced: (}, ()][, ([]{[])}, (()). Our task is to develop an algorithm that will read strings composed only of the six given characters and will report whether the string is balanced or not. Try to think of an algorithm that does not use stacks to solve this problem. It is not easy. Now try to think of an algorithm that does use stacks.

An algorithm using stacks is straightforward. Every time a left parenthesis of any kind is input, push it on the stack. If a right parenthesis is input, examine the element on top of the stack. If it is the corresponding left one, pop it off. It is clear that this algorithm will correctly recognize balanced strings. How will it report strings that are not balanced? First of all, if all the input has been read and the stack is not empty then some left parenthesis never saw its corresponding right parenthesis so the input is not balanced. Similarly, if the stack is empty and a right parenthesis is seen, then a corresponding left parenthesis has not been read, else it would still be on the stack, so this string is not balanced. Finally, if the top of the stack does not properly match the right parenthesis (as discussed before) then the nesting is not right and again the string is not balanced. Let's assume that stacks have been implemented for us already in Pascal and see what the program looks like. You will be able to figure out exactly how many arguments each stack function and procedure takes and what types they are by looking at how they are used in this function (Figure 3.1). We will implement stacks soon and discuss these issues in more detail then.

```
function balanced : boolean;

{ There are no arguments to this function because we will }
{ assume it gets the string by reading input. Also, we     }
{ assume all input will be one of the six parenthesis.     }
{ This function does not check for illegal characters.     }

var s : stack of char;    { Pretend this is legal }
    ch : char;
    result : boolean;
begin
    init(s);
    result := true;              { assume balanced and try }
                                 { to prove otherwise        }
    while (not eoln) and result do begin { data remains and }
                      { haven't proven not balanced yet }
        read (ch);
        if ch in [ '[', '{', '(' ] then      { is it a left paren? }
            push(ch, s)
        else                          { it must be a right paren }
            if empty(s) then
                result := false; { No matching left parenthesis }
            else
                case ch of
                    ')' : if top(s)  =  '(' then
                             pop(s)
                          else
                             result :=  false { Improper nesting }
                    ']' : if top(s)  =  '[' then
                             pop(s)
                          else
                             result :=  false { Improper nesting }
                    '}' : if top(s)  =  '{' then
                             pop(s)
                          else
                             result :=  false { Improper nesting }
                end
    end;
    if empty(s) and result then
        balanced := true   { could not prove otherwise }
    else
        balanced := false { either already shown not to be }
                          { balanced or missing right paren }
end;
```

Figure 3.1. A Pascal Function That Uses Stacks

3. THE BASIC METHOD

Now that you see how stacks work, how do you think they help us to implement recursion? The basic idea is simple to state, though the details can get a bit tedious. In a nutshell, every time a recursive call is made, store the current program status on the stack. The current status includes things like the values of local variables and which statement the procedure is currently executing. Next, set the values of the parameters to be passed to the recursive procedure. Then branch to the top of the procedure as if to start up a new recursive call. Whenever we would return from a recursive call, get the pertinent information off the top of the stack, which amounts to restoring the former status of the program and then resume executing where it left off. That's basically it. Every time you call the procedure, push; every time you return, pop. Intuitively this makes a lot of sense. Whenever the program returns from a recursive procedure call it wants to return to the most recently active procedure, the one that made the procedure call. Since the statuses are saved on a stack the last procedure status that was placed on the stack will be the first one restored.

Before we look at an example, let's discuss in a little more detail exactly what needs to go on the stack. We need to put enough information on the stack so that when we return to the procedure after having made a recursive call we can resume execution of this procedure as if we had never left it. But the recursive call probably changed a lot of things. These things that might change must be put on the stack before they are changed so that when we return from the call the original values can be recovered. As mentioned earlier, we certainly need to put the values of the local variables onto the stack. This is because when we simulate a recursive call we will be using the same local variables in the next and subsequent incarnations of the recursive procedure and the values of these variables are likely to be different and changeable. We need to be able to recover the current values of these variables when we return from the recursive calls.

By this reasoning we see that not only the variables that are declared locally in the procedure need to be saved, but also the values of the formal parameters, that is, the actual parameters. When making recursive calls we know that some values passed to the procedure will be changing (otherwise the problem won't be getting easier) so again we must recover the original values of the parameters when we return from the recursive call.

Besides the values of the parameters and the local variables, there is one more thing that determines the current status and so needs to be saved on the stack. We also need to remember where we are in the procedure. Certainly we know we are about to make a recursive call so we need to return to the point immediately following this call. Of course, if there is only one recursive call in the procedure we know that when we return from a recursive call it must be to the statement following that recursive call.

However, if there is more than one recursive call in the procedure we must remember which recursive call was made so that we can return to the proper place. So, we will save some kind of marker on the stack that will remind us exactly where we should return. You will see the details shortly.

3.1. An Example — Output An Array

It's now time to look at an example. Reproduced below is Figure 1.15 (3.2), one of the recursive procedures that outputs an array.

Our rules for simulating recursion are simple, so let's follow them to the letter. As we come to understand the rules better we will see shortcuts and simplifications. We first notice that the stack will have to store five different items: the only local variable, *mid;* the values of the three formal parameters, *nums, left*, and *right;* and which recursive call is being made. We will store this last item on the stack as either a 1 or a 2, depending on whether we are at the first or second recursive call. The best way to keep track of all of this is in a record, so we will define a record to contain exactly those types we just described and then we will define our stack to be a stack of those records. You might want to peek ahead to see this.

We are going to have to introduce some *GOTOs* and labels in our program so that we may simulate the process of starting up a new recursive procedure (i.e., *GOTO* the top) and returning from a procedure (i.e., *GOTO* where we left off last time). Also, we are going to have to somehow recognize the difference between a simulated return from a recursive call and a honest to goodness return from the entire procedure back to the main

```
procedure out_array(nums : array_type; left, right : integer);
var mid : integer;
begin
   if left > right then      {easiest case — an empty array}
                             {nothing to do                 }
   else begin
       mid := (left + right) div 2; {find the middle of the array}
       out_array(nums, left, mid − 1);
           { output the left half of the array }
       write(nums[mid]);
           { output the middle element }
       out_array(nums, mid + 1, right)
           { output the right half of the array }
       end
end;
```

Figure 3.2. Figure 1.15 Again

program. This turns out to be easy. If the stack is empty, then this means that there are no suspended procedures waiting to be resumed, so it means that it is time to return to the main program. If there is still something on the stack, then it must be the status of some previous call to this procedure so we must return to it before we return to the main program.

Recall that we said that before we actually branch to the top of the procedure we must set the values of the parameters. Since there are three formal parameters, we will play it safe for now and set all three of them. We know what values to set them to by looking at the recursive call that we are replacing. The first argument in the recursive call gets assigned to the first formal parameter, the second to the second, etc. We might get some silly looking statements, but for now we are blindly following the rules. We incorporate all of the above ideas into the nonrecursive version seen below (Figure 3.3).

3.2. Implementation of Stacks

We need to do one more thing to finish this example. We need to implement stacks. There are certainly many ways to do this, but one of the most straightforward is to use an array and a pointer into the array. The array will store the stack elements and the pointer will point to the top of the stack. We will put both of these items into one record since the stack must have both and neither makes sense without the other. Since we are using an array we can only fit so many elements into it. As a result we have added one more stack function called *full*. Full reports whether or not there is room in the stack (implemented as an array) for more elements. The other functions and procedures operate as described before.

In case an error occurs, like trying to pop from an empty stack or trying to push onto a full stack we output an error message and call the procedure *halt*. Though not standard Pascal, its meaning should be clear and it is provided by most Pascal compilers. *Halt* has the effect of stopping the entire program at the point it is called. Nothing else happens after a *halt* is encountered. It is a reasonable thing to do here. If, for example, you try to push onto a full stack, there will be no room for the element being pushed so your program can no longer be expected to behave properly. If you continued executing, you may not get an error immediately, but sooner or later something would have to go wrong. After all, something that was supposed to be on the stack isn't. Why wait for disaster? Immediately report the error so the user will know exactly what went wrong.

3.3. The Finished Example

We have chosen to put the entire implementation of stacks inside the procedure *out_array*. The reason is that these particular stacks are not

```
procedure out_array(nums : array_type; left, right : integer);
label start, 1, 2;
type saver    = record                 {-------------------------------------}
           mid, left, right : integer;  {-- the record which --}
           nums : array_type;           {--    saves all the   --}
           returnpt : 1 .. 2;           {--   local variables  --}
           end;                         {-------------------------------------}
var mid : integer;
      tempholder : saver;
      s : stack of saver; {-- pretend this is legal for now --}
begin
      init(s);            {-- initialize the stack, one time only --}
start:
      if left > right then      {easiest case--an empty array}
                                {nothing to do               }
      else begin
         mid := (left + right) div 2; {find the middle of the array}
         tempholder.mid := mid;        {-------------------------------------------}
         tempholder.nums := nums;      {----   save everything   ----}
         tempholder.left := left;      {----        on the       ----}
         tempholder.right := right;    {----        stack        ----}
         tempholder.returnpt := 1;     {----                     ----}
         push(tempholder, s);          {-------------------------------------------}
         nums := nums;                 {--- assign the three ---}
         left := left;                 {--- formal parameters ---}
         right := mid − 1;             {-------------------------------------------}
         goto start;                   {--- begin executing recursively ---}
         {out_array(nums, left, mid − 1);-- the way it used to be }

1:       { output the left half of the array }
         write(nums[mid]:3);
         { output the middle element }
         tempholder.mid := mid;        {-------------------------------------------}
         tempholder.nums := nums;      {----   save everything   ----}
         tempholder.left := left;      {----        on the       ----}
         tempholder.right := right;    {----        stack        ----}
         tempholder.returnpt := 2;     {----                     ----}
         push(tempholder, s);          {-------------------------------------------}
         nums := nums;                 {--- assign the three ---}
         left := mid + 1;              {--- formal parameters ---}
         right := right;               {-------------------------------------------}
         goto start;                   {--- begin executing recursively ---}
```

Figure 3.3. Removing Recursion From Figure 1.15

```
            {out_array(nums, mid + 1, right);-- the way it used to be}

2:          { output the right half of the array }
            end;
        if empty(s) then
            { No recursive calls pending. Return. }
        else begin
            top(s, tempholder);            {----------------------------------}
            pop(s);                        {--    recover the      --}
            mid := tempholder.mid;         {--    status of the    --}
            nums := tempholder.nums;       {--    procedure that   --}
            left := tempholder.left;       {--    called this one  --}
            right := tempholder.right;     {----------------------------------}
            if tempholder.returnpt=1 then  {--    decide where     --}
                goto 1                     {--    to resume        --}
            else                           {--      executing      --}
                goto 2                     {----------------------------------}
            end
end;
```

Figure 3.3. (Continued)

going to be useful anywhere else. Only this procedure will be using them. It is usually wise to define your procedures and functions within the structure that will be using them. Otherwise, someone else reading your program might get the wrong idea (e.g., if stacks were declared globally one would be likely to jump to the conclusion that stacks are being used by a number of subsequent procedures or functions). You may want to take another peek ahead to see the details of the implementation, but before we display the final version of the procedure, let's discuss a few ways to clean it up.

First, we notice that where we assigned the formal parameters, they often already had the correct values. If this is the case, there is no need to reassign them with the same value. This has the side benefit of removing the statements *nums := nums* which are not standard Pascal because standard Pascal does not allow the assignment of one array to another in one statement—a loop must be used. In fact, notice that the variable *nums* never changes so there is really no need to put it on the stack at all. Remember, the point of the stack is to save the values of the local variables. But if *nums* never changes it will always have the same value, so there is no need to save it. This has the same side benefit of removing statements like *nums :=* *tempholder.nums* which are also not standard Pascal for the same reason.

In a similar vein, we notice that the variable *left* is never used after the first recursive call. You can see this most convincingly by looking at the original recursive procedure. If we never need it again, why save it? So, we can remove it from the stack as well. After implementing stacks (containing only the information really needed) and making the other changes just suggested, the final version of the recursive algorithm implemented without using Pascal's recursion looks like Figure 3.4.

4. RECURSIVE FUNCTIONS

Recursive functions work very much like recursive procedures only a little more work is necessary to see that the proper value is ultimately returned by the function. What we must do is introduce another local variable to store the result of the function call so that when we return from the function we can use that variable in the place where the recursive function would have appeared. Let's look at an example. Rather than use the same old functions we've been looking at until now, let's look at something new. In the exercises to Chapter 1, we looked at a couple of ways to recursively multiply two integers. Here is another. For the sake of this example only whenever I write $\frac{a}{2}$ I will mean integer division, that is, if a is odd we lose the fractional part. This, of course, is exactly how Pascal's *div* works. We can now define $a \times b$ recursively as follows: if a is odd then $a \times b = \frac{a}{2} \times b + \frac{a}{2} \times b + b$; if a is even then $a \times b = \frac{a}{2} \times b + \frac{a}{2} \times b$. Of course the easiest case is when $a = 0$. Using this idea we come up with the following Pascal function (Figure 3.5):

You probably expected the first two lines in the *else* (where *total* is assigned twice) to be written a little differently. You will soon see that it is harder to deal with two recursive calls on the same line, so for the sake of a clear example it is broken up into two lines. You also might object that the second recursive call is unnecessary and therefore, is probably doing nasty things to the complexity. Again, I plead guilty and ask you to tolerate an inefficient algorithm for the sake of a nice example.

To write this without using recursion in Pascal, we proceed as we did in the last example, except now we introduce another variable called *result* that will return the value of a recursive call to *mult*. The idea is that whenever we return from a recursive call we can assume that the variable *result* has the result of the recursive call, so we can use that variable wherever we previously had the recursive call. In this case, this means that in any statement before a recursive call we simulate a recursive call as we did for procedures, then use *result* where we previously used the recursive call itself.

Recall that, ordinarily, the result of the function is assigned into the name

```
procedure out_array(nums : array_type; left, right : integer);
label start, 1, 2;
type saver = record              {--------------------------------------}
        mid, right : integer;    {--   record saving    --}
        returnpt : 1 .. 2;       {--   local variables   --}
        end;                     {--------------------------------------}
    stack = record               {-- define the stack --}
        item : array[1..max_stack] of saver;
        toppt : integer
        end;
var mid : integer;
    tempholder : saver;
    s : stack;
procedure init(var s : stack);   {--  If the stack's toppt is   --}
begin                            {-- 0 then the stack is empty. --}
    s.toppt := 0                 {-- No need to clear out the --}
end;                             {--          item array.        --}
function empty(s : stack) : boolean;
begin                            {-- If the toppt is 0 then --}
    empty := s.toppt = 0         {--   the stack is empty,   --}
end;                             {--   otherwise, it's not   --}
function full(s : stack) : boolean;
begin
    full := s.toppt = max_stack {-- same idea as empty --}
end;
procedure push(data : saver; var s : stack);
begin
    if full(s) then begin
        writeln('Pushing onto a full stack!');
        halt
        end
    else with s do begin
        toppt := toppt + 1;
        item[toppt] := data
        end
end;
procedure top(s : stack; var data : saver);
begin
    if empty(s) then begin
        writeln('Trying to top an empty stack!');
        halt
        end
```

(continued on next page)

Figure 3.4.   The Final Version with Recursion Removed

```
        else
            data := s.item[s.toppt]
end;
procedure pop(var s : stack);
begin
    if empty(s) then begin
        writeln('Trying to pop an empty stack!');
        halt
        end
    else
        s.toppt := s.toppt - 1
end;
begin
    init(s);              {-- initialize the stack, one time only --}
start:
    if left > right then        {easiest case — an empty array}
                                {nothing to do               }
    else begin
        mid := (left + right) div 2; {find the middle of the array}
        tempholder.mid := mid;      {--------------------------------------}
        tempholder.right := right;  {-- save needed local --}
        tempholder.returnpt := 1;   {-- variables on stack --}
        push(tempholder, s);        {--------------------------------------}
        right := mid - 1; {-- set formal param that changes --}
        goto start;          {--- begin executing recursively ---}
        {out_array(nums, left, mid − 1);-- the way it used to be}

1:              { output the left half of the array }
        write(nums[mid]:3);
            { output the middle element }
        tempholder.mid := mid;      {--------------------------------------}
        tempholder.right := right;  {-- save needed local --}
        tempholder.returnpt := 2;   {-- variables on stack --}
        push(tempholder, s);        {--------------------------------------}
        left := mid + 1; {-- set formal param that changes --}
        goto start;          {--- begin executing recursively ---}
        {out_array(nums, mid + 1, right);-- the way it used to be}

2:              { output the right half of the array }
        end;
    if empty(s) then
        { No recursive calls pending. Return. }
    else begin
```

Figure 3.4. (Continued on next page)

```
        top(s, tempholder);              {-----------------------------------}
        pop(s);                          {--      recover the       --}
        mid := tempholder.mid;           {--           status       --}
        right := tempholder.right;       {-----------------------------------}
        if tempholder.returnpt=1 then    {-- decide where --}
            goto 1                       {--   to resume  --}
        else                             {--   executing  --}
            goto 2                       {-----------------------------------}
        end
end;
```

Figure 3.4.   (Continued)

of the function, in this case *mult*. So now wherever we used to assign to
mult , we assign to the variable *result* instead. This will guarantee that when
we simulate the return from the recursive call, *result* will have the value the
function was supposed to return. All that remains is to decide when to
assign to *mult*. We only want to do this when we are returning back to the
main program, in other words, when the stack is empty. All of this can now
be seen in the finished product (Figure 3.6).

In this example we notice that *arg2* never changes. We pointed out earlier
that if a parameter never changes from one recursive call to the next we
don't have to bother saving it on the stack. After a recursive call has
completed, the stack allows the program to recover the status it had before
the recursive call had been made. If a local variable or a parameter never

```
function mult(arg1, arg2 : integer) : integer;
var total : integer;
begin
    if arg1 = 0 then
        mult := 0
    else begin
        total := mult(arg1 div 2, arg2);
        total := mult(arg1 div 2, arg2) + total;
        if odd(arg1) then
            mult := total + arg2
        else
            mult := total
        end
end;
```

Figure 3.5.   A Pascal Function to Multiply Integers

```pascal
function mult(arg1, arg2 : integer) : integer;
type
    saver  =  record                    {-- The record              --}
        total, arg1, arg2 : integer;     {-- containing all of       --}
        returnpt : char;                 {-- the local information --}
        end;
    stack  =  record
        item : array[1..100] of saver;
        toppt : integer
        end;
label start, a, b;
var total, result : integer;
    tempholder : saver;
    s : stack;
{------------------------------------------------------------------}
{-- The actual implementations of the --}
{-- stack operations are exactly as    --}
{-- before, so they have been omitted  --}
{-- to cut down on the clutter.        --}
{------------------------------------------------------------------}
begin
    init(s);                            {-- Initialize the stack once --}
start:
    if arg1 = 0 then
        {mult} result := 0
    else begin
        tempholder.total := total;      {-----------------------------------------}
        tempholder.arg1 := arg1;        {--                                     --}
        tempholder.arg2 := arg2;        {-- Save the current       --}
        tempholder.returnpt := 'a';     {-- status and simulate --}
        push(tempholder, s);            {-- a recursive call       --}
        arg1 := arg1 div 2;             {--                                     --}
        goto start;                     {-----------------------------------------}
a:      total := {mult(arg1 div 2, arg2)} result;
        tempholder.total := total;      {-----------------------------------------}
        tempholder.arg1 := arg1;        {--                                     --}
        tempholder.arg2 := arg2;        {-- Save the current       --}
        tempholder.returnpt := 'b';     {-- status and simulate --}
        push(tempholder, s);            {-- a recursive call       --}
        arg1 := arg1 div 2;             {--                                     --}
        goto start;                     {-----------------------------------------}
b:      total := {mult(arg1 div 2, arg2)} result + total;
        if odd(arg1) then
```

Figure 3.6. A Pascal Function to Multiply Integers with Recursion Removed (continued on next page)

```
            {mult} result := total + arg2
        else
            {mult} result := total
        end;
    if empty(s) then        {-- Stack is empty, so return --}
        mult := result   {-- to the calling program      --}
    else begin
        top(s, tempholder);                 {-------------------------------}
        pop(s);                             {--                           --}
        arg1 := tempholder.arg1;            {-- Retrieve old   --}
        arg2 := tempholder.arg2;            {-- status and     --}
        total := tempholder.total;          {-- return to      --}
        if tempholder.returnpt = 'a' then   {-- previous       --}
            goto a                          {-- recursive call --}
        else                                {--                --}
            goto b                          {-------------------------------}
        end
end;
```

Figure 3.6. (Continued)

changes it won't be forgotten so there is no need to save it. This means that in this example we didn't have to have *arg2* in the record which gets pushed on the stack. You might want to convince yourself that this is true by actually making the change and running the program. We did this same sort of thing in the previous example.

5. TAIL RECURSION

There is a special case where the stack may be eliminated entirely. This occurs when there is only one recursive call in a procedure and it is the last statement in the procedure. Recursive procedures that look like this are called *tail-recursive*. Since nothing else happens after the recursive call, there is no need to remember anything. To remove the recursion, simply set the formal parameters and *GOTO* the start of the procedure. Since we don't need the stack we won't need to do any popping or pushing. Let's look at a simple example. One of our procedures for outputting an array looked like Figure 3.7.

To remove the recursion from this procedure, at the point of the recursive call we simply set the formal parameters (notice only one needs to be set since the other two don't change) and branch to the top of the procedure. It will look like Figure 3.8.

```
procedure out_array( nums : array_type; left, right : integer);
begin
    if left > right then {there are no elements in the array}
        { so there is nothing to do }
    else begin
        write(nums[left]);              {output the first element}
        out_array(nums, left + 1, right)   {output the rest}
    end                                 { of the array  }
end;
```

Figure 3.7.   The Output Procedure of Figure 1.11

```
procedure out_array( nums : array_type; left, right : integer);
label 1;
begin
1: if left > right then {there are no elements in the array}
        { so there is nothing to do }
    else begin
        write(nums[left]);              {output the first element}
        left := left + 1;                 {output the rest}
        goto 1                          { of the array  }
        end
end;
```

Figure 3.8.   The Output Procedure of Figure 1.11 with Recursion Removed

But now that the stacks are gone and there is only one *GOTO* statement, it is easy to tidy this procedure up even more. First you can flip the sense of the *if* so that an *if-then* without an *else* is created. After doing that, you will be left with something that looks a lot like a *for* loop. Writing it that way you will discover that you have created the natural iterative algorithm. This is typical of what happens when recursion is removed from a tail-recursive procedure.

It should be noted that functions are never tail-recursive. This is because by their very nature functions expect something to happen *after* they have been called. Since a function returns a value, it is expected that that value is going to be used and so it will be used after the function is called. This means that the function call cannot be the very last thing done in the function and so the function cannot be tail-recursive.

6. SUMMARY

We hope that this chapter has shown you that recursion is really not all that mystical and, in fact, works in a fairly simple way. We will occasionally find it useful knowing how recursion works because it helps us describe the workings of some of our algorithms. For example, to explain some algorithms we need to have an idea of how deeply nested our recursive calls have become. This idea does not fit neatly into our simple scheme of taking a hard problem and making it easier. However, now we know exactly what that means. Also, it sometimes helps to be able to discuss various invocations of a recursive procedure, for example, we might need to talk about the currently active procedure as well as the inactive procedure that called the one that is active. If you understand what we did in this chapter, these sort of ideas should be quite simple for you now.

In order to discuss the workings of recursion we had to use stacks. The beginning of this chapter hinted at an important fact: stacks are ubiquitous in computer science. You will find stacks not only useful for solving the kind of problem we discussed in the second section and for implementing recursion, but also for many other interesting applications whose list is too long to even consider trying to write. Stacks are also important in more theoretical areas of computer science. For example, a discussion of how stacks can rearrange objects leads to the important Catalan numbers and an abstract computing device called a *push-down automaton* that has been heavily studied the last few decades is based on stacks. So, stacks are more than just a simple little data structure for solving little toy problems and for implementing recursion.

Having made it through these three chapters you may now consider yourself a amateur recursive programmer. You know the basic rules for creating recursive algorithms, you know how efficient your algorithms are, and you know how they work. You have all the basics under your belt. It is now time to become a professional. Recursion is useful for solving an incredible variety of problems. The next chapter will focus on problems dealing with dynamic data structures like linked lists and trees. The final chapter will look at a variety of different kinds of problems. These two chapters will teach you the true power of recursion and help you make the transition from amateur to professional.

7. EXERCISES

1. By this time we have seen many recursive algorithms, especially in Chapter 1 and the exercises for Chapter 1. Take a few of your favorites and rewrite them in Pascal without using recursion but using the techniques

developed in this chapter. Do not try to find new, nonrecursive algorithms. You should implement the original recursive algorithm. The point of this problem is to show that you can simulate recursion using Pascal.

2. Suppose we first code a recursive algorithm directly into Pascal and then code it into Pascal without using recursion directly but by simulating it using the techniques of this chapter. How do the complexities compare between the two implementations?

3. What is the complexity of the multiplication algorithm seen in this chapter? It was pointed out that the algorithm was intentionally inefficient so that the mechanisms of recursion could be better demonstrated. Improve the algorithm and analyze the complexity of the improved algorithm.

4. It was pointed out in the chapter that the stack used in the multiplication example contained some unnecessary elements. Remove all unnecessary elements from the stack and run the program to show that it still works correctly. Now return to the programs you wrote for Exercise 1 above and make the stacks there as small as you can. Remember that if there is only one recursive call there will be no need to save the current location of execution since there is only one place a recursive call could be made. Compare running times of the two versions to see how much faster the program runs with the smaller stack. Has the big-oh time complexity improved? Pay attention to tail recursion so that you can completely remove the stack when appropriate.

4

Dynamic Data Structures

1. LINKED LISTS

Algorithms that work on dynamic data types are often recursive because most dynamic types are themselves defined recursively. For example, in the first part of this chapter we will be working with linked lists. A linked list, by definition, is an element (of the list) followed by a smaller list. Clearly, this is a recursive definition. As a result, you would have to expect many algorithms to take advantage of this recursive structure. In fact, the vast majority of the algorithms on linked lists that we will be looking at will use this intuitive recursive definition. These algorithms will first do something to the first element of the list and will then recursively work on the remaining smaller list.

Let's begin by recalling the basics of Pascal linked lists. For the sake of most examples in this chapter we will assume we have linked lists of integers. This will mean that our linked lists will be typed like the following.

```
type nodeptr = ^node;

    node = record
        item : integer;
        next : nodeptr
        end;
```

The lists themselves will be variables of type *nodeptr*. This means that what we call a list is actually a pointer to a node which contains two things: the first element of the list and a pointer to the rest of the list. The smallest list is a list with no elements and so is a pointer which points to nothing. In Pascal this is denoted as *nil*. For example, to test if a list is empty, or put another way, to test if a pointer points to the empty list you would write a statement like

if pt = nil then ... ,

where *pt* is declared of type *nodeptr*. Also recall that to get new nodes in Pascal the procedure *new* is used. For example, the statement *new(pt)* is like an assignment statement to *pt*. Whatever value *pt* used to have is lost and it now points to a brand new record of type *node*. Each call to *new* provides a new record that has never before been used in the program. This means that the more calls to *new* that are made, the more memory is used. Of course the big advantage is that *new* need not be called until the record is actually needed. This is in contrast with arrays where the size of the array is fixed before the program begins execution.

1.1. A Simple Example – Counting

Let's begin by looking at a simple example. Let's write a function to count the number of elements in a linked list. The algorithm is straightforward. The number of elements is 1 plus the number of elements in the smaller list pointed to by the first element's pointer. The empty list has no elements. In pseudocode, it looks something like Figure 4.1.

This is trivial to implement in Pascal. (See Figure 4.2.) Recall that *list^.next* is the list excluding the first element; the tail of the list; the "rest" of the list.

What is the complexity of this function? First of all, the size of a linked list is best measured by counting the number of elements in the list. In other words, a list with n elements has size n. So, in this case, we notice that the function does a constant amount of work and makes one recursive call to a list one smaller than the original list. So, the recurrence relation is $T(n) = 1 + T(n - 1)$. We have see this one before but even if you hadn't it is easy to solve. We conclude that the complexity of this algorithm is $O(n)$. This is intuitively satisfying since you would not expect such a simple problem to take any longer than that. Had we come up with a larger complexity we would have been obliged to at least try to find a more efficient algorithm.

---

if the list is empty then
    the count is 0
else
        the count is 1 + the number of elements in the tail (the rest of the list)

Figure 4.1. Pseudo-code for Counting the Elements in a Linked List

```
function count(list : nodeptr) : integer;
begin
    if list = nil then          { the empty list has no elements }
        count := 0
    else
        count := 1 + count(list^.next)
end;
```

Figure 4.2.   Pascal Function for Counting the Elements in a Linked List

On the other hand, we cannot expect to do any better that $O(n)$ since we cannot know how many elements are on a list until we have visited every element, and there are n elements.

1.2. Output a Linked List

We should look at a few more easy examples before we proceed to some more challenging ones. In the spirit of Chapter 1, we should be sure we can output a linked list. We can pretty much just steal one of the algorithms from Chapter 1 that worked on arrays. But we must be a little careful. The only algorithms we can steal are those that made the problem easier by first working on the first element and then working on the rest of the array. This is due to the way linked lists are built. An algorithm that cuts an array into two halves is not much use to us with linked lists because, in general, it is too much trouble finding the middle of a linked list. So, the basic algorithm must look like this. First, output the first element of the linked list, then output the rest of the list. An empty list has nothing to output, so nothing needs to be done. The procedure looks like Figure 4.3.

Clearly, the complexity of this procedure is $O(n)$. The recurrence relation for this algorithm is the same as the one for the last one.

How hard is it to output a linked list backwards? At first you might be tempted to say that it is hard because the first element you must output is

```
procedure out_list(list : nodeptr);
begin
    if list = nil then        { nothing to do }
    else begin
        write(list^item);          { output the first element }
        out_list(list^next)        { output the rest of the list }
        end
end;
```

Figure 4.3.   Pascal Procedure to Output a Linked List

at the end of the list, and you must proceed backwards from there. If this is what you decided, you still are not thinking recursively. We had a discussion similar to this in the first chapter. To output the list backwards, first, output the rest of the list backwards and then output the first element. You might want to review that part of Chapter 1 to convince yourself that it is a good algorithm and that it applies equally well to arrays and linked lists. Notice how easy it is to implement in Pascal (Figure 4.4).

1.3. Tougher Examples – Tail Insert and Tail Delete

Now let's try something a little harder. Suppose we want to add an element to a linked list. There are two natural places on the list to do this. Depending on the application you may want to add the element to the front or head of the list, or you may want to add the element to the end or tail of the list. There is a simple $O(1)$ algorithm to add an element to the front of a list (find it) so let's discuss how we might add an element to the end of a linked list.

This algorithm will look simple, but don't be fooled. It will, in fact, use recursion in a very clever way. Before you read on, I encourage you to first try to find the algorithm on your own. If you are unable to come up with the algorithm, don't give up and just read my solution. Read the first part of my solution, then sit down and try to fill in the details. Read just enough about my algorithm so that you can finish it on your own and then compare yours with mine. You will get much more out of this discussion, and future discussions, if you think about the algorithms before reading my solution. You will get more out of my solutions that way and you may find better ones.

Adding to the tail of an existing linked list just modifies the list. It does not require anything to be returned, so we should write a procedure rather than a function. What information needs to be passed to this procedure? Again, it would depend on the actual application but let's assume that, in this case, it makes sense to pass to the procedure the linked list and the integer to be added on to the list. Do any of the parameters need to be *var* parameters? Intuitively, since the list is changing you would expect that it

```
procedure out_back(list : nodeptr);
begin
    if list = nil then        { nothing to do }
    else begin
        out_back(list^.next)      { output backwards the rest }
        write(list^.item);        { output the first element }
        end
end;
```

Figure 4.4. Pascal Procedure to Output a Linked List Backwards

should be *var*. As we continue evolving this algorithm you should be thinking about whether or not it must be *var* or not. Of course the integer being added to the end of the list should not be *var*.

The algorithm can be stated quite simply. To insert an integer at the tail of a list, insert it at the tail of the smaller list pointed to by the first node of the list. The easiest case is inserting the integer into an empty list. In this case a new node must be created and the integer must be placed into this node. Figure 4.5 shows the Pascal version.

Did you notice how we used *list?* There was no need to create another local variable. The statement *new(list)* made *list* point to a new node and the next two statements simply filled in the proper values for that node. This means that the list that used to be an empty list is now a one-element list with the proper integer for its *item*.

But can it really be this simple? (Yes.) Even though this procedure does seem to capture the spirit of the algorithm as described in English, which list really gets changed in the easiest case? Do we actually wipe out the original list and always end up with a one-element list? (No.) Does the original list actually change at all? (Yes.)

To see that this does work properly, let's look at a few examples. First, suppose that a call to the procedure is made from the main program that looks like this: *tail_insert(ptr, 8)* and further suppose that *ptr* is an empty list, that is, *ptr* has the value *nil*. In the procedure, *list* will have the value *nil* and since it is a *var* parameter any change to *list* will actually change *ptr*. This means that when *list* ends up pointing to a new node and this node gets filled with the appropriate values, creating a one-element list, all of this will really be happening to *ptr*, so *ptr* will end up pointing to the correct one-element list so *tail_insert* does work properly when passed an empty list.

Now suppose that *ptr* is already a one element list and the call *tail_insert(ptr, num)* is made. In this case *list* will not be *nil* because it points

```
    procedure tail_insert(var list : nodeptr; num : integer);
    begin
        if list = nil then begin              { easiest case }
            new(list);
            list^.item := num;
            list^.next := nil
            end
        else
            tail_insert(list^.next, num)
    end;
```

Figure 4.5. Pascal Procedure to Insert at the Tail of a Linked List

to a nonempty list, so the recursive call will be made. In this second incarnation of *tail_insert* we must be careful to understand exactly what *list* is. Since *list* is a *var* parameter, we must see what argument was passed into *tail_insert* because this is what *list* really is. Looking at the recursive call we see that the argument being passed in is *list^.next*. This means that any reference to *list* in this second incarnation is really referring to *list^.next* in the first incarnation. Since we started with a one element list, we know that this value is *nil*. So, we will be dealing with the easiest case and the second *list* will end up pointing to a new one element list. But recall that *list,* being a *var* parameter, is really the previous *list^.next* so, in fact, this is the pointer that will end up pointing to the new one-element list and this is precisely the pointer we want. The Figure 4.6 demonstrates the continuation of this reasoning on a two element list.

You should now be able to convince yourself that this procedure does indeed work for linked lists of any size. It should also be clear that the recurrence relation for this procedure is $T(n) = 1 + T(n - 1)$, so the complexity is $O(n)$.

Now that we completely understand *tail_insert,* it should be easy to write *tail_delete*, a procedure that will delete the last element of a linked list. In order to be able to present clear algorithms in this and future examples when we delete or remove from a dynamic structure, like linked lists, we will not bother trying to reuse the deleted node later. There are many ways to reuse nodes that are temporarily not needed but these techniques only detract from the beauty and simplicity of the recursive algorithms, so for this reason they will not be presented. So, to delete the last node from a linked list we simply delete the last node from the smaller linked list pointed to by the first node in the list. The easiest case is the empty list when we simply . . . , simply what? What does it mean to delete the last node from an empty list. It does not make sense. If there are no nodes present, it is impossible to delete anything, so the easiest case is not the empty list but a one-element list. (This means that any procedure that calls this procedure is responsible for making sure that an empty list is never passed to it.) Deleting the last element from a pointer pointing to a one-element list means to simply change the value of the pointer to *nil* so that the list is now an empty list. All of this translates easily to Pascal as in Figure 4.7.

Certainly, the complexity here is the same as it was in *tail_insert*, namely, $O(n)$. As we did for *tail_insert* you should try a small example, say a three-element list, and carefully trace how the procedure will execute so that you are convinced that it really works properly.

1.4. Reversing a List

1.4.1. A slow example. Suppose we have a linked list of integers and we would like to reverse that list. This is similar to the problem of outputting

original list

call tail_insert(ptr, 8)
list is a var parameter,
so it is ptr

list ≠ nil so recursive call
tail_insert(list^.next, 8)
this list is the previous
list^.next

list ≠ nil so another recursive
call tail_insert(list^.next, 8)
again, this list is the previous
list^.next

list = nil so change it accordingly
this means the previous list^.next
changes

return from 3 calls to tail_insert,
leaving the new list

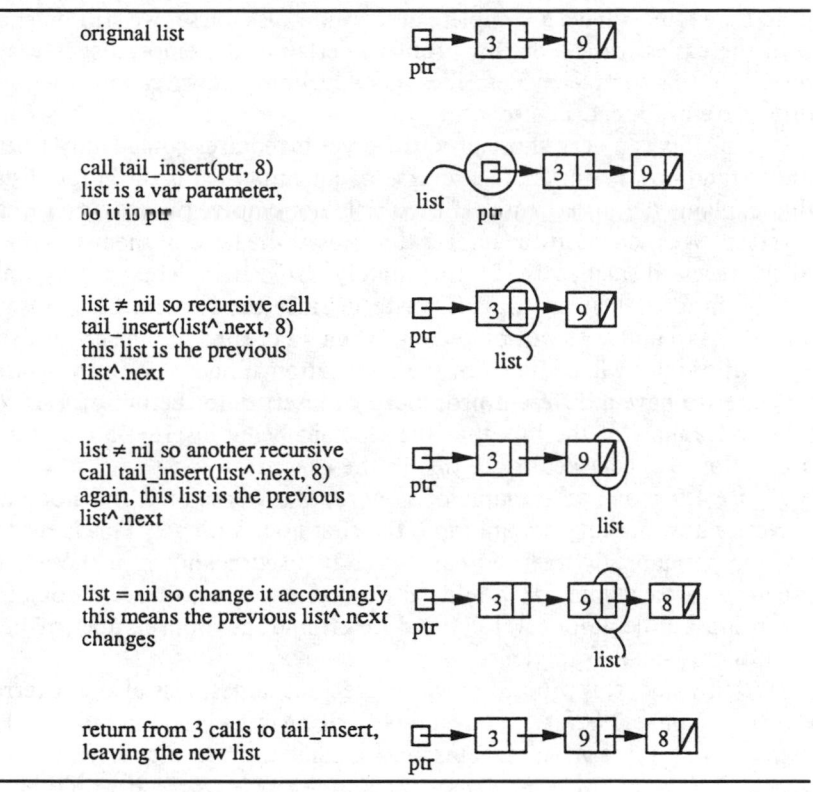

Figure 4.6.   Step-by-Step Example of Tail_Insert

```
procedure tail_delete(var list : nodeptr);
begin
    if list^.next = nil        { a one element list }
        list := nil
    else
        tail_delete(list^.next)
end;
```

Figure 4.7.   Pascal Procedure to Delete the Last Element of a Linked List

a list backwards. We must first reverse the rest of the list and then we must
do something with the first element of the list. In the case of outputting
backwards it was enough to just output the remaining element. Now we
must somehow attach this element somewhere to the reversed part of the
rest of the list. Where does it belong? At the end of the newly reversed list.
We already have a procedure that adds to the tail of a list, so if we borrow

it here we almost have a complete algorithm. Of course, we still must deal with the easiest case. For this problem certainly the empty list is easy to reverse so this completely describes the algorithm and we can now write the procedure in Pascal (Figure 4.8).

Again, this is a very short procedure yet it requires some study to truly understand how it works. The reverse of an empty list is the empty list, so that explains the easiest case. If the list is not empty, the rest of the list is reversed. We then insert the integer that was at the head of the list to the tail of the reversed smaller list. Unfortunately, *tail_reverse* creates a new node for the inserted element. This is wasteful since the element being inserted already has a node. As we pointed out when we created *tail_insert*, for some applications this will be fine. For the application at hand, however, it would be better to have a different procedure to insert onto the tail of a list that takes advantage of the fact that the element being inserted already has a node. You will be asked to do this in the exercises.

Figure 4.9 shows an example of how *reverse* works on a five-node list.

Notice how nothing is pointing to the first node with a 2. This means this node is permanently lost and can never be used again, even though it is pointing to something. It would be a good exercise to trace through the algorithm a little more carefully and determine the total number of nodes lost for this small example.

Not only does this procedure waste precious nodes, it is also not terribly efficient. Notice that after the recursive call we must insert to the tail of the list, but this takes n steps. This means that the recurrence relation for *reverse* is $T(n) = T(n - 1) + n$ so the complexity is $O(n^2)$. It would be nice to find a way to improve on this complexity.

1.4.2. A faster method. The most direct way to improve the complexity is to get the n out of the recurrence relation. In other words, we must find a way to hook the first element of the list on to the end of the reversed list in a constant number of steps rather than in n steps. One way to do this is

---

```
procedure reverse(var list : nodeptr);
begin
    if list = nil then
        { the reverse of an emtpy list is still empty }
    else begin
        reverse(list^.next);        { reverse the rest of the list}
        tail_insert(list^.next, list^.item); { add to end of list }
        list := list^.next          { return head of reversed list }
        end
end;
```

Figure 4.8. A Slow Pascal Procedure to Reverse a Linked List

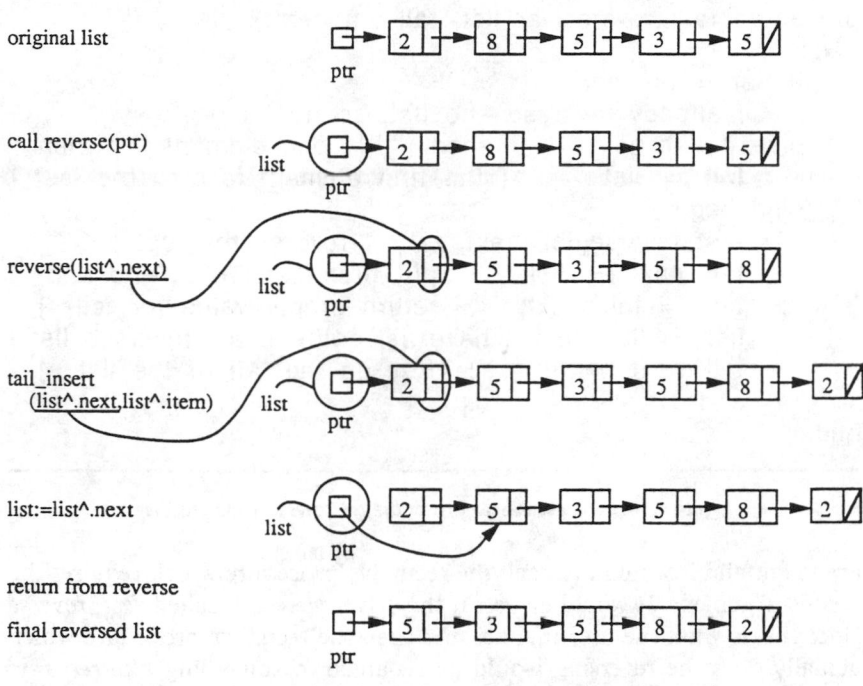

Figure 4.9. Step-by-Step Example of Reverse

to have the recursive procedure not just return a pointer to the front of the reversed list, but also return a pointer to the last element of the reversed list, so that we can quickly attach the original first element to the tail of the reversed list. Figure 4.10 displays how it might look.

Notice we needed to have two easiest cases. The empty list has no elements so it is already reversed and since there are no elements in an empty list it doesn't make sense to have *tail* point anywhere since *tail* is supposed to point to the last node in the list. A one-element list is also already reversed, but in this case the last element of the list is defined; it is the only element of the list. The recursive part is reasonably straightforward. Figure 4.11 is a small example to help you see how it works.

From a stylistic point of view there is one bad feature of *fast_reverse*. Anyone who uses this procedure is required to provide two arguments whenever it is called like we did in the above example when we called it *fast_reverse(ptr, dummy)*. The first argument is the list, which is okay, but the second argument will return the last element in the reversed list which is not something that is usually needed nor would a user expect to have to provide for. For this reason, *fast_reverse* would be best written with a *driver* procedure around it. This driver would only require the list as

```
procedure fast_reverse(var list, tail : nodeptr);
begin
    if list = nil then
        { already reversed — no list, so no tail }
    else if list^.next = nil then { if a one element list then }
        tail := list        { the first element is also the last }
    else begin
        fast_reverse(list^.next, tail); { reverse the rest }
        tail^.next := list;    {   put first element at end and   }
        tail := tail^.next;    {   return proper value for tail   }
        list := list^.next; { have list point to the reversed list }
        tail^.next := nil     {   tidy up the tail of the list   }
        end
end;
```

Figure 4.10. A Fast Pascal Procedure to Reverse a Linked List

argument and it would then call the recursive procedure which requires the second argument. It would be best if the driver were still called *fast_reverse* since this is what the user invokes and then the recursive procedure which actually does the reversing would be renamed to something like *rec_rev*. Figure 4.12 is what all this might look like.

Of course this second version has the same complexity as does the first, both of which are $O(n)$.

1.5. Copying a List

Another handy thing to do with linked lists is to make an exact copy of an existing linked list. This is different from just having two pointers point to the same linked list. If we have two distinct copies of the same list, a change to one of the lists will not affect the other, but if we have two pointers pointing to the same list, since there is only one list, a change to that list will mean both pointers now point to the changed list. The algorithm is actually simple. It just follows the basic form we have been discussing: do something to the first node of the list and then recursively work on the rest of the list. In this case, we simply make a copy of the first node of the list and then copy the rest of the list. The easiest list to copy is certainly the empty list and the complexity is $O(n)$, which is easily verified.

When implementing this in Pascal we have to decide whether to write a function or a procedure. Since the idea is to create a brand new list (the copy of the original) it seems most natural to write a function that returns apointer to the new list. Let's take a look at the function (Figure 4.13). We will see it used a little later.

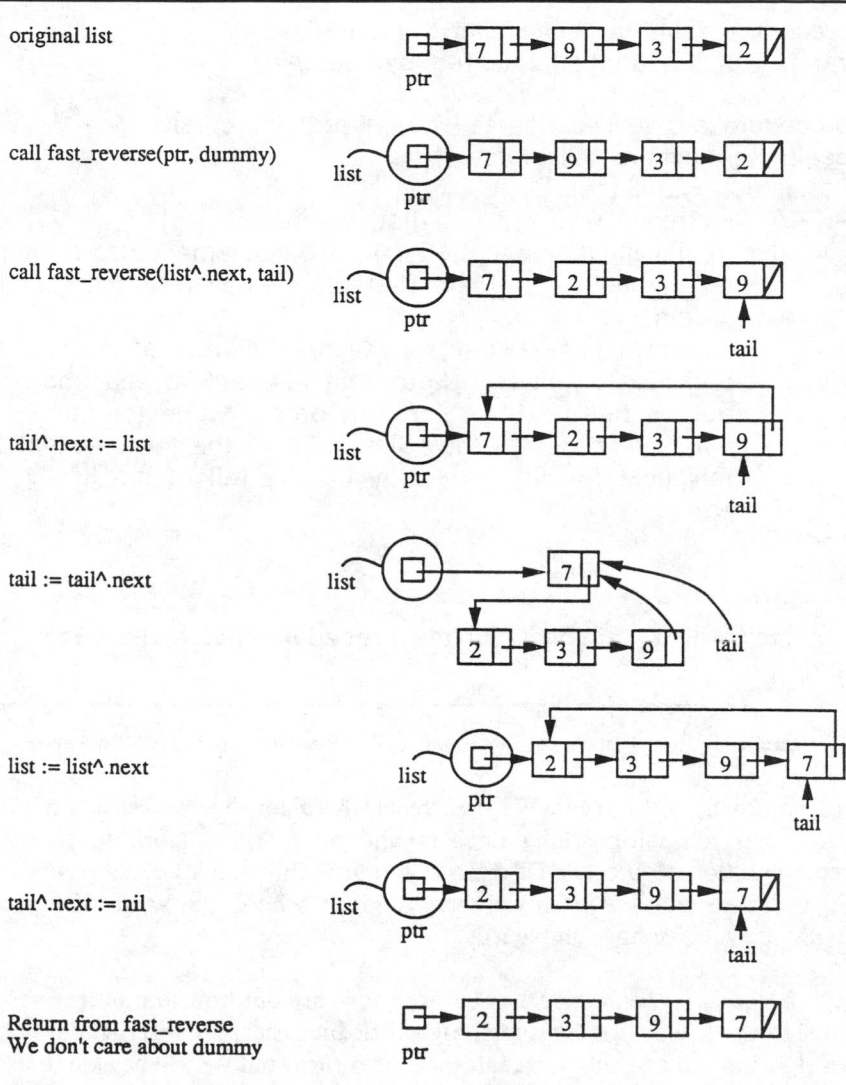

original list

call fast_reverse(ptr, dummy)

call fast_reverse(list^.next, tail)

tail^.next := list

tail := tail^.next

list := list^.next

tail^.next := nil

Return from fast_reverse
We don't care about dummy

Figure 4.11. Step-by-Step Example for Fast Reverse

1.6. Multiplying Big Numbers

Now let's tackle a more interesting and more challenging problem. Have you ever wanted to multiply 14,159,265,358,979 by 3,238,462,643,383 but realized you couldn't because your computer didn't allow integers to get this large? A natural way to solve this kind of problem is to use linked lists. The basic idea is to put one digit in each node of a linked list so that the entire

```
procedure fast_reverse(var list : nodeptr);
var tail_pt : nodeptr; { required by rec_rev }

procedure rec_rev(var list, tail : nodeptr); { recursive }
begin { procedure to reverse a list }
    if list = nil then
        { already reversed—no list, so no tail }
    else if list^.next = nil then { if a one element list then }
        tail := list          { the first element is also the last }
    else begin
        rec_rev(list^.next, tail);  { reverse the rest of the list }
        tail^.next := list;     { put first element at end and }
        tail := tail^.next;     { return proper value for tail }
        list := list^.next; { have list point to the reversed list }
        tail^.next := nil       { tidy up the tail of the list }
        end
end;

begin
    rec_rev(list, tail_pt) { call the procedure that really does it }
end;
```

Figure 4.12. The Fast Pascal Procedure to Reverse a Linked List with a Driver Procedure

list represents one integer. We then recall the algorithm we learned many years ago to multiply long integers and apply that algorithm to our representation of integers. Of course, you probably didn't learn a recursive algorithm to multiply when you were in grade school, but you'll wish you had once you see how simple it is.

1.6.1. Adding big numbers. Before we figure out how to multiply very large integers, let's first try something a little bit easier. We will first develop an algorithm to add very large integers. As it turns out we will be able to use this algorithm in our algorithm for multiplying, so our time won't be wasted.

Let's look at an example and use it try to find a recursive algorithm to add two very large integers. Suppose we wish to add 123,456,789 and 97,531. Of course you might not call these two numbers *very* large, but the algorithm we develop should work with integers of any size, including small ones and very large ones. How do you usually add such numbers using pencil and paper? Probably you first add the 9 and the 1, get 10, write down the 0 and carry the 1. You then continue working your way backwards down the number, next adding the 3 and the 8 and the carried 1. Unfortunately, this

```
function copy(list : nodeptr) : nodeptr;
var newnode : nodeptr;
begin
      if list = nil then          { Easiest case. The copy }
          copy := nil             { is also nil.            }
      else begin
            new(newnode);                      { copy the first   }
            newnode^.item := list^.item; { node of the list }
            newnode^.next := copy(list^.next); { copy the rest }
            copy := newnode          { return the new list }
            end
end;
```

Figure 4.13. A Pascal Function to Copy a Linked List

is not a recursive algorithm, but it's a good starting point. It is probably the algorithm you learned in grade school.

To find a recursive algorithm we have to find a smaller addition to do and use that result for calculating the original addition. Let's suppose that someone has already added 12,345,678 and 9,753 for you. That sum turns out to be 12,355,431. How can you use this information to calculate the sum of the original numbers? All you have to do is add the two remaining digits, the 9 and the 1 and write that answer next to 12,355,431. Well, almost. You can't write a 10. What you have to do is write the 0 and then propagate the carry (the 1) across the answer you have already been given. Propagating the carry simply means adding 1 to that number. So, in this case you know the last digit of the answer is 0 and the rest of the answer is 1 plus the answer already calculated, namely, 12,355,431. In general, then, the recursive algorithm for adding two integers is to first add the two smaller integers by ignoring the last digit of the two original numbers, add the last two digits that were ignored and if this sum is greater than 9 add one to the first sum calculated. The easiest case will correspond to the situation where one of the integers is as small as possible. Since we already know we will be representing integers as linked lists, the natural choice for the smallest integer is the empty list. Adding an empty list to some other integer requires no adding at all. The answer is simply that other integer.

We can't quite write this in Pascal yet, because we still don't know how to propagate the carry. A recursive algorithm that does this is simple to find. We simply add 1 to the last digit of the number. If this sum is less than 10 we are done, otherwise we recursively add 1 to the smaller integer without the last digit and make the last digit a 0. There are actually two easiest cases here. We already described one of them. If the sum is 9 or less we are done. The other easiest case corresponds to the situation where we are doing a carry to the smallest possible integer. This case comes up, for example, when we carry 1 to a number like 99. Following the algorithm for 99, you see that we come to a point where we still need to carry the one but there is no more integer left. In a sense, this is the smallest possible integer; it is no integer at all. In this case, since we are trying to carry where there is no integer we must extend the length of the integer by adding one more node and put the carry (the 1) in this newly created node.

We are almost ready to do this in Pascal. We have already said that we will put one digit of the integer in each node of the list. This means that our Pascal procedures must always create linked lists with this property. We don't want any of our results to suddenly have more than one digit in a node. But we have two choices as to how to represent an integer using a linked list. For example, with the number 97,531 you would expect the head of the list to point to 9, which, in turn, would point to 7, etc. However, there is no reason not to represent the integer so that the head points to the last digit, 1, which in turn points to 3, etc. In essence, the integer is being stored backwards. If you look at the algorithms we've developed for adding and carrying, you should, in fact, notice that this second representation is the more natural one. This is because both of the algorithms do things to the last digit and recursively work on the rest of the integer to the left. If the linked list starts with the last digit, we then have easy access to both the last digit and the rest of the integer without the last digit.

Finally, we need to discuss whether to write functions or procedures and how many parameters are necessary. As always, there are many different possibilities here. For the sake of example, I have chosen to write both as procedures but there is no claim here that this is the best way to do it. The procedure for carrying will modify the integer passed into it, so only one parameter is necessary. The integer passed in will be modified so that it will be 1 larger when it is returned. The procedure for adding will also take two parameters with the first one always changing to be the sum of the original values. This means that this procedure implements an assignment statement like $num1 := num1 + num2$. The reason for this seemingly strange choice is that it turns out to be natural when we need to use addition for multiplication.

Having specified the details of the implementation, we are ready to see it in Pascal (Figure 4.14).

Did you notice that we were able to use the copy function we developed earlier? You will be asked in the exercises why a call to *copy* is necessary. The rest of the procedure is a direct implementation of the algorithm as discussed above.

1.6.2. The complexity of adding.   What is the complexity of *add*? Since *add* uses *carry*, we must first calculate the complexity of *carry*. For an n element list the recurrence relation is $T(n) = T(n - 1) + 1$ so the complexity of *carry* is $O(n)$. For future reference it is worth noting that the

```
procedure add(var num1 : nodeptr; num2 : nodeptr);

procedure carry(var num : nodeptr);
begin
    if num = nil then begin { Easiest case. An empty list. }
        new(num);           { Create a one element }
        num^.item := 1; { list and put a 1 in    }
        num^.next := nil{ it.                     }
        end
    else begin
        num^.item := num^.item + 1;       { add the carry }
        if num^.item < 10 then
            { easiest case—nothing left to do }
        else begin
            num^.item := 0;             { propagate the carry}
            carry(num^.next)            { if necessary       }
            end
        end
end;

begin
    if num2 = nil then
        { easiest case--nothing to add, answer already in num1 }
    else if num1 = nil then
        num1 := copy(num2) { easiest case--put answer in num1 }
    else begin
        add(num1^.next, num2^.next); {add smaller numbers}
        num1^.item := num1^.item + num2^.item;
                                        {add the last digits}
        if num1^.item > = 10 then begin { propagate the carry }
            num1^.item := num1^.item - 10; { if necessary }
            carry(num1^.next)
            end
        end
end;
```

Figure 4.14. A Pascal Procedure to Add Two Long Integers

worst case only occurs for numbers like 9,999, that is, integers that are all 9's. For any other integer the recursive calls stop when a digit other than 9 is seen so all *n* recursive calls will not be made.

Since *add* has two arguments we should use both of them in calculating the complexity. Let's assume the first list has *n* elements and the second has *m*. In the worst case each recursive call does a constant amount of work plus one call to *carry* on a list of size $n - 1$, one smaller than the original first list. Since the complexity of *carry* is $O(n)$, the recurrence relation for add looks like this: $T(n, m) = (n - 1) + T(n - 1, m - 1)$. It is not hard to show that the solution to this recurrence relation is

$$\sum_{k=max(0,n-m)}^{n} k = O(n^2 + m),$$

where *max* means you are to take the larger of the two values. Before you waste too much time pondering this recurrence relation and the resulting complexity let's make two quick observations. First, if $m = n$ then the complexity is $O(n^2)$. Second, what two numbers can you add to actually achieve our supposed worst case? The worst case was based on the fact that we had to call *carry* every recursive call and that each call to *carry* was itself a worst case for *carry*. It turns out that this is impossible. Suppose we are inside the *add* procedure and we make a recursive call to *add*. Further suppose the recursive call required a call to *carry*. For example, suppose we are adding 9,999 and 9,999. The recursive call that adds 999 and 999 will require a call to *carry* because 9 plus 9 generates a carry. However, the final sum generated by the recursive call is 1,998. Notice that the last digit is an 8. Upon returning from the recursive call and adding the last two digits of the original four digit number (9 and 9) we will not have a worst case for *carry* because the next digit is an 8, not a 9. In fact, we will have an easiest case because *carry* will only have to add 1 to the 8 and will not have to make any recursive calls. So, not only is it true that two consecutive calls to *carry* cannot both achieve the worst case but, in fact, the total work of all the calls to *carry* during the entire addition cannot be greater than $2n$. Another way to see this is to note that during an addition, a carry cannot take place in the same location more than once. This is because the largest value that can be produced by a position that created a carry is 8 and so will never be able to produce another carry. Thus, the complexity calculated based on the recurrence relation was too pessimistic. That result was based on our incorrect assumption on the total amount of work *carry* was doing through the course of the entire addition. We now see that *carry* does a total of $O(n)$ work. Let's recalculate the total amount of work done by everything in *add*. *Carry* takes at most $2n$ steps. When $m > n$ *copy* takes $m - n$ steps. (If $m \leq n$ *copy* is not called at all.) Finally, the actual number of additions done is the smaller of n and m or $min(n, m)$. So when $m > n$ we get a total of $2n + m - n + min(n, m) = 2n + m$ and when $m < n$ we get a total of $2n + min(n, m) = 2n + m$. In either case, the complexity is then $2n + m = O(n + m)$, which is intuitively correct since you would expect to visit every node exactly one time. For example, this means that when $n = m$ the complexity is actually much better than the $O(n^2)$ that we first thought. It is simply $O(n)$.

You may be concerned that we did this calculation somewhat informally.

The problem is that the argument concerning the total work done by *carry* is actually quite subtle and would be quite difficult to express in terms of a recurrence relation. Now that you are becoming quite expert in recursive algorithms and their complexities I hope you will find such arguments convincing nevertheless.

1.6.3. The multiplication algorithm. It is now time to do what we set out to do, which was to multiply. As we did for addition, we must find a way to break down a hard multiplication into some easier multiplications. The best way to do this is to look at an example. Suppose we wish to do the following multiplication:

$$\begin{array}{r} 123456789 \\ \times \quad 13579 \\ \hline \end{array}.$$

As you well know, the usual way to do such a multiplication is like this:

$$\begin{array}{r} 123456789 \\ \times \quad 13579 \\ \hline 1111111101 \\ 864197523 \\ 617283945 \\ 370370367 \\ 123456789 \\ \hline 1676419737831 \end{array}.$$

This suggests one way of doing it recursively. Recursively multiply 123,456,789 by 1,357; multiply the result by 10 and then add to it the result of multiplying 123,456,789 by 9. This works because

$$\begin{array}{r} 123456789 \\ \times \quad 13579 \\ \hline \end{array} = \begin{array}{r} 123456789 \\ \times (1357 \times 10) + 9 \\ \hline \end{array}$$

$$= \begin{array}{r} 123456789 \\ \times 1357 \\ \hline \end{array} \times 10 + \begin{array}{r} 123456789 \\ \times 9 \\ \hline \end{array}$$

$$= \left(\begin{array}{r} 123456789 \\ \times 1357 \\ \hline \end{array} + \begin{array}{r} 123456789 \\ \times 9 \\ \hline \end{array} \right) \times 10$$

The problem with this approach is that we still have the problem of multiplying 123,456,789 by 9. This would require, perhaps, another recursive algorithm. We made the multiplier smaller but the multiplicand stayed the same size and so the entire multiplicand has to be dealt with separately.

A better approach would be to make both the multiplier and the multiplicand smaller. This would then require four multiplications rather than the two that were needed above. However, the easiest case is much easier to deal with now. In this case, (a) we multiply 12,345,678 by 1357, (b) we multiply 12,345,678 by 9, (c) we multiply 9 by 1,357, and (d) we multiply 9 by 9. Graphically, it looks like this:

```
    123456789
×     13579
_____

16753085046   (a)
  111111102   (b)
      12213   (c)
         81   (d)
_____

1676419737831
```

The reason this works can be seen by this simple equation:

$$(10a + b) \times (10c + d) = 100ac + 10ad + 10bc + bd,$$

where ac corresponds to (a), ad to (b), bc to (c), and bd to (d). Hence, the result of multiplication (a) must be multiplied by 100 and the results of multiplications (b) and (c) must both be multiplied by 10. We can then use the addition algorithm developed earlier to add together the four pieces.

What is the easiest case? Multiplication (d) is just part of the algorithm so we cannot really call it an easiest case. However, if either argument is *nil* then there is nothing to multiply, so that is certainly an easiest case.

For this example we have decided to do it as a function. Figure 4.15 is the final result.

A few observations are in order. There was no reason to write *mult10* recursively since there is a straightforward algorithm that works in constant time. Also, rather than write a separate procedure to multiply by 100, it is simpler to simply call *mult10* twice. Finally, add is the same procedure we developed earlier.

What is the complexity of *mult?* Assume that we are multiplying two integers with m and n digits. Clearly, we need to express the recurrence relation in terms of both sizes. There are three recursive calls and three calls to *add*. The four subproducts *prod1, prod2, prod3,* and the first value assigned to *result* have lengths approximately $n+m$, n, m, and 2, respectively. (Look again at the example.) Thus, the three calls to *add* require a total of about $2n + 2m + 2$ steps so the recurrence relation is:

$$T(m,n) = T(n - 1, m - 1) + T(n - 1, 1) + T(1, m - 1) + 2n + 2m + 2.$$

You will be asked in the exercises to show that the solution to this recurrence relation is $O(n \times m)$.

```
function mult(num1, num2 : nodeptr) : nodeptr;
var rest1, rest2, prod1, prod2, prod3, result : nodeptr;

    procedure mult10(var num : nodeptr);
                                        { Multiply the integer by  }
    var zero : nodeptr;                 { 10 by adding a zero to   }
    begin                               { the end of the list.     }
        if num < > nil then begin       { Don't forgot that tho    }
            new(zero);                  { pointer points to the    }
            zero^.next := num;          { last digit of the number,}
            zero^.item := 0;            { not the first.           }
            num := zero
            end
    end;

begin
    if (num1 = nil) or (num2 = nil) then    { Easiest case. Nothing }
        mult := nil              { to multiply, so return nothing. }
    else begin
        rest1 := num1^.next;
                            { Break both numbers into two parts: }
        rest2 := num2^.next;    { the last digit and the rest of the }
        num1^.next := nil;      { integer.                         }
        num2^.next := nil;
        prod1 := mult(num2, rest1); { Multiply the last digit of }
        mult10(prod1);              { num2 by the rest of num1, }
        prod2 := mult(num1, rest2);   { the last digit of num1 by }
        mult10(prod2);                { the rest of num2, the rest }
        prod3 := mult(rest1, rest2); { of num1 and num2, scaling }
        mult10(prod3); mult10(prod3); {the results along the way. }
        num1^.next := rest1;          { Put num1 and num2 }
        num2^.next := rest2;          { back together again. }
        new(result);
        result^.item := num1^.item * num2^.item;
                                        { Multiply the last }
        if result^.item < 10 then       { two digits.       }
            result^.next := nil
        else begin
            new(result^.next);
            result^.next^.next := nil;
            result^.next^.item := result^.item div 10;
            result^.item := result^.item mod 10;
            end;
```

(continued on next page)

Figure 4.15. A Pascal Function to Multiply Two Long Integers

```
        add(result, prod1);          { Add together the four pieces }
        add(result, prod2);          { to get the final answer.      }
        add(result, prod3);
        mult := result
        end;
end;
```

Figure 4.15.   (Continued)

2. BINARY TREES

Another common dynamic data type is the binary tree. It has myriad uses. Binary trees can be used to implement efficient search, insert, and delete operations on ordered data. They can be used to concisely represent arithmetic expressions and are useful for evaluating them as well. The list goes on and on.

The binary tree has a natural recursive definition and so will lend itself to recursive algorithms. A binary tree is an element with two (smaller) binary trees hanging from the left and right sides. In Pascal this will be represented using a record that will store the element and the two smaller binary trees. For all of the examples we will be doing in this chapter, the element will be an integer so the declarations look like this:

```
type nodeptr = ^node;
     node = record
         item : integer;
         left, right : nodeptr
         end;
```

The *left* and *right* pointers point to smaller trees that are often called *subtrees* of the original tree while the node itself is referred to as the *root*. Other nodes are *interior* nodes. Notice that it is important to distinguish the left subtree from the right one. Two trees that are identical except that their left and right subtrees are exchanged are considered to be different trees. For example, these two binary trees are different:

They both have two nodes and both have a root labeled 6. However, the first one has a left subtree of size one and an empty right subtree, while the second one has an empty left subtree and a right subtree with one element. The importance of this will become clear when we discuss binary search trees.

Let's look at a slightly bigger tree to be sure we understand the terminology and to define a few more terms.

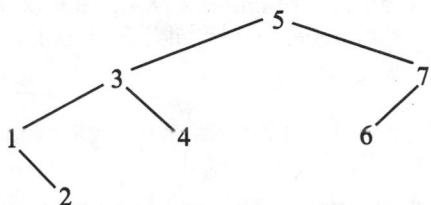

This tree has root labeled 5, while its left subtree has its own root labeled 3. The two (or sometimes one) nodes directly beneath a node are called the *children* of the node. Conversely, the node directly above another node is called that node's *parent*. The node labeled 5 has children labeled 3 and 7, and so the nodes 3 and 7 both have the same parent, 5. The node labeled 1 has only has one child, 2. The nodes labeled 2, 4, and 6 have no children. Any node with no children is called a *leaf*. Conversely, the node with no parent is the root.

2.1. Counting Nodes

First, let's begin by looking at some simple algorithms that operate on binary trees. As we did with linked lists, a natural place to start is to write a function that will count the number of nodes in a binary tree. Since the size of a binary tree is the number of nodes in the tree it is a useful number to know. I'm sure you've already thought of a nice recursive algorithm, but in case not, here is one idea. The nodes in a binary tree include: the root node, all the nodes in the left subtree, and all the nodes in the right subtree. The simplest binary tree is the tree with no nodes, that is, the *nil* tree. This should sound a lot like the algorithm for counting the nodes in a linked list. The only difference now is that we have two smaller structures to visit instead of just one. In Pascal, it looks like Figure 4.16.

```
function count(tree : nodeptr) : integer;
begin
    if tree = nil then      { the empty tree has no elements }
        count := 0
    else
        count := 1 + count(tree^.left) + count(tree^.right)
end;
```

Figure 4.16.   A Pascal Function to Count the Nodes of a Binary Tree

As simple as this algorithm is, it is irritatingly hard to find the complexity using recurrence relations. If the number of nodes of the tree is n, it must be the case that the complexity of *count* is $O(n)$, yet how do we prove it? Let's defer this question for a moment so we may first look at some more similar algorithms.

2.2. Output

2.2.1. Parentheses notation.   The next thing we would probably like to do with a binary tree is output it. But how do we want to output it? A tree is inherently a two-dimensional structure, yet we are used to doing output one dimensionally, that is, on a single line. For example, let's consider the following binary tree.

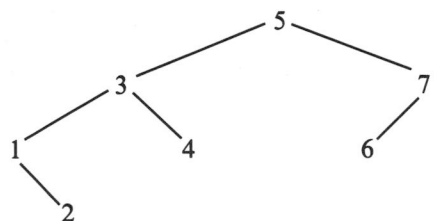

One way to output it would be to use *parenthesis notation*. For example, the above tree using parenthesis notation looks like: $(((1(2))3(4))5((6)7))$. Do you see what is happening here? For any node the parenthesis output is described recursively as follows: inside a pair of parentheses output three things — the parenthesis notation for the left subtree, the node itself, then the parenthesis notation for the right subtree. If you look real hard you can see the original tree. Numbers all alone must be leaves of the tree. A number directly touching the convex part of one of the parentheses from a leaf must be the parent of that leaf. Similarly, its parent is touching the convex part of its parenthesis. And so on.

Since the description of parenthesis notation was recursive, the recursive algorithm to actually output the tree follows immediately in Figure 4.17. Again, for an n node tree the complexity is clearly $O(n)$ but let's wait a bit longer before we prove it.

You must admit that this is a fairly simple algorithm but the readability of the resulting output is difficult at best. Some ways of improving it are discussed in the exercises but we must question the whole idea of parenthesis output. We need to find something better. Another idea is to try to turn the tree on its side by rotating it 90 degrees counterclockwise and output it this way. Our sample tree output this way (without the helpful lines) will look like this:

```
procedure parenout(list : nodeptr);
begin
    if tree = nil then
        { the empty tree requires no output }
    else begin
        write( '(' );
        parenout(tree^.left);
        write(tree^.item);
        parenout(tree^.right);
        write( ')' )
        end
end;
```

Figure 4.17. A Pascal Procedure to Output a Binary Tree in Parenthesis Notation

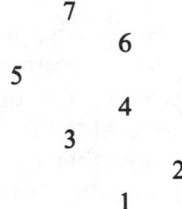

At this point, it would be fairly easy to manually add the lines that connect nodes with their parents and the tree becomes quite readable. In this case, however, the algorithm is not quite as simple as it may seem.

A first try at an algorithm might be: Output the right subtree one line per node, output the node on a new line, and then output the left subtree one line per node. Do you see what is missing from this algorithm? No mention is made of doing the indenting properly. It will simply output the tree one node per line all lined up in the first column. We need to incorporate the idea that subtrees of a node must be output further to the right than the node itself. The correct algorithm looks something like this: Output the right subtree one line per node and three spaces to the right of where the node will be output, output the node on a new line, and then output the right subtree one line per node and three spaces to the right.

Doing this in Pascal poses one problem. For any given node, how do we know how far to indent it? One possible answer is to tell the procedure by passing along a value that reports how far the node should be indented. Then, when the recursive calls are made, we send a larger value effectively saying that the subtrees must be indented further than the parent was. Let's take a look at the procedure in Figure 4.18.

```
procedure outtree(tree : nodeptr; indent : integer);
var i : integer;
begin
    if tree  =  nil  then
        { nothing  to  output }
    else begin
        outtree(tree^.right, indent  +  1);
        for i := 1 to indent do
            write('   ');
        writeln(tree^.item);
        outtree(tree^.left, indent  +  1)
        end
end;
```

Figure 4.18.   A Pascal Procedure to Output a Binary Tree "Sideways"

Notice the *for* loop that properly indents the node. Rather than indent one space per level I chose three because it makes it easier to connect the nodes with their parents. Also, when calling the procedure from the main program you must provide an initial value for *indent*. The natural choice is 0, but you have the option of indenting the whole tree by choosing a different value. If this seems a bit unnatural to you, you may choose to use a driver procedure, as we did in some previous examples, that takes a single argument, the tree, and, in turn, calls the recursive procedure that takes two arguments. This frees the user of having to worry about deciding on an initial value for indenting.

There is another way to view the *indent* variable that is important to understand. It can be thought of as the number of other calls to *outtree* that were made leading to this call. It is not the total number of recursive calls made before this one was made. Rather, it is how deeply nested this recursive call is among other recursive calls. More to the point, perhaps, *indent* is the current depth of the stack as described in Chapter 3. In later examples we will find it useful to know how deeply nested our recursive calls are getting and so we will employ something like the *indent* variable.

2.3. A New Technique for Finding the Complexity

The complexity of *outtree* is surely $O(n)$. Even though it is intuitively obvious (since each node of the tree is visited exactly once and nothing else is done) it is a little tricky to prove using recurrence relations. The main problem is that we really don't know how big our smaller problems are because the remaining nodes could be distributed in many different ways between the two subtrees. For example, both subtrees could be about the same size or one could be much larger than the other. In fact, this problem often makes calculating the complexity of tree algorithms very difficult and sometimes forces us to resort to the kind of argument that was used parenthetically at the start of this paragraph. Another method that can prove useful in these cases is to guess the answer to the recurrence relation and then check to see if the guess is a good one. Let's try that method for this algorithm.

First we must find the correct recurrence relation. The easy part is noticing that there is a constant amount of work being done in the procedure in addition to two recursive calls. But how big are these recursive calls? Even though we don't know how big each subtree is, we do know how big both subtrees are. That is, the total number of nodes in both subtrees is clearly $n - 1$. So if we just use a variable, k, to describe how many nodes are in the left subtree, we can say that the right subtee must have $n - k - 1$ nodes. Hence, our recurrence relation looks like $T(n) = 1 + T(k) + T(n - k - 1)$. What we now do is guess what the solution to the equation is and see if it works. For the fun of it, let's first guess wrong and see what happens. Let's guess that $T(n) = 2n^2$. Substituting this solution back into the original equation gives us

$$2n^2 = 1 + 2k^2 + 2(n - k - 1)^2.$$

Multiplying this out and subtracting $2n^2$ from both sides of the equation gives us

$$0 = 3 + 4k^2 + 4k - 4n - 4kn.$$

Clearly this equation is not always true (try $k = 1$) so our original guess must have been wrong.

You may object that the last guess may have been bad because we chose $2n^2$ rather than something like $3n^2$. One way around this kind of problem is to guess an^2 and see if there is a way to make it work for any value of a. Let's try this technique with our next guess. This time we will guess that the solution is an for some a. Substituting this back into the original recurrence relation we get:

$$an = 1 + ak + a(n - k - 1).$$

Collecting terms and cancelling the an that appears on both sides of the equation we get: $0 = 1 + ak - ak - a$ or $0 = 1 - a$. This means that if $a = 1$ everything works and so we can conclude that the solution to the recurrence relation is $T(n) = an$ where $a = 1$ and so indeed the complexity is $O(n)$.

3. BINARY SEARCH TREES

3.1. Why Do We Need Them?

Suppose that you have a large collection of integers that you would like to keep track of. For example, you might need to store the identification numbers of all the students in your university. Further suppose that numbers are sometimes removed from this list, numbers are sometimes added to the list, and sometimes you simply need to search for a particular number on the list. For this example, this might correspond to students leaving the university (ideally by graduating), students matriculating, and the chair of the department searching to see if students she believes to still be majors are still in the university. How should these data be stored? Let us look at two possibilities.

The first idea that comes to mind is to simply store all of the numbers in an array. As new numbers are added to the list, add them to the end of the array. When a number is removed from the list, simply shift all the other numbers to the left to fill in the hole created. To determine if a number is in the list, the list must be scanned from left to right, possibly scanning the whole list in case the number is not on the list. How good of an implementation is this? We answer this question by looking at the complexities of the three operations that are performed on the data. Assuming that in addition to the array itself we keep track of its size, n, it is clear that inserting an element into the list is a constant-time operation. Simply insert it into the next available spot and increment n. Unfortunately, things do not work out so well for the other operations. Removing an element from the list involves shifting all elements to the right of the removed element and so, in the worst case, this could involve $O(n)$ shifts. Also, searching to see if a certain element is in the list could require the entire list to be traversed, so this too is a $O(n)$ operation. In summary, inserting, deleting, and searching take times $O(1)$, $O(n)$, and $O(n)$ respectively.

Let us look at another possible method of storing the data. Suppose we store the numbers in a sorted array instead. Remembering binary search from the first chapter we realize we can search for an element in $O(\log n)$ time. Inserting an element requires two steps: finding the spot where the element belongs and shifting elements to the right to make room for the new element. Finding the spot can be done using the idea of binary search and so takes time $O(\log n)$ but we might have to shift n elements to make room for the element and this would require $O(n)$ steps. This means that inserting requires $O(n)$ steps. Finally, deleting an element requires finding the element to be deleted and then shifting elements to the left to fill the hole created. As with insert, this will also require $O(n)$ steps. Comparing this with the unordered array, we see that insertion is $O(n)$ compared to $O(1)$, deletion is $O(n)$ for both, and searching is $O(\log n)$ compared to $O(n)$. This second implementation has saved us time searching while costing us extra time while inserting. So which is better? Well, it really depends. If you expect not to do much searching, but a lot of inserting and deleting, then you will probably choose to use an unordered array. On the other hand, if you expect to do a lot of searching relative to the number of insertions then the ordered array is better.

Suppose there were another implementation where inserting, deleting, and searching could all be done in *O(log n)* time. Unless the application requires a lot of insertions compared to the other operations this new implementation would probably be preferred. The rest of this chapter is devoted to finding a way to do this with the help of binary trees.

3.2. Definition and Examples

The data structure we will be using is called a *binary search tree.* A binary search tree is a special kind of binary tree that is best described recursively. All of the nodes of the left subtree of the root of a binary search tree have values that are less than the root and all of the nodes of the right subtree have values that are greater than the root. The left and right subtrees of the root are also binary search trees. To keep things simple, for now, we will assume that no value appears more than once in a binary search tree. As you can well imagine, this recursive definition begs us to use recursive algorithms when working on binary search trees. A sample binary search tree is seen below. We will be referring to it often in our examples that follow.

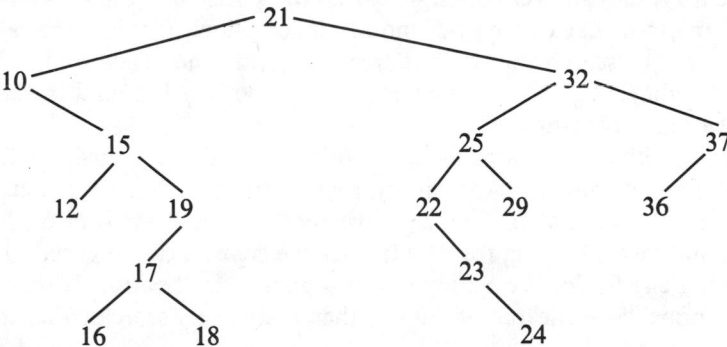

We will soon discover that the shape of a binary search tree is very important in determining how efficiently our three operations of insertion, deletion, and searching can be performed. However, from the user's point of view, he couldn't care less what the shape of the tree is. He only wants to use the tree as a data structure for storing information and accessing information. For this reason, there is no good reason to write a procedure to output a binary search tree in the shape of a tree. However, it might be useful to be able to output all of the values of a binary search tree. Let us discuss this problem before we go on to the three main operations.

3.3. Output

Given the structure of a binary search tree you should expect that it will be easy to output all the values in increasing order. The recursive structure forces this recursive algorithm to: recursively output all of the small values which are in the left subtree, output the value of the root, and recursively output all of the large values which are in the right subtree. That's all there is to it! The easiest case, of course, is an empty tree where there is nothing to output. Figure 4.19 shows it in Pascal:

The analysis of our earlier output routine applies here, too, so the complexity of *outbst* is $O(n)$.

3.4. Searching

Searching for an element in a binary search tree is equally easy. However, we must decide whether to write a procedure or a function and we must decide what parameters are necessary. Since we don't plan to modify the tree during the search and since the result of a search is a single entity (just what will be determined next) a function seems most appropriate. But what should the function return? A boolean value is a possibility. If we find the value we return *true* and if not we return *false*. This choice is not entirely satisfactory, though. Very often we search for a node because we want to do something to it, like delete it, or modify it somehow. If this is the case, we would have to search through the tree a second time. Therefore, a better choice might be to return a pointer to the node if it is found in the tree, otherwise simply return *nil*.

The algorithm for searching for a node is straightforward. In fact, it should remind you a lot of binary search from the first chapter. It is essentially the same algorithm. First we check to see if the root of the tree is the node we are looking for. If it is, then we have an easiest case, for there is nothing else to do. We simply return a pointer to the root. If the root is not the node we are searching for, we then recursively search either the left

```
procedure outbst(tree : nodeptr);
begin
    if tree = nil then
        { nothing to output }
    else begin
        outbst(tree^.left);      { output the small values }
        write(tree^.item);       { output the root }
        outbst(tree^.right)      { output the large values }
        end
end;
```

Figure 4.19. A Pascal Procedure to Output the Nodes of a Binary Search Tree in Order

subtree or the right subtree, depending on whether the element we are looking for is less than or greater than the root. The other easiest case is when the tree is empty, for then we certainly will not find the element we are searching for and so we return *nil*. Figure 4.20 shows this in Pascal:

The complexity of *bstsearch* depends on the shape of the tree. If we do as we did before and let k be the number of nodes in the left subtree then $n - k - 1$ is the number of nodes in the right subtree. Since we only make one recursive call, to get the worst case we must always make this recursive call on the larger subtree. Hence, the recurrence relation is $T(n) = 1 + max(T(k), T(n - k - 1))$ where *max* takes the larger of the two values. In fact, this should be easy to visualize. The worst case comes about when we are searching for an element as far away from the root as possible. This means the element must be a leaf and it must be the furthest leaf away from the root.

If the binary search tree has the property that each node has one nil child and one other child, like:

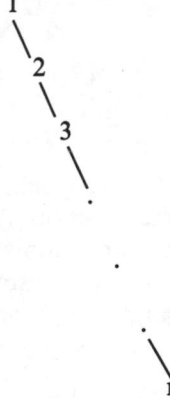

```
function bstsearch(tree : nodeptr; x : integer) : nodeptr;
begin
    if tree = nil then        { easiest case--no tree at all }
        bstsearch := nil
    else if tree^.item = x then    { x is here }
        bstsearch := tree
    else if x < tree^.item then    { check the left subtree }
        bstsearch := bstsearch(tree^.left, x)
    else                          { check the right subtree }
        bstsearch := bstsearch(tree^.right, x)
end
```

Figure 4.20. A Pascal Function to Find an Element in a Binary Search Tree

then if we are searching for n, it clearly requires n steps so the complexity is $O(n)$. Looking at the recurrence relation this corresponds to the case where $k = 0$. We then get

$$T(n) = 1 + max(T(0), T(n - 0 - 1)) = 1 + T(n - 1)$$

whose solution we know is $O(n)$.

On the other hand, if we have a tree that is "bushy," this means that no node is too far away from the root and we might expect the complexity of *bstsearch* to be better. A bushy tree would be one where for each node in the tree the number of nodes in the left subtree is about the same as the number of nodes in the right subtree. A bushy tree is sometimes called *balanced* because neither the left nor the right subtrees at any node is much "heavier" than the other. An example of a bushy tree follows.

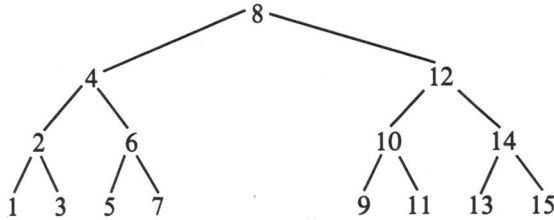

Is it obvious what the complexity of *bstsearch* is in such a tree? When in doubt, we can always solve the recurrence relation. As we said before, for a tree to be bushy each subtree must have approximately the same number of nodes. In other words, the tree must be reasonably well balanced. Recalling the original recurrence relation: $T(n) = 1 + max(T(k), T(n - k - 1))$ this will correspond to the situation where $k = \frac{n}{2}$. Hence, the recurrence relation is

$$T(n) = 1 + max(T(\tfrac{n}{2}), T(\tfrac{n}{2})) = 1 + T(\tfrac{n}{2})$$

and we remember from Chapter 2 that the solution to this is $O(log\ n)$.

Clearly, a bushy tree gives a much faster search. At this point you are probably thinking: "Hold everything here! I thought you said the complexity was based on the *worst* case. What right do you have to say that the tree might be bushy. In the worst case the tree won't be bushy and so the complexity is $O(n)$, period."

You have a point. After all, it is certainly possible for a tree to look like that spindly one we saw before, so what right do I have to be talking about bushy trees? I have no right, yet. But suppose I could find a way to be sure that my trees were always bushy. Then I'd be on to something because then I would know I would never have a scrawny tree and I'd know my searches (and inserts and deletes, for that matter) would be very fast; $O(log\ n)$ to be exact. So, as we continue our discussion about binary search trees we should be thinking of ways to keep the trees bushy. I will eventually tell you a way.

3.5. Inserting

The way trees get built up, of course, is through insertions, so let us see how to insert into a binary search tree. The algorithm is very much like the one for searching only now we modify the tree in one case. If the element we are inserting is less than the root we must, of course, insert it into the left subtree (which we do recursively), if it's greater than the root we must insert it into the right subtree and if it equals the root, it's already in the tree so there is nothing to do. Depending on the particular application, if the element that is being inserted is discovered to already be in the tree you may choose to do something more than what we are doing here, which is nothing. For example, thinking of the student list discussed earlier, if we try to add a student and he is already on the list we may have given him a bad number and so an error message might be the most appropriate. However, for now let's just do nothing.

As usual, the easiest case is when the tree is empty. In this case we modify the tree so it becomes a one-element tree containing the value that is being inserted (Figure 4.21).

Notice that the basic structure of this procedure really is the same as *bstsearch*. In particular, the recurrence relation will be the same here as it was for *bstsearch* and so everything we said about the complexity also applies

---

```
procedure bstinsert(var tree : nodeptr; x : integer);
begin
      if tree = nil then begin     { Easiest case--no tree at all. }
            new(tree);             { Return a one node tree        }
            tree^.item := x;       { whose item is the inserted    }
            tree^.left := nil;     { value.                        }
            tree^.right := nil
            end
      else if x < tree^.item then { insert into left subtree   }
            bstinsert(tree^.left, x)
      else if x > tree^.item then { insert into right subtree  }
            bstinsert(tree^.right, x)
      else                         { inserting element is here }
            { nothing to do }
end
```

Figure 4.21. A Pascal Function to Insert into a Binary Search Tree

here. Also, the spirit of *bstinsert* is much the same as it was for our algorithm for inserting into a linked list. You may want to review that algorithm and its Pascal program to help you convince yourself that the element here is really getting inserted as a leaf into the proper location in the tree. In summary, *tree* is a *var* parameter so this means that when we make the call *new(tree)* the variable *tree* that used to be nil and is now changing is actually either the *left* or *right* pointer of the parent of this nil pointer. This, in fact, is the pointer we really want to change so everything is working just fine.

Since this is where a binary tree actually gets built, it is instructive to see what sequence of data gives bushy trees and what gives spindly ones. We have seen an example of a spindly tree with *n* nodes earlier. Assuming we begin with an empty tree, how can this terrible tree be built? It is not to hard to see that if the numbers are inserted from smallest to largest, this worst case tree will be created. Of course there are many other equally bad trees. Try inserting nodes in decreasing order and see what happens.

3.5.1. Building bushy trees. To get a bushy tree with the numbers 1 through *n* follow this simple rule: Pretend zero and *n* + 1 are already in the tree, even though we will never put them in. Continue inserting elements into vacant intervals, that is, find *i* and *j* that are in the tree while no value between *i* and *j* is, and insert *(i + j)div* 2 into the tree where *div* is the same as standard Pascal *div*. For example, suppose *n* = 15. Since we pretend 0 and 16 are already in the tree at the beginning, the only element we are allowed to insert is (0 + 16)*div*2 = 8. Once 8 is in the tree you have the choice of inserting either 4 or 12. Suppose you choose to insert 12 next. You now have the choice of inserting either 4, 10, or 14. Continue in this way until all of the elements are inserted. Try it. It's fun! This method gives many different ways of getting a bushy tree since you may feel free to choose whatever vacant interval you like at any step. However, you will always end up with the same bushy tree.

Of course, the above sequences of insertions are a bit artificial. In practice you would not expect any of the above sequences, good or bad, to actually occur. It might be reassuring to know, however, that on average, if data are inserted into a binary tree in random order then the tree will end up fairly bushy. However, we need to keep thinking about ways to guarantee bushiness. This will mean that we will have to be able to somehow reorganize the tree during or after the insertion process since the current scheme gives us no choices as to where we can insert an element. Reorganizing a tree might sound terribly complicated, but it need not be so bad. We can get an early taste for it by looking at the last of our basic algorithms, deletion.

3.6. Deleting

Suppose we wish to delete an element from a binary search tree. Certainly we can't just pluck it out of the tree, for there would be a gaping hole left.

This means the tree must somehow be modified. We will try to find another element from the tree to replace it with. There are two natural choices, both equally good. We could replace it with the largest of all the small elements, that is, the largest element in the left subtree, or we could replace it with the smallest element in the right subtree. For the sake of being specific, let us assume we will always choose the largest element of the left subtree. We should be sure that if we move this element, we still end up with a binary search tree. Being the largest element of the left subtree, it could serve as the root of that tree since now everything remaining in the left subtree will be smaller than that largest element. Also, everything in the left subtree is less than everything in the right subtree so since the element is coming from the left subtree it will be smaller than every element of the right subtree. This means that it is, indeed a fine replacement, because when it replaces the deleted element it will preserve the binary search tree property.

For example, suppose we wish to delete the 32 from our first example of a binary search tree. In this case we would replace it with the 29. Since 29 is a leaf it would be easy to remove and move to where the 32 used to be. This example makes it look a little easier than it really is, however. Suppose we wish to delete the 21. In this case we would replace it with the 19 which is not a leaf, thus, when we move the 19 to where the 21 used to be another hole is created. Fortunately, this second hole is easier to plug. Since we know that 19 is the largest element in the left subtree we know there can be no right subtree, for a right subtree would mean there were elements larger than 19. We also know that every element (if there is any) of the left subtree of 19 is greater than 19s parent (15), because they are all in the right subtree of 19s parent, 19 being the root of its parent's right subtree. So we simply have the right subtree of the parent become the left subtree of the element that is moving up. You should convince yourself that this argument works in general, not just for the example being discussed. For this example, the resulting tree looks like this:

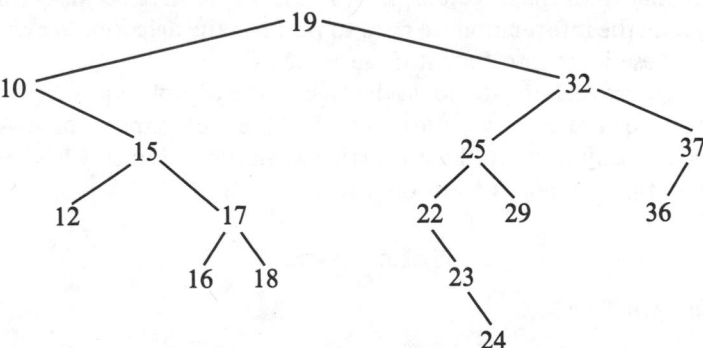

There is one final complication. Looking again at the original example, suppose we wish to delete 10. What does our algorithm tell us to do? We must replace 10 with the largest element of the left subtree. Unfortunately, there is no left subtree in this case. However, you should notice that this case is similar to the case of moving the largest element of the left subtree. In both cases the node being removed had only one child so in such cases we can just replace the element with its only subtree. When deleting 10, we have the left subtree of 21 start at 15, like the following:

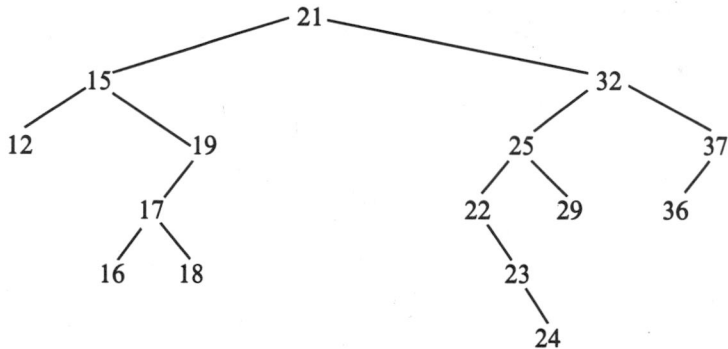

We now need to formulate these ideas more precisely and, of course, recursively. Finding the element to be deleted can be done (recursively) in exactly the same way it was done for *bstsearch*. Deciding if there is a left subtree is a constant-time operation that requires no recursion. Finding the largest element of the left subtree can be done recursively. The largest element of a tree is the largest element of its right subtree. The easiest case is when a tree has no right subtree, in which case it must be the largest element. Finally, once we have the node to be deleted and the node that will replace it, we must do the appropriate assignments to accomplish this. Notice there are two different recursive algorithms here. We will implement these by having the procedure that finds the largest element inside the searching algorithm. The actual tree rearrangement will take place in the procedure that finds the largest element in the left subtree because it is here that we get all the information we need to perform the deletion. We can now put all of these ideas into Pascal (Figure 4.22).

Every recursive call moves down the tree so the complexity is $O(h)$ where h is how far down the tree we must go to find the replacement for x. Again, if the tree is bushy, this will be no further than $log\ n$, but if it is spindly it could be as far as n nodes from the root.

4. SPLAY TREES

4.1. What Are They?

As has been pointed out a number of times, the algorithms presented so far that search for an element, insert an element, and delete an element in a

```
procedure delete(var tree : nodeptr; x : integer);

procedure replace(var going, rep : nodeptr);
    { rep node will replace going node }
var gone : nodeptr;    { temporary ptr to save going node }
begin
    if rep^.right = nil then begin { move up to where going is }
        gone := going;
        going := rep:          { move replacing node up }
        rep := rep^.left;      { remove rep from old location }
        going^.left := gone^.left; { connect the node moved }
        going^.right := gone^.right { up to its children      }
        end
    else    { we must replace with the largest element }
        replace(tree, rep^.right)
end;

begin
    if tree = nil then
        { x not in the tree, nothing to delete }
    else if x < tree^.item then { x is in the left subtree }
        delete(tree^.left, x)
    else if x > tree^.item then { x is in the right subtree }
        delete(tree^.right, x)
    else                        { x will be deleted from this spot }
        if tree^.left = nil then { no left subtree           }
            tree := tree^.right { so replace with right subtree }
        else                   { replace with largest of left subtree }
            replace(tree, tree^.left)
end
```

Figure 4.22. A Pascal Procedure to Delete From a Binary Search Tree

binary search tree all require time $O(n)$. However, the motivation for using binary search trees was the expectation that these operations can be completed in $O(log\ n)$ time. It is indeed true that, on the average, binary search trees end up fairly bushy and so there is usually no real need to use any algorithms other than the ones presented. However, since we emphasize the worst case in this book, and since it is often important to have good worst case performance, we need to find a way to search, insert, and delete in $O(log\ n)$ time.

The usual approach to guaranteeing fast worst case behavior is to keep the binary search tree *balanced*. This means that at each node the left subtree should be about the same size as the right subtree, which means the tree will be bushy. How is the tree kept balanced? Whenever the shape of the tree changes, in other words after every insertion and deletion, the tree has to be rearranged so that good balance is maintained. This is done to assure the tree never gets too out of balance and so that no operation ever takes more than $O(log\ n)$ time. To accomplish all of this, extra information is usually stored at each node to keep track of the current balance status and as the tree changes this information is updated.

There is another technique for reorganizing binary search trees called *splaying*, requiring no extra information stored at each node, and operating by moving a chosen element to the root of the tree. Trees that are maintained using splaying are called *splay trees*. Splay trees are rearranged after every insertion, deletion, and search where most other balancing schemes rearrange only after insertions and deletions. For example, when performing a search in a splay tree, the element being searched for is splayed to the root of the tree when it is found, meaning that it is moved to the top of the tree. In the process of moving the node, the tree is made bushier. If the element is not found, some other element at the bottom of the tree is splayed to the top, again making the tree bushier.

Splay trees have a peculiar property. It is possible for some searches (or insertions or deletions) to take $O(n)$ time, however, it can be proved that over a long enough sequence of worst case operations the total time taken is $O(log\ n)$ times the number of operations. This means that the performance measured after many operations are performed is as good as can possibly be expected and so is as good as any other balancing scheme. When complexity is computed in this way (i.e., the time per operation is averaged over a worst case sequence) it is referred to as *amortized* time complexity. Calculating amortized complexities can be very complicated, as is the case for splay trees, so we will content ourselves with studying the algorithms and understanding intuitively why they perform so well.

4.2. Searching and Inserting

The algorithm for searching in a splay tree contains all the major ideas used in splay trees. The insertion algorithm turns out to just be a simple extension of the search algorithm, so a thorough understanding of the search procedure will make insertion (and deletion, for that matter) easy to understand. A search actually comprises two steps: (a) find the element in the tree, and (b) splay that element to the root. By now we understand how to find an element so all that remains is to describe how to splay an element to the top of a tree.

For the sake of this discussion, let's assume the element being searched for and splayed is 25, we always have a pointer to this node called x, and *tree* is a pointer to the root of the (sub)tree that *search* is currently searching. A call to *search* will find the node containing a 25, make sure *x* points to it, and will move the node closer to the root. Hence, from within *search,* upon returning from such a recursive call, the procedure must then move 25 closer to the root. As you will see next, this is done by sometimes having *tree* point to *x* and rearranging the tree accordingly and at other times by doing nothing at all.

Splaying works by moving a node towards the root two nodes at a time. This means that after a recursive call to *search,* two cases have to be considered. The simpler case is when *x* is found to be a child of *tree.* Since the major splay operation wants to move the 25 up the tree two steps, but it is currently only one step away from *tree,* nothing has to be done. We know that upon returning from this recursive call 25 will then be a grandchild of *tree* in the previous *search* and so will be properly handled there. There is one exception, however. If there is no previous call to *search,* then this must be the first call and so *tree* is actually the root of the entire binary search tree and not just the root of one of the subtrees from a recursive call. In this case, 25 must be moved the final step up so that it may become the root. Consider the following example.

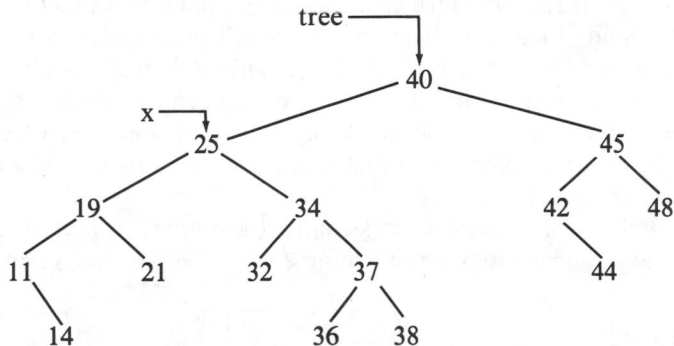

If 25 is going to move to the root, we must rearrange some of the subtrees. The three important subtrees are $x^\wedge.left,$ $x^\wedge.right,$ and $tree^\wedge.right,$ which correspond to subtrees rooted at 19, 34, and 45, respectively. Notice what must happen if 25 is going to become the root. Node 40 must become the right subtree of 25 (i.e., $x^\wedge.right$ must get the value *tree.*) All that remains is to figure out how to hook subtrees on to the two nodes 25 and 40. Clearly, 19 becomes the left subtree of 25, 34 the left subtree of 40, and 45 the right subtree of 40. But 19 ($x^\wedge.left$) and 45 ($tree^\wedge.right$) are already properly connected, so only 34 needs to be moved. Think about how you might do all of this in Pascal. If you peek ahead, you will see that I was able to do this using just three assignment statements. For this example, the resulting tree is:

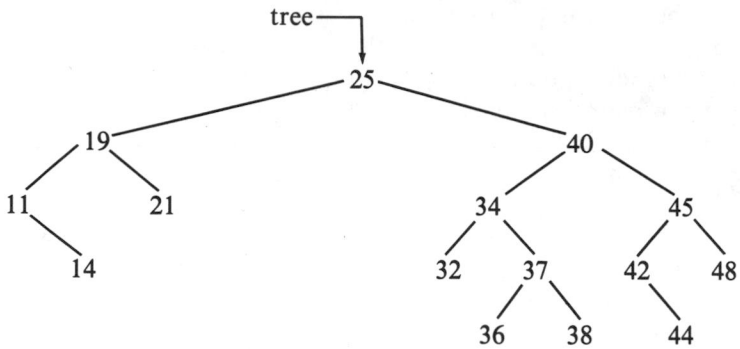

Let's review what we have done so far. We are working on Case 1, where *x* is pointing to a node that is a child of *tree*. If *tree* is not the root of the entire tree, we do nothing. If *tree* is the root, then we move it to the root, as seen in the example. The example only covered the case where *x* was on the left. We can use the same example to demonstrate what happens if *x* is on the right. We will use the last diagram above as the starting point, and assume that 40 needs to be splayed to the root. The first diagram below shows the result. In other words, the two operations are inverses of each other. Splaying 40 to the root will give us back the original tree we had before we splayed 25. Study these two diagrams. They will prepare you for Case 2.

Summarizing Case 1, *x* is a child of *tree* and there are four possibilities corresponding to whether or not *x* is a left or right child and corresponding to whether or not *tree* is the root of the entire tree or not. When *tree* is not the root there was nothing to do and the other two possibilities were just reverses of each other.

The second case also has four possibilities, but now *x* is a grandchild of *tree*. Let's look immediately at an example where we are still splaying 25.

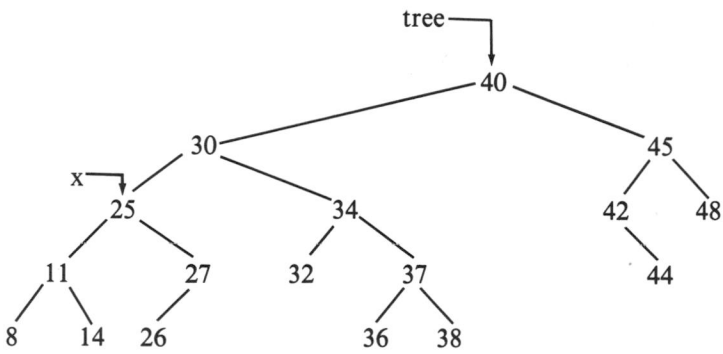

Our goal is to get 25 to the top of the tree. If we move 25 to the top, then 30 and 40 must go down the right side, like this:

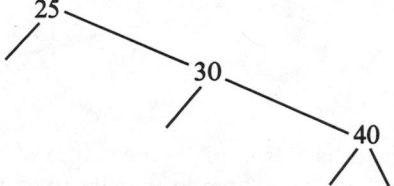

As we did before, we have to figure out how to hook up the subtrees, this time rooted at 11, 27, 34, and 45. If we just hook them up left to right in the only legal way everything works. That is, 11 to the left of 25, 27 to the left of 30, 34 to the left of 40, and 45 to the right of 40. The resulting tree looks like this:

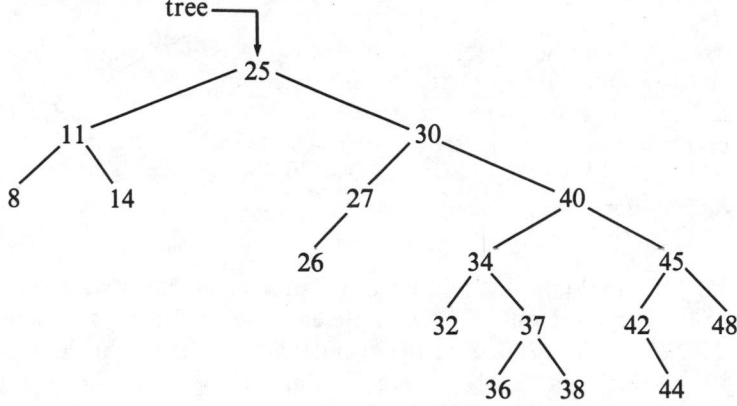

In this case 25 just hopped along the left edge and so is referred to as a *zig-zig* step. The other case on the left side is called a *zig-zag* step and is demonstrated by the following example.

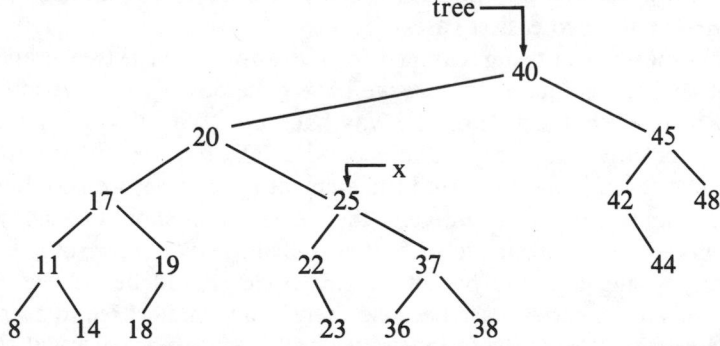

If 25 is going to move to the top of the tree, the resulting tree will have to have this structure:

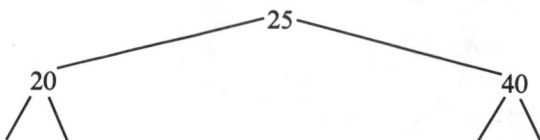

and we are again going to have to replace the subtrees. I bet you're getting the hang of this by now, aren't you? Node 17 will come off the left of 20 and 22 will come off of the right. Node 37 will come off the left of 40 and 45 will come off of the right. The resulting tree, after the zig-zag, looks like this:

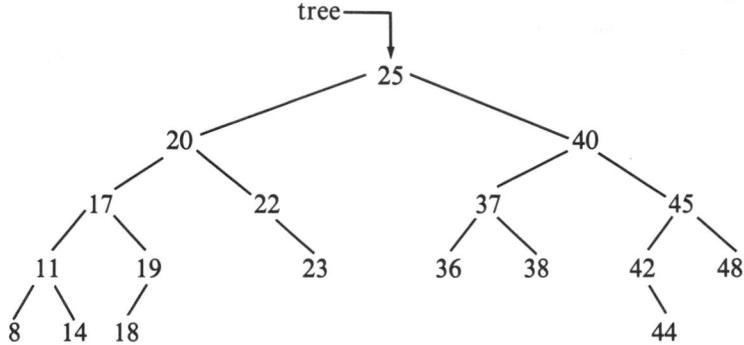

Again, you should think about what assignment statements are necessary to actually carry this out. This completes Case 2, the zig-zag step, for grandchildren on the left side. If the grandchild is on the right side instead, exactly the same ideas apply. There, again, will be a zig-zig case and a zig-zag case and they will be treated the same as they were on the left side. If you like, you may want to peek ahead to the actual Pascal procedure so that you can actually see the similarities. This nearly completes the recursive algorithm for searching in a splay tree. There is one final detail to consider. Do you know what it is? The easiest case, of course! For this algorithm, there are actually two easiest cases.

What if the element being searched for is not found in the tree at all? The spirit of splaying is that as long as we have gone down a tree we might as well try to balance it a little on the way back up. (We still don't have any intuition for why splaying does any good at all, but we will get to that shortly.) So, even if we don't find the element in the tree, we should splay something up to the top. Intuitively, the element that should be splayed is the last node visited. Recursively, if we search at the *nil* tree, we must return something saying that the parent of this node should be splayed. This corresponds to an easiest case because there is no smaller tree to search in than the *nil* tree. We use the following trick. We have said that x will always point to the node that was searched for, which is the node being splayed. We need to extend the use of x a little so it can be used when the searched for element is not found. If we are searching at the *nil* tree, we have *x* point to *nil* which acts as a signal that we don't know what should be splayed yet. In general, when we return from a recursive call to *search* we check to see if *x* is *nil*. If it is, it means that we just visited the *nil* subtree and so the node we are now at is the node that should be splayed and so we should assign *tree* to *x*. Of course, if *x* has a value other than *nil* then that is the node that is being splayed.

The other easiest case corresponds to the situation that the node being searched for and being splayed is the node at *tree*. Since the node is already at the root, the only other thing that needs to be done is to correctly assign *x*. That these are the two easiest cases should not surprise you since they are the same two that appeared in the binary search tree search algorithm without splaying.

We have now described the entire algorithm. Let's look at it in all of its Pascal glory (Figure 4.23).

Notice that we have used the idea of a driver procedure here. One would expect *search* to have only two parameters, so that is how it is written. What are the two extra parameters for in the recursive version, *search1*? If you look at the declaration of *search1* you will see. The extra *nodeptr* corresponds to *x*; the pointer to the element being splayed. The boolean parameter is used to tell us when we are really at the root. It is set to *true* the first time we call *search1* (because that is when we are at the root) and is set to *false* thereafter.

Even though we presumably understand the algorithm for searching it would still be nice to see some examples on bigger trees where the recursive step is applied more than once. Before we do this, however, I ask you to bear with me and see how insertion works first. This we can do quickly since it is really just a simple extension of the algorithm for searching. Then, we can look at some interesting examples.

One simple way to perform an insertion is to simply insert the element using the standard method for binary search trees and then search for that element, splaying it up to the root. We can, of course, be a little more efficient about it. With regular binary search trees *insert* was a simple extension of the *search* algorithm. The same is true here. The only difference between *search* and *insert* in splay trees is that when inserting we must create a new node and splay that one up the tree instead of one that already exists in the tree. If an element to be inserted is already found in the tree, the correct course of action depends on the particular application. In the case of binary search trees, we simply chose to leave the already existing element alone rather than, say, report an error. To keep in the same spirit with splay trees, we should not report an error but we should splay that element to the root of the tree. Given this information and the Pascal procedure for searching a splay tree you should find it easy to write *insert*

```
procedure search1(var tree, x : nodeptr; val : integer;
                                         root : boolean);
var child, temp : nodeptr;
begin
    if tree = nil then    { val is not in the tree }
        x := nil          { nothing to splay yet }
    else if val = tree^.item then { an easiest case –        }
        x := tree                  { element is already at root }
    else if val < tree^.item then begin
        search1(tree^.left, x, val, false);
        if x = nil then { val not found so splay the parent }
            x := tree
        else begin
            child := tree^.left;
            if x = child then { case 1 – element is left child }
                if root then begin
                            { case 1a – move it to the root }
                    tree^.left := x^.right;
                    x^.right := tree;
                    tree := x
                    end
                else { case 1b – not a splay step }
            else begin { case 2 – splay left }
                temp := tree;
                tree := x;
                if child^.left = x then begin { case 2a – zig-zig }
                    child^.left := tree^.right; { left step      }
                    temp^.left := child^.right;
                    tree^.right := child;
                    child^.right := temp
                    end
                else begin                    { case 2b - zig-zag }
                    child^.right := tree^.left; { left step      }
                    temp^.left := tree^.right;
                    tree^.right := temp;
                    tree^.left := child
                    end
                end
            end
        end
end
```

Figure 4.23. A Pascal Procedure to Search and Splay

```
        else { val > tree^.item } begin
            search1(tree^.right, x, val, false);
            if x = nil then { val not found so splay the parent }
                x := tree
            else begin
                child := tree^.right;
                if x — child then
                        { case 1 — element is right child       }
                    if root then begin
                            { case 1c — move it to the root }
                        tree^.right := x^.left;
                        x^.left := tree;
                        tree := x
                        end
                    else            { case 1d — not a splay step }
                else begin { case 2 — splay right }
                    temp := tree;
                    tree := x;
                    if child^.right = x then begin
                                        { case 2c — zig-zig }
                        child^.right := tree^.left; { right step     }
                        temp^.right := child^.left;
                        tree^.left := child;
                        child^.left := temp
                        end
                    else begin              { case 2d — zig-zag }
                        child^.left := tree^.right; { right step     }
                        temp^.right := tree^.left;
                        tree^.left := temp;
                        tree^.right := child
                        end
                    end
                end
            end
end;

procedure search(var tree : nodeptr; val : integer);
var dummy : nodeptr;
begin
    search1(tree, dummy, val, true)
end;
```

Figure 4.23. (Continued)

yourself. In fact, you are asked to do this in the exercises. Now let's look at some examples.

4.2.1. Examples.   For this first example we will start with a tree that only has right children. We will search for the largest element in the tree, the only leaf. This means that we will recursively call search at each node until we get to that leaf. Let's see what happens then.

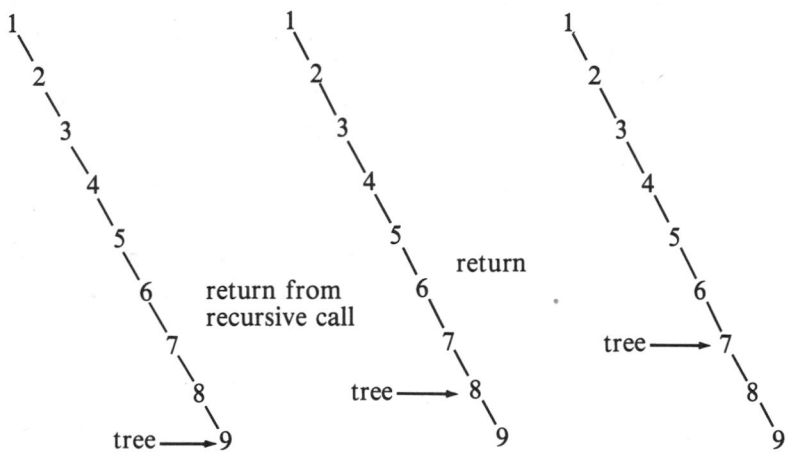

Easiest case. Element   not a splay step   zig-zig splay
searched for is the root.

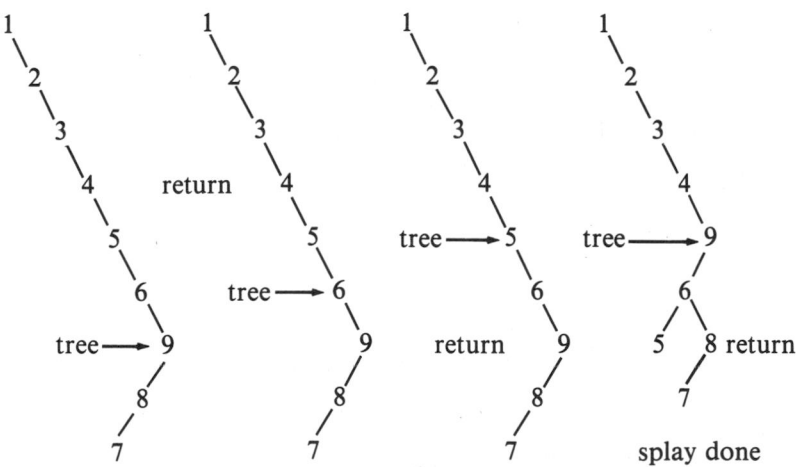

splay done   not a splay step   zig-zig splay

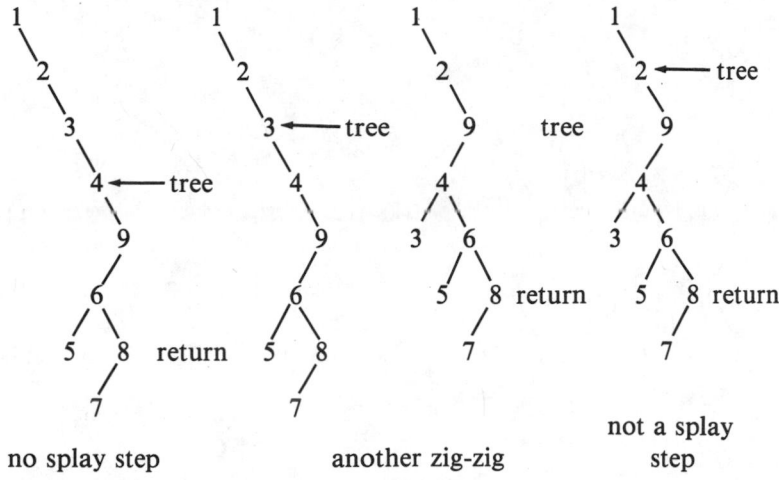

no splay step   another zig-zig   not a splay
                                                                  step

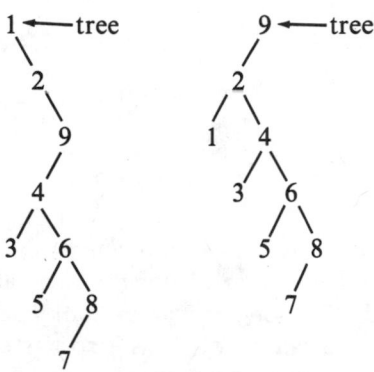

a final zig-zig step

   In this example searching for 9 took a long time because the tree was very
spindly and 9 was far away from the root. However, by the end of the
search the tree was much bushier because the path that 9 followed on its way
up the tree was made about half as long as its original length. Let's look at
another example where the main activity is zig-zag steps. Let's be more
concise this time and only look at the tree after each splay operation is
performed. In this example the last splay step corresponds to Case 1a, that
is, the element is a child but is still moved because its parent is the root of
the tree. In this case we are searching for 4.

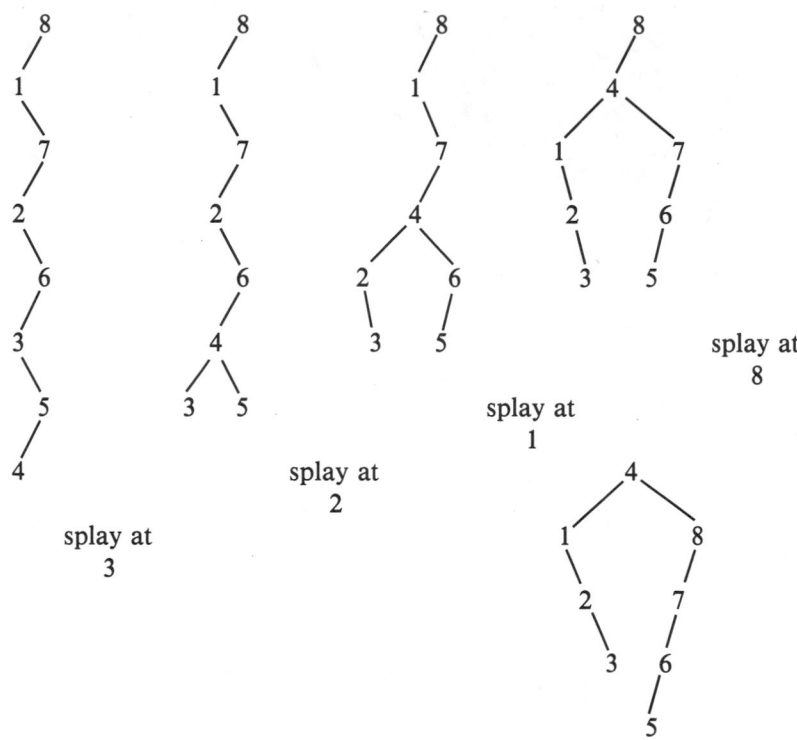

splay at
3

splay at
2

splay at
1

splay at
8

As in the previous example, the spindly tree has been made bushier. In general, you should be noticing that the old path along which all the splaying is being done is made about half as long as it was. Look back on how splay search is accomplished and you can see why this is so. On either a zig-zig or a zig-zag step one element is removed from the path and moved to another branch of the tree. In total, half of the elements are relocated so that path is made half as long. Meanwhile, the paths that are made longer are only made longer by a constant amount of one or two. You can see, then, that it is possible for a search to have a very positive effect in making a tree bushy by taking a long path and making it half as long, while the worst damage it can do is take a long path and make it 2 longer. These ideas can, in fact, be formalized to prove an amortized worst case for splay trees of *O(log n)* per operation, but the mathematics gets a bit too complicated for our purposes here.

Lets look at one last example of a slightly more general nature. Our diagrams will start at the point where the procedure finds the correct place for insertion and we will only show the tree after each splay operation. In this example we would like to insert a 13.

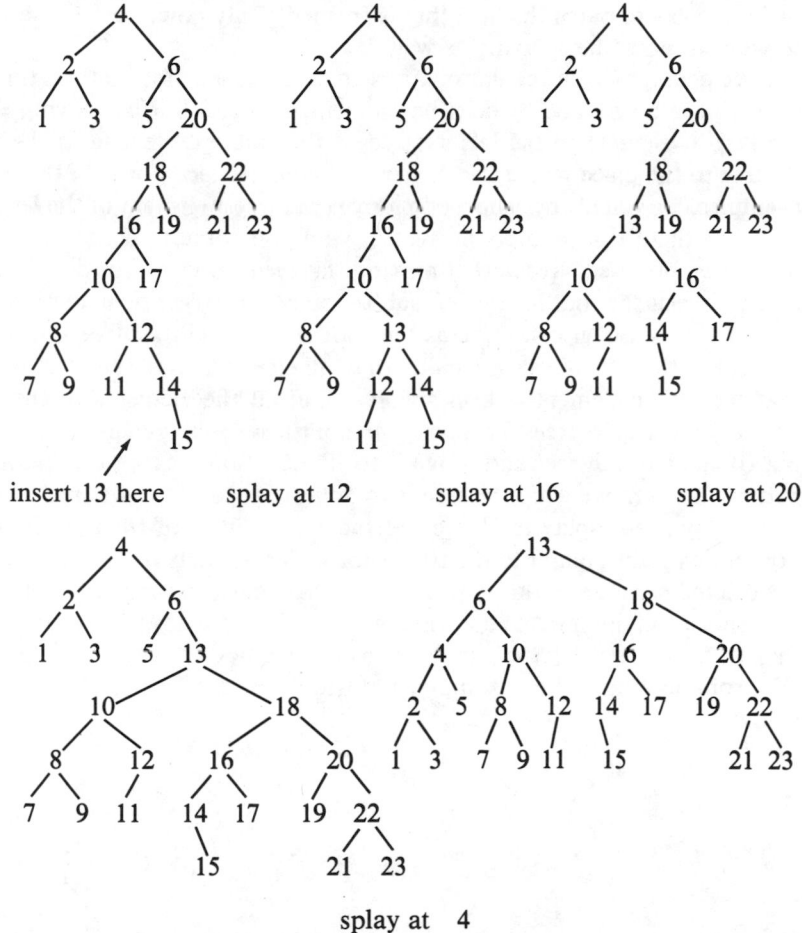

splay at   4

Take a good look at this example to be sure you understand exactly how the tree is rearranged by splaying. You should go back to the *search* procedure and convince yourself that the code there really does rearrange the tree as was done in this example. All that remains for us to do in this chapter is to see how deletion is accomplished in splay trees.

4.3. Deleting

Now that we have a good understanding of how to insert into and search a splay tree, we should find deleting fairly easy. The only problem we are going to have is the same problem we had when we deleted from an ordinary binary search tree. If an element is about to be taken out of a tree we need to find a way to patch the hole that is formed. Only now, we are also going to want to do some splaying as well.

Here again, as with regular binary search trees, the most natural thing to do with the hole made by deleting an element is to fill it by moving either the largest element in the left subtree or the smallest element in the right subtree to the place where the element is being deleted. For the sake of our examples, we will always choose to move the largest element of the left subtree, but there is absolutely no reason why you couldn't choose the other one if you prefered. Recall that moving this element is appropriate because it can serve as the root for the left subtree since it is larger than anything else in that tree. Also, it can serve as the root for the right subtree since every element in the left subtree is smaller than all elements in the right subtree so that particular element is also smaller than all the elements in the right subtree. With splay trees, however, we don't just forcibly yank that element out of the left subtree, and move it to its new home as we did before. A better way to move it up the tree is to splay. Specifically, we treat the left subtree by itself, splay the largest element to the top of the tree, hook its now empty right pointer to the right subtree, and finally hook the parent of the deleted node up to this new node that has replaced the deleted element. To continue in the spirit of splaying, as long as we are down in the tree now, the last step is to splay the parent of the deleted node to the top of the tree. It's probably time for an example. We will delete the 14 from the first tree below.

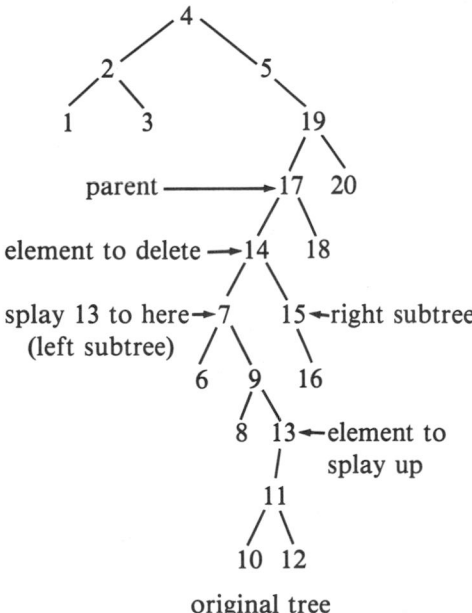

original tree

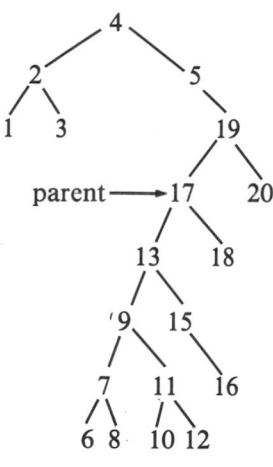

tree after 13 is splayed,
right subtree is connected,
and 13 hooked back to parent

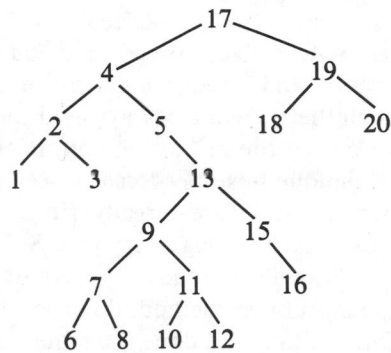

final tree after parent (17) is splayed to root

You can see that deleting an element from a splay tree only uses ideas that have already been programmed in other parts of this book. In the order of use in this algorithm, these are: (a) find an element (that will be deleted), (b) find the largest element (of the left subtree), (c) splay an element (the one found in Step b) to the root (of the left subtree mentioned in b), (d) rearrange a few pointers (see the example), and (e) splay another element (the parent this time). Since each step by itself is actually quite simple, I will leave the programming of it to you as an exercise. In fact, at this point you have seen more than enough examples of splay trees so it is time to look back on what all we did in this chapter.

5. SUMMARY

A lot of information has been covered in this chapter. Most of it can be distilled into an aphorism: if the data structure is recursive, algorithms that work on the data structure should be recursive also. Of course this is an oversimplification, but look at how much we were able to do recursively. Practically any problem we could think of for linked lists or binary trees had a natural recursive algorithm that was efficient as well.

One useful technique also stands out and is most clearly demonstrated in the tail insertion and tail deletion algorithms for linked lists. This is the technique of passing the object to be worked on, like a linked list, say, as a *var* parameter so that the easiest case works directly on the part of the data structure that is changing. This is the most natural way to implement many algorithms, yet is irritatingly hard to understand. Once you develop skills in determining exactly what is changing in the easiest case it becomes much easier to use. I hope you are at this stage now and are discovering the beauty and power of this simple technique.

Most of the examples in this chapter are well-known and should be part of any computer scientist's problem-solving arsenal. You have probably seen many of these examples in other places already and you will surely need to be able to use them again, and often, in the future. There is one exception, however. Although there are many ways used to balance binary search trees, splaying is not one of the more common. Probably the main reason for this is that the technique has only recently been discovered and the other more well-known methods are already firmly rooted in the literature and in existing code. Don't let this worry you. Splaying has many advantages over the more traditional approaches. It requires no additional information in the nodes like most older methods do. The balancing scheme used when splaying is uniform in that it is done the same way regardless of the size or shape of the tree. As we have seen, it is reasonably easy to program. Splay trees have been proven to perform very well and have been conjectured to be as good as any balancing scheme that might ever be devised. This last statement is a little hard to state formally here, especially since we did no complexity analysis on splay trees, but you probably have some sense of what this means in terms of big-oh complexity and you can see the potential that splaying offers.

At this point you should be getting pretty good at coming up with recursive algorithms. Because of this, the emphasis is going to shift a little bit in the next chapter. Up until now we have been dealing with fairly easy problems that allowed fairly easy recursive algorithms to solve them so that we could focus on the fundamentals of recursion. In the next chapter we will look at some harder problems and find some more sophisticated recursive algorithms so we can develop a deeper appreciation for the true power of recursion.

6. EXERCISES

1. Write a function that will return the sum of all the elements in a linked list of integers. What is the complexity of your function?

2. Write a function that will return the sum of the positive elements in a linked list. Negative elements in the list should be ignored. What is the complexity of your function?

3. Write a Pascal procedure that will output a linked list followed by a carriage return. Try to write a Pascal procedure that will output a linked list backwards followed by a carriage return. What difficulties do you encounter? How are these difficulties overcome? Hint: Try using a driver procedure.

4. You probably realize that *tail_insert* as presented in the chapter will not work if *list* is not passed as a *var* parameter. Explain why this is so.

5. The following procedure is very similar to the one in the text that inserts an element at the end of a list. Is this a better or worse way to do it?

```
procedure tail_insert(var list : nodeptr; num : integer);
var small_list : nodoptr;
begin
    if list = nil then begin { easiest case }
        new(list);
        list^.item := num;
        list^.next := nil
        end
    else begin
        small_list := list^.next;
        tail_insert(small_list, num)
        end
end;
```

6. Write a recursive procedure that will take a list and a node and will insert the node at the end of the list. Use this procedure to write another $O(n^2)$ procedure to reverse a list.

7. Write recursive procedures that will input and output long integers as done in this chapter. Write a main program that will be menu driven that will allow a user to easily add and multiply integers that can be arbitrarily large.

8. The addition algorithm developed in the chapter contained the statement *num1 := copy(num2)*. Why is it important to copy *num2?* Provide a sequence of *add* operations (one is not enough) that shows the pitfall of not using *copy*.

9. Show that the solution of

$$T(m,n) = T(n - 1,m - 1) + T(n - 1,1) + T(1,m - 1) + 2n + 2m + 2 \text{ is } O(n \times m).$$

Hint: $O((min(n,m)^2 + m \times n) = O(m \times n)$.

10. Draw a binary tree where the root is also a leaf.

11. The following is supposed to be an improvement over the algorithm given in the chapter to do a parenthesis output of a binary tree. Carefully describe excactly how the output from this algorithm will differ from that of the one in the chapter. Is it an improvement?

```
procedure parenout(list : nodeptr);
begin
    if tree = nil then
        write( '()' )
    else begin
        write( '(' );
        parenout(tree^.left);
        write(tree^.item);
        parenout(tree^.right);
        write( ')' )
    end
end;
```

12. Explain why the following is not a binary search tree:

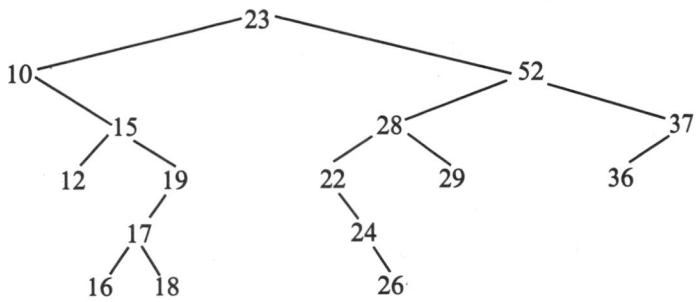

13. Write a procedure to output the contents of the nodes of a binary search tree in decreasing order.

14. The *height* of a binary search tree is the length of the longest path in the tree. For example, the height of the tree in Problem 12 is 6. The height of the empty tree is 0. If you recall the discussion we had concerning the complexity of searching in a binary search tree you can see that the complexity of searching corresponds to the height of the tree. Write a Pascal function to find the height of a binary search tree. What is the complexity of your function? Remember our rule of thumb that says that you should minimize the number of recursive calls a function makes? Be sure you do that here or you may end up with an unnecessarily large complexity.

15. Describe the tree that is obtained if the numbers from 1 to n are inserted into a binary search tree in the following order: 1, n, 2, $n - 1$, 3, $n - 2$, 4, $n - 3$, ... Describe another way to insert the integers 1 through n into a binary search tree to end up with a worst case tree. How many different worst case trees are there?

16. You have been given a method of inserting elements into a binary search tree that will provide a very bushy tree. Show the tree that is obtained when the Elements 1–20 are inserted into a binary search tree using the given

method. Is it possible to get a bushier search tree containing the Elements 1–20 by inserting in some other order? More formally, explain what is meant by the intuitive phrase *bushiest binary search tree.*

17. Given the following splay tree, show the resultant trees after the following elements are searched for: 25, 22, 40, 45, 14, 38, 44, 21, 35, and 43.

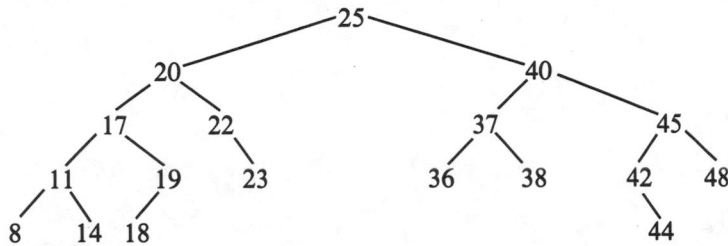

18. Find a tree and an element in that tree so that splay searching for that element in that tree actually makes the height of the tree greater. (Recall the definition of *height* from Problem 14.) Try to give a general description of what a tree must look like and where the searched for element must be in that tree so that the height of the tree will increase after a search.

19. Write a Pascal procedure that inserts an element into a splay tree. If the element being inserted is found to be in the tree already, do not do anything drastic; just splay it to the root of the tree. You should be able to do this by just making a few changes to the search procedure for splay trees that appears in this chapter.

20. What tree is formed after the numbers 1, 2, . . . , *n* are inserted into a splay tree. Does this tree contradict the supposed speed of splay trees? How long did it take to insert the *n* elements? Next, how long does it take to search for 1? After this search, how long does it take to search for 3? After this, how long to search for 5? How is the tree starting to look? How many searches need to be made before the height of the tree is *log n?*

21. Write a procedure that will delete an element from a splay tree. Even though in this chapter I claimed it is very easy to do, there are a couple of things you have to be careful of. In particular, it is a little tricky recognizing the parent of the node that is deleted. You will probably need to pass along another argument to the procedure to do this properly. Similarly, if the node to be deleted is the root it will have no parent and so your procedure had better be ready for this case. Finally, if the left subtree of the deleted node is nil, you will have to treat this case separately. You might want to go back and see how this was handled for the case when we deleted from a binary search tree.

5

Advanced Topics

1. MORE SORTING ALGORITHMS

In Chapter 1, we studied two similar sorting algorithms: insertion sort and selection sort. Recall that the difference between these two algorithms was just a matter of timing. With insertion sort we first made the recursive call (on an array one smaller than the original array) then we produced a sorted array by inserting the remaining element into the sorted smaller array. Selection sort was just the opposite. In this case, we first put the largest element into its proper place in the array and then we sorted the remaining array. In this section, we will just extend these ideas slightly to get two more very important sorting algorithms. The difference will be that instead of having to try to put together a recursively sorted smaller array with $n - 1$ elements and a single element from the array, we will put together two recursively sorted arrays with $\frac{n}{2}$ elements in each. If you think about it, the two approaches are very similar. In both cases you are dealing with two smaller sorted arrays. The difference is that, in this chapter the two sorted arrays will be about the same size, while in Chapter 1, the two sorted arrays were of quite different sizes since the two sizes where $n - 1$ and 1. (An array of size one is sorted, of course.)

Again there will be two possibilities depending on whether the recursive call comes first or last. If we sort the two smaller arrays first and then put them together into one large sorted array, this is called *mergesort*. With insertion sort we only had to sort one of the two smaller arrays since the other smaller array, the one of size 1, was already sorted. On the other hand, if we separate the array in such a way that the larger elements are in one half and the smaller elements are in the other half and then sort the two halves, this is called *quicksort*. With selection sort there was only one half to sort because the largest element by itself, the other "half," was already sorted.

We will start by first studying mergesort, then look at the more practical but slightly more complicated quicksort. We will also study a third sorting algorithm called *heapsort* which is unique in its own right. I think you will find it interesting. The complexity analyses of all three algorithms will also turn out to be interesting, each for quite different reasons.

1.1. Merge Sort

Let's start by immediately looking at the Pascal procedure for mergesort (Figure 5.1). See if you can guess what the procedures *copy* and *merge* are supposed to do.

Recall that mergesort is supposed to recursively sort the left and right halves and then put the two parts together. Looking at Figure 5.1, it is easy to see the two recursive calls and further, *merge* must be written so that the two sorted halves are put back into *a*. The process of combining two sorted arrays into one large sorted array is called *merging,* hence, the name of the procedure. We will discuss merging shortly, but first what is *copy* all about?

To help you appreciate *copy,* pretend we don't need it. This would imply that after the two recursive calls, the first half of *a* would contain a sorted array and the second half would contain another sorted array. Now how do

```
procedure mergesort(var a : arraytype; size : integer);
var lefthalf, righthalf : arraytype;
begin
    if size < = 1 then
        { 1 or 0 element arrays are already sorted }
    else begin
        copy(a, 1, size div 2, lefthalf);
        copy(a, (size div 2) + 1, size, righthalf);
        mergesort(lefthalf, size div 2);
        mergesort(righthalf, (size + 1) div 2);
        merge(lefthalf, righthalf, a,
            size div 2, (size + 1) div 2)
        end
end;
```

Figure 5.1.   High-Level Pascal Description of Merge Sort

we put the two halves together? Think hard about it before you read on. We have big problems. For example, suppose the smallest element is the first element in the second half. To move it to the front of *a* where it belongs would mean that we would have to do something to the current first half of *a*. But what are you going to do with it? Shift it over to the right? This would be much too inefficient (see the exercises). Copy it into another array? I thought we were trying to avoid doing a *copy*. It turns out to be impractical not to copy. The best solution to this problem is to have a third array to merge the two halves into. We do this by putting the two sorted halves into temporary arrays and then merge these back into the original array. We put the two different halves into temporary arrays using the *copy* procedure. The arguments being passed to it are clear and it should be easy for you to write *copy*. You can see how I did it a bit later when I show you all the pieces of my mergesort Pascal procedure.

It is, or course, clear that the size of the left half of the array is *size div* 2, but it may not be so obvious why the size of the right half is (*size* + 1) *div* 2. I'm going to let you figure this out for yourself, however, let me give you a hint. There are really just two different cases to consider: *size* is even or *size* is odd. Try a few examples of both cases and you should quickly see what is going on.

All that remains is to figure out how to merge the two halves together into one magnificent sorted array. Let me suggest a recursive (of course) way to go about it. You can fill in the details by looking at the Pascal code that follows. The basic idea is very simple. Look at the first element of the two sorted arrays and choose the smaller. This will be the smallest element so put it in the beginning of the third array and then recursively merge the two sorted arrays, where one of them is now one smaller, into the third array making sure the merging in the third array begins to the right of where the element was just placed. You should be able to figure out the easiest case(s). Before you look at *copy* and *merge* in Figure 5.2 and 5.3 shown below, try it yourself. Notice that *merge* is just a driver procedure for the recursive merging algorithm. This is because the recursive version requires more parameters than one would naturally expect to use when naively calling merge.

To find the complexity of *mergesort* we must first figure out the complexities of *copy* and *merge*. Since *copy* is just a simple loop, it is clearly $O(n)$. When merging we start with two arrays of size l and m and end up with a merged array of size n, where $l + m = n$. If we focus on n, the size of the merged array that is created, and looking at the merge procedure, above, we can say that to create the merged array of size n we must do a constant amount of work (check to see if either l or m is 0, find the smaller of two values, etc.) and then create a merged array of size $n - 1$. In other words, the recurrence relation for *merge* is: $T(n) = 1 + T(n - 1)$. We've seen this

```
procedure merge(a1, a2 : arraytype; var a3 : arraytype;
                size1, size2 : integer);

  procedure recursivemerge(a1 : arraytype; left1, right1 : integer;
                           a2 : arraytype; left2, right2 : integer;
                           var a3 : arraytype; left3 : integer);
  begin
    if (left1 > right1) and (left2 > right2) then
      { easiest case— nothing to merge }
    else if left1 > right1 then begin { elements only in a2 }
        a3[left3] := a2[left2];
        recursivemerge(a1, left1, right1, a2, left2 + 1, right2,
                       a3, left3 + 1)
      end
    else if left2 > right2 then begin { elements only in a1 }
        a3[left3] := a1[left1];
        recursivemerge(a1, left1 + 1, right1, a2, left2, right2,
                       a3, left3 + 1)
      end
    else { elements in both a1 and a2 }
      if a1[left1] < a2[left2] then begin { find next element }
        a3[left3] := a1[left1];              {       for a3       }
        recursivemerge(a1, left1 + 1, right1, a2, left2, right2,
                       a3, left3 + 1)
      end
      else begin
        a3[left3] := a2[left2];
        recursivemerge(a1, left1, right1, a2, left2 + 1, right2,
                       a3, left3 + 1)
      end
  end;

begin
  recursivemerge(a1, 1, size1, a2, 1, size2, a3, 1)
end;
```

Figure 5.2.   Pascal Procedure to Merge Two Sorted Lists

one many times in the past and so we know that the complexity of merge is
$O(n)$. You probably suspected this all along since intuitively you could see
that each element in the two arrays gets "processed" exactly once. When
calculating complexities it's important to try to get the mathematical analysis
to agree with your intuition. If they don't agree, one of them has to be wrong.

```
procedure copy(a : arraytype; left, right : integer;
                                var b : arraytype);
var ct, i : integer;
begin
     ct := 1;
     for i :- left to right do begin
          b[ct] := a[i];
          ct := ct + 1
          end
end;
```

Figure 5.3. Pascal Procedure to Copy One Array to Another

So, to do a mergesort on an n-element array we must sort two smaller arrays of size $\frac{n}{2}$ and also do n additional steps corresponding to the copying and the merging. We can now figure out the complexity of mergesort.

$$T(n) = 2T(\tfrac{n}{2}) + n \qquad \text{as described above}$$

$$= 2[2T(\tfrac{n}{4}) + \tfrac{n}{2}] + n \qquad \text{expanding } T(\tfrac{n}{2})$$

$$= 2^2 T(\tfrac{n}{2^2}) + n + n \qquad \text{distributing the 2}$$

$$= 2^i T(\tfrac{n}{2^i}) + in \qquad \text{recognizing the pattern}$$

$$= n + (log n)\, n \qquad \text{choosing } i = log_2 n$$

$$= O(n\ log\ n)$$

Notice that this is considerably better than either of the other two sorting algorithms we did early, since they both had complexity $O(n^2)$. There is one wrinkle in all of this, however. So far we've never said anything about *space* complexity because all of our algorithms so far have used little extra space beyond what is input to them. This algorithm is an exception, however. Looking back at the Pascal procedure *mergesort* you will notice that there are two local variables of type *arraytype* to hold the copies of the left and right halves of the original array, *a*. Even if Pascal were clever enough to only make the two arrays exactly the size that's needed (which it isn't) everytime *mergesort* is called an additional n memory locations are needed.

Even if this procedure were called only once, this would roughly double the amount of memory needed, and that is usually unacceptable. However, it gets worse. A little thought should convince you that *mergesort* can call itself a total of *log n* times, each time requiring half the extra memory than the previous time, meaning that, in all, *mergesort* requires about triple the amount of memory that the original problem required. And that was assuming Pascal was smart with its memory. Since it's not, each recursive calls produces local arrays of exactly the same size and so *log n* times more memory is actually needed. This is a lot of extra memory. For this reason and some others discussed in the exercises, mergesort is not often seen in practice.

1.2. Quicksort

As we discussed earlier, in the case of quicksort all the extra work is done before the two recursive calls. What we need to do is to find a way to divide the array into two partitions so that all of the elements in the first partition are smaller than all of the elements in the second one. Then recursive calls to each partition will complete the sort.

As it turns out, it is easy to have the partitioning procedure do just a bit more. We will have it partition the array so that when it is done we will get back the modified array and a pointer to the location of a special element called the pivot. Everything to the left of the pivot element will be less than or equal to it, while everything to the right will be greater than or equal to it. In some sense, then, this is the middle of the partition. This means that the recursive calls to quicksort need not include the pivot element since it is already in the proper place. That is, the pivot element should not be included in either of the partitions that are recursively sorted. The Pascal procedure for quicksort looks like Figure 5.4.

All that remains is to come up with an algorithm to do the partitioning. Not surprisingly, one of the simplest algorithms to do this is recursive. The idea is to partition all but the first element of the array and then make sure the first element is correctly located. Since the recursive call to the partitioning algorithm returns a pointer to the pivot element, if the first element is less than that element, it is already in the correct partition and so we are done. If, however, that first element is greater than the pivot element then it must somehow be moved over to the right partition. This means that the left partition is actually one element too big and the right one is one too small. So the pivot must be moved over to the left, the first element fills the gap left by the pivot element moving out and the element replaced by the pivot (the one originally to the pivot's left) replaces the first element.

This is all actually quite simple. To help convince you, let's look at two

```
procedure quicksort(var a : arraytype; left, right : integer);
var mid : integer;
begin
    if left  > =  right then
        { 0 and 1 element arrays are already sorted }
    else begin
        partition(a, left, right, mid);
        quicksort(a, left, mid  −  1);
        quicksort(a, mid  +  1, right)
        end
end;
```

Figure 5.4. Pascal Procedure for Quicksort

examples corresponding to the two cases just described. This first example shows what happens when nothing has to happen after the recursive call.

23 12 56 67 32 35 41 89 76 74 49 ◄—— original array

23│ 12 56 67 32 35 41 89 76 74 49 ◄—— ignore first element and
                                                partition smaller array

23│ 12 35 41 32 49 56 67 89 76 74 ◄—— smaller array partitioned,
             ↑   procedure returns pointer
            mid   to pivot element

23 12 35 41 32 49 56 67 89 76 74 ◄—— first element < pivot so done
             ↑
            mid

The next example requires elements to be moved after the recursive call because the first element of the array is larger than the pivot element,

51 12 56 67 32 35 41 89 76 74 49 ◄—— original array

51│ 12 56 67 32 35 41 89 76 74 49 ◄—— ignore first element and
                                                partition smaller array

51│ 12 35 41 32 49 56 67 89 76 74 ◄—— smaller array partitioned,
             ↑   procedure returns pointer
            mid   to pivot element

51 12 35 41 32 49 56 67 89 76 74 ◄—— first element > pivot so move
             ↑   elements as indicated
            mid

32 12 35 41 49 51 56 67 89 76 74 ◄—— partitioned array
             ↑
            mid

Since we want our partitioning algorithm to return a pointer to the pivot element, it would not make sense to try to partition a zero-element array as there would be no pivot element available. Thus, the easiest case for this algorithm is a one-element array. Also, the complexity is clearly $O(n)$ since the recurrence relation for this algorithm is $T(n) = T(n - 1) + 1$. Figure 5.5 shows the algorithm in Pascal.

Now that we have seen the Pascal code for quicksort, all that remains is to figure out the complexity. But the argument that we used for mergesort should work here just as well, right? The array is partitioned into two halves in $O(n)$ steps and then each half is sorted recursively. So, the recurrence relation is the same as it was for mergesort, namely $T(n) = n + 2T(\frac{n}{2})$, right? And so, if you look back in the last section (or if you remember), you can see that the complexity of quicksort is $O(n \ log \ n)$. Right?

Wrong! We have made a big assumption here that is not always correct. Can you find it? Read that last paragraph again and figure out where we went wrong before you read on. Did you figure it out? We made the assumption that *partition* would always partition the array into two equal halves. This simply is not true. For example, take an array that happens to

```
procedure partition(var a : arraytype; left, right : integer;
                                        var pivot : integer);
var temp : integer;
begin
    if left = right then { easiest case – nothing to }
        pivot := right { partition }
    else begin
        partition(a, left + 1, right, pivot); {partition all but 1st}
        if a[left] > a[pivot] then begin { if first element is not }
            temp := a[pivot]; { in the correct partition then }
            a[pivot] := a[left]; { move it there by shifting a few }
            a[left] := a[pivot - 1];
                        { elements around, including the   }
            a[pivot - 1] := temp;
                        { pivot element which must get     }
            pivot := pivot - 1
                        { shifted to the left to make room }
        end             { for the first element, a[left]   }
    end
end;
```

Figure 5.5. Pascal Procedure to Partition an Array

be sorted and apply the partition algorithm to it. What happens? The array remains unchanged and the last element in the array turns out to be the pivot. This means that the first "half" of the partition has $n - 1$ elements in it and the second "half" has no elements at all. Hence, we cannot assume that the array is always partitioned into two equal halves.

So what is the complexity, then? The last paragraph suggests to us that an array that is already sorted is probably going to be the worst case because then we will recursively sort an array with $n - 1$ elements (and an array with zero elements which we don't even have to bother counting). So, the recurrence relation is really $T(n) = n + T(n - 1)$ which we know implies that $T(n) = O(n^2)$. So it looks like quicksort is a misnomer in that it is no better than insertion or selection sort and is worse than mergesort. Well, not really. Even though we said we would only be interested in the worst cases of algorithms, this will be our only exception. It turns out that in practice quicksort does very well. This is because the worst case doesn't seem to come up that often. When the data is random the partitioning algorithm actually does very well and usually splits the array into two fairly equal-sized pieces. This means that the first recurrence relation we came up with really does apply and so quick sort will act like a $O(n \ log \ n)$ algorithm. In fact, among all of the sorting algorithms known, quicksort or some simple modification of it (see the exercises) is usually the best algorithm to use if you know nothing in advance about what your data might look like. You will be asked in the exercises to convince yourself of this by writing programs for the different sorts and testing them on various data. But first, lets look at our last and probably most exotic sorting algorithm.

1.3. Heap Sort

From the last chapter we know that binary search trees, especially when they are well balanced, can provide data structures for very efficient algorithms. This applies to sorting as well. If we are using balanced binary search trees we know that insertions take $O(log \ n)$ time, so an entire binary search tree can be built in $O(n \ log \ n)$ time. We can then "output" this binary search tree into an array in linear time. Hence, we have sorted the data in $O(n \ log \ n)$ time. Is this, therefore, a good sorting algorithm? Of course it depends on the situation, but usually the answer is "no." The reason is the same as it was for mergesort. Both of these sorts are fast, but both of them use too much extra memory. If we were to use binary search trees for sorting we would need all the extra memory that would be required for the tree as well as the memory for the array. This would more than double the memory requirements and so, for most applications, is simply not acceptable.

Let's not give up on the idea of using trees, however. What we would like to do is to find a way to use trees without using extra memory. What this means is that we need to find a way to view an array not just as a linear data structure but as some kind of tree as well. Let's look at an example of what we are planning to do.

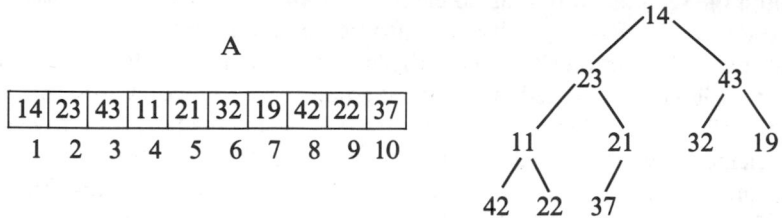

The array, *A*, on the left has been reshaped to look like a tree on the right. We simply wrote down the array one element at a time from top to bottom, left to right. in other words, *A*[1] (14) is the root, *A*[2] (23) and *A*[3] (43) are the children of *A*[1]. *A*[4] (11) and *A*[5] (21), are the children of *A*[2], etc. *A*[6] through *A*[10] are the leaves.

All of this will be quite useless if we have no natural way to move about the tree, but, fortunately, it is very easy to move up and down this kind of tree. Do you see how? Pause for a minute and assume you are at some arbitrary element in the array, say *A*[*i*]. What is the parent of *A*[*i*] and what are its two children? Do you see it? No matter how big the array is, *A*[*i div* 2] will always be the parent of *A*[*i*] while *A*[*i* * 2] and *A*[*i* * 2 + 1] will be the children. Check to make sure this really works on the ten-element example above. What is the parent of *A*[1]? We said that *A*[1] is the root so it should have no parent. According to the rule, the parent of *A*[1] is *A*[0] but there is no element 0 in the array (it is indexed from 1 to 10) so indeed it has no parent, so it is the root. Similarly, what are the children of *A*[7]? The rule says the two children are *A*[14] and *A*[15] but again, since the array is only indexed up to 10, it means that *A*[7] has no children (i.e., it is a leaf). So, we have a very simple way to view an array as if it were a tree that allows us to move up and down the tree very easily. Now what?

We need to use this idea to help us sort. As you might expect, there is no simple way to use this tree structure to have the array behave like a binary search tree. This is because the shape of a binary search tree changes during insertions and deletions while the shape of the tree using this technique is fixed. What we need is some kind of tree whose shape doesn't change too much even when elements are inserted and deleted and yet is somehow useful for sorting. What we will be interested in is a tree where each element on the tree is larger than all of its progeny. We will call such a tree a *heap*. For example, this would mean that the largest element in a heap is the root of the tree (i.e., *A*[1]). We are often interested in the largest element when we are sorting so a heap just might be useful for sorting.

We can define heaps recursively. The empty tree is a heap. The root of a heap is greater than its children and both children are the roots of heaps (almost). There are shape constraints to heaps that are not captured in this definition. However, since most algorithms will not be interested in the shape anyway, the recursive definition will provide the clue to many algorithms using heaps. In this book, we will only be interested in using heaps for sorting, but there are many other uses for heaps that you will probably learn about in your advanced algorithms and data structures class.

So, what does a heap look like? The example above is not a heap, but the following is.

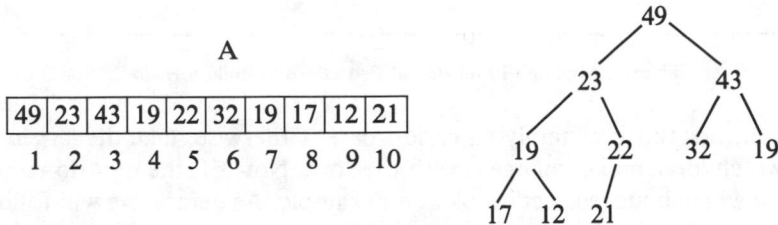

At this stage there should be two things concerning you. The first has to do with the fact that when you look at the Heap A in the above example, it doesn't look terribly well sorted yet. In fact, since we usually sort from smallest to largest, we seem to be in especially bad shape since some of the largest elements are near the front of the array, in particular, the largest element is first in the array even though we would eventually like to see it at the end of the array. You are probably also concerned about creating heaps. How can one build a heap and how quickly can it be done? First we will discuss the process of building a heap.

Having seen the recursive definition of a heap you should not be too surprised to find out that there is a simple recursive algorithm for building a heap. The gist of the algorithm is to make a heap of the left subtree, make a heap of the right subtree, and then take the element at the root and place it so that the entire tree is a heap. This, of course, is the tricky step since recursive calls are easy to make.

This process of moving the root of a tree with two heaps as children to form a large heap is called *sifting*. Before we figure out how to sift let's look at the Pascal procedure, Figure 5.6, to build a heap.

Pay particular attention to how we decide if an element is a leaf. The *bottom* variable tells us where the last element in the array is to be found so if the left child of a node is found, to be past the last element then there is no left child, so there are no children at all (i.e., it is a leaf).

Now we have to figure out how to sift. Sifting has a natural recursive algorithm: If the root is larger than its children, then we have an easiest case because this means the tree is already a heap. If the root has no

```
procedure buildheap(var a : arraytype; top, bottom : integer);
begin
   if 2*top > bottom then
      { just one element — already a heap }
   else begin
      buildheap(a, 2*top, bottom);        { make heap of left child  }
      buildheap(a, 2*top + 1, bottom); { make heap of right child }
      sift(a, top, bottom) { make whole thing a heap }
      end
end;
```

Figure 5.6. High-Level Pascal Procedure to Build a Heap

children, then this is certainly an easiest case. Otherwise, take the larger of
the two children and exchange it with the root. Now sift the root down the
subtree where it moved. Let's look at an example. As before, we will follow
along watching the data as a heap as well as a linear array. We will show
what happens during each recursive call so that you can watch the whole
process.

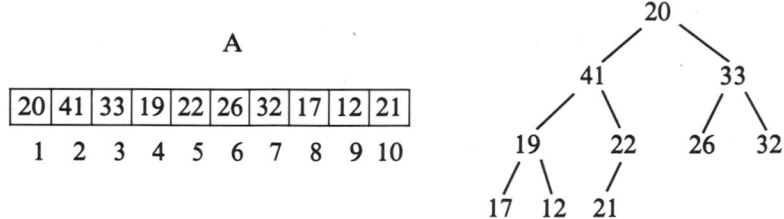

The original array. Left and right children of root are heaps. Must sift
the root (20). First, exchange the root with its larger
child.

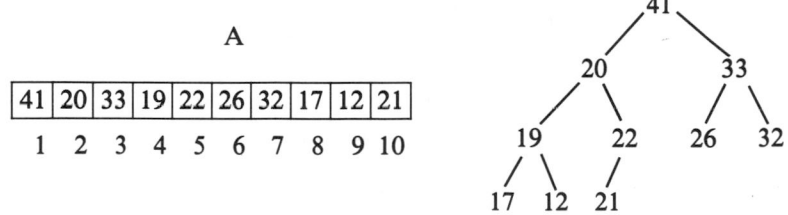

The root is now correct. Now sift the 20 again in this subtree.

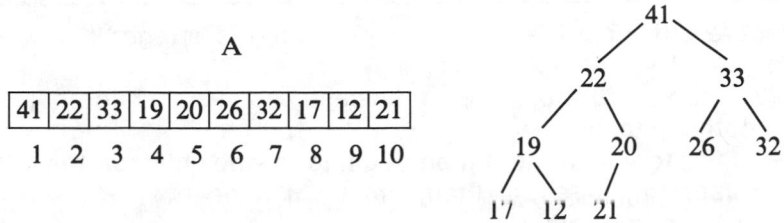

Again, recursively sift the 20. Note that there is only one child this time. Our Pascal procedure will have to watch for this special case.

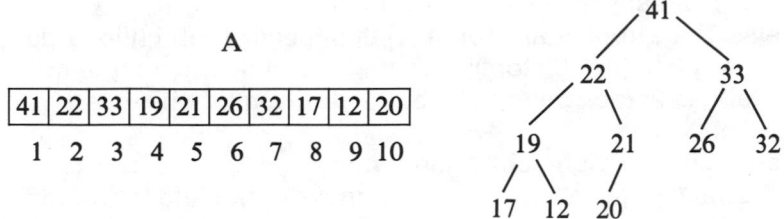

20 is now a leaf so we are done and the entire array is a heap.

We are now ready to look at the Pascal procedure in Figure 5.7.

This recursive procedure does exactly what we said had to be done. Reading it is almost like reading English. I will assume you can write the procedure *swap* that exchanges two values. Before we go on to the actual sorting there are two questions we should probably ask first. Just what are the complexities of *sift* and *buildheap?* The answer to one of these questions is actually quite long, so if you are impatient you might want to skip ahead to see what all of this has to do with sorting. The Pascal procedure *heapsort* will make it all clear.

The recurrence relation for *sift* is $T(n) = T(\frac{n}{2}) + 1$. This is because a call to *sift* does a constant amount of work (mainly just a couple of conditionals) followed by a recursive call to *sift* on a subtree that we know is about half the size of the original tree. (The fact that the subtree is half the size of the original tree is fairly obvious, but I will ask you to convince me, anyway, in the exercises.) This is a familiar recurrence relation whose solution we know is $log_2 n$ so the complexity of *sift* is $O(log\ n)$.

Now that we know the complexity of *sift,* we see that the recurrence relation for *buildheap* is $T(n) = 2T(\frac{n}{2}) + log\ n$ because there are two recursive calls to *buildheap* on children about half the size and one call to *sift*. Let's solve this recurrence relation.

```
procedure sift(var a : arraytype; top, bottom : integer);
begin
  if (2 * top) > bottom then { easiest case − no children }
    { nothing to do }
  else if (2 * top) = bottom then begin {only one child (on the left)}
    if a[bottom] > a[top] then { make it a heap }
      swap(a[top], a[bottom])
    end
  else { find largest among root and two children }
    if (a[top] > = a[2*top]) and (a[top] > = a[2*top + 1]) then
        { already a heap − done }
    else if a[2*top] > a[2*top + 1] then begin { left child largest }
      swap(a[top], a[2*top]); { move left child up to the top }
      sift(a, 2*top, bottom) { build the rest of the heap }
      end
    else begin { right child largest }
      swap(a[top], a[2*top + 1]); { move right child to the top }
      sift(a, 2*top + 1, bottom) { build the rest of the heap }
      end
end;
```

Figure 5.7. Pascal Procedure to Sift an Element Down a Heap

$$T(n) = 2T(\frac{n}{2}) + log(n) \qquad \text{as described above}$$

$$= log(n) + 2log(\frac{n}{2}) + 4T(\frac{n}{4}) \qquad \text{expanding } T(\frac{n}{2})$$

$$= log(n) + 2^1 log(\frac{n}{2^1}) + 2^2 log(\frac{n}{2^2}) + \ldots$$

$$+ 2^k log(\frac{n}{2^k}) + (k + 1)T(\frac{n}{2^{k+1}}) \qquad \text{recognizing the pattern}$$

$$= \sum_{i=0}^{log\,n} 2^i log(\frac{n}{2^i}) \qquad \text{choosing } k = log\,n$$

$$= \sum_{i=0}^{log\,n} 2^i log(n) - \sum_{i=0}^{log\,n} 2^i log(2^i) \qquad \text{expanding the log}$$

$$= log\,n \sum_{i=0}^{log\,n} 2^i - \sum_{i=0}^{log\,n} i2^i \qquad \text{more fiddling}$$

We are now left with two summations. We know how to do the one on the left. Unfortunately, we have never seen one like the one on the right before. We now have three choices. In increasing order of preference we can: (a) give up because we don't know how to do that second summation, (b) look up the formula for the second sum, or (c) figure out how to add up that second summation ourselves. Let's choose the hardest, but most satisfying approach, the third one.

What we need to do is find a way to sum the series $\sum_{i=0}^{k} i2^i$. Since we don't know how to sum up this series, sometimes it helps to write it out in a more expanded form to help see what is going on. Let's write it out in the form of a table where each row corresponds to a different i. Note that the case $i = 0$ adds nothing to the sum so we won't bother including that in the table. This means that the first row of the table will correspond to $i = 1$, the second to $i = 2$, etc. This table is presented in Figure 5.8.

The trick now is to notice that the *columns* of the table are easy to sum. Each column is of the form $\sum_{i=j}^{k} 2^i$ which is the same as $\sum_{i=0}^{k} 2^i - \sum_{i=0}^{j-1} 2^i$. But we know how to sum both of these so we can conclude that the sum of any column is

$$\sum_{i=0}^{k} 2^i - \sum_{i=0}^{j-1} 2^i = 2^{k+1} - 1 - (2^j - 1) = 2^{k+1} - 2^j.$$

So, when we pick $j = 1$ we get the sum of the first column, $j = 2$ gives us the sum of the second column, and so on until $j = k$ gives the sum of the last column. If we add this up for all j from 1 to k we will have the sum of the entire table. In other words

$$+ \ 2^1$$
$$+ \ 2^2 + 2^2$$
$$+ \ 2^3 + 2^3 + 2^3$$
$$+ \ 2^4 + 2^4 + 2^4 + 2^4$$
$$\cdot \quad \cdot \quad \cdot$$
$$+ \ 2^k + 2^k + 2^k + 2^k \ ... \ 2^k$$

Figure 5.8. The Secret to Finding the Value of $\sum_{i=0}^{k} i2^i$

$$\sum_{i=0}^{k} i 2^{i} = \sum_{j=1}^{k} 2^{k+1} - 2^{j}$$

$$= k2^{k+1} - \sum_{j=1}^{k} 2^{j}$$

$$= k2^{k+1} - (2^{k+1} - 2)$$

$$= (k - 1)2^{k+1} + 2$$

Wasn't that fun? By using a little ingenuity and a few things we already knew we were able to find the sum of something that looked like it might be tough. We can now use this to finish solving the recurrence relation. Let's pick up where we left off.

$$T(n) = \log n \sum_{i=0}^{\log n} 2^{i} - \sum_{i=0}^{\log n} i 2^{i}$$

$$= \log n(2^{\log n+1} - 1) - ((\log n - 1)2^{\log n+1} + 2)$$

$$= \log n(2n - 1) - ((\log n - 1)2n + 2)$$

$$= 2n\log n - \log n - 2n\log n + 2n - 2$$

$$= 2n - \log n - 2$$

So, after a little bit of effort, we are able to conclude that *buildheap* is a linear algorithm. This is actually quite surprising when you consider how well organized the data are inside a heap. When we first began our discussion on heaps I bet you didn't think we could build one in $O(n)$ steps.

Now that we know how to sift and how to build a heap and how long these things take we are ready to finish up and take a look at heapsort. Once we have a heap, how can we use it to sort? Certainly the element that is at the top of the heap needs to go to the end of the array. So if we just exchange these two elements and sift down the new root into the heap excluding the last element in the array (which is no longer part of the heap but part of the sorted array) we are left with the largest element in the last position and a heap that is one element smaller. We just repeat this process with the next largest element and so on until we are done. Of course this last part could also be done recursively but it would be a bit more awkward because we only have to build a heap once and so that part of the algorithm should not appear in the recursive procedure. I'll leave the details of getting it all right as an exercise. Figure 5.9 is the heap sort procedure.

We can now ask the $64,000 question. What is the complexity of *heapsort*? Actually, it is very easy to calculate. We know that *buildheap* takes $O(n)$ steps. The loop is executed n times (*size* times) and each time through the loop a constant amount of work is done for the swap and $O(\log$

```
procedure heapsort(var a : arraytype; size : integer);
var i : integer;
begin
    buildheap(a, 1, size);
    for i := size downto 2 do begin
        swap(a[1], a[i]); { move large element to bottom of heap }
        sift(a, 1, i – 1) { and then rebuild the heap           }
        end
end;
```

Figure 5.9. The Pascal Heapsort Procedure

n) work is done for the sift. This means that the total work done by the loop is $O(n \log n)$ and so the entire algorithm has complexity $O(n \log n)$.

This completes our look at three interesting sorting algorithms. The heapsort algorithm was especially interesting in that it looked like no other algorithm we had seen before. The idea of finding a tree structure inside an array is quite clever. And even though large elements start out getting pushed to the front of the array, they eventually end up at the rear where they belong. Also, we got to look at some interesting complexity analyses and even figured out how to sum a series we had never seen before.

The mergesort algorithm was a straightforward enough algorithm and even though it seems to have a great deal of potential because of its speed and simplicity, it just isn't used much because of its demands on memory. Quicksort, on the other hand, did not have a great worst case complexity yet I claimed it is still a very good algorithm to use in general. In fact, the only problem we had with quicksort was that the partitioning did not always go well. If we could somehow find a way to partition the array quickly so that half of the elements go in each partition, we'd really be on to something because then the worst case for the sort would drop down to $O(n \log n)$. (Do you see why this is so?) Of course, the key word here is "quickly." It turns out that the reason quicksort is so good in practice is that there is not much unnecessary overhead, so as soon as you start adding things to the algorithm to improve its worst case behavior you hurt its practical value by adding to the overhead. Nevertheless, the problem of trying to find a fast way to divide an array evenly is an interesting problem and is the subject of the next section.

2. FINDING THE MEDIAN

Given an array with n elements, what is the kth smallest element in the array? This is a general problem that has many interesting special cases. For example, when $k = 1$ we are simply asking for the smallest element in the array. Similarly, when $k = n$ we are requesting the largest element in the array. When $k = (n + 1)$ *div* 2 we are asking for the median. That is, we are looking for an element in the array such that half of the elements are greater than it and half are less. Of course, if n is even there is one less element in the smaller "half" than in the larger "half," but let's not quibble over one element. Also, if there are duplicates in the array we have to be a little careful about how we make our definitions. To avoid a lot of nit-picky details about definitions and to simplify the forthcoming algorithms, we will assume throughout this section that there are no duplicates in the array. The algorithms we develop can be easily modified to include arrays with duplicates, but I will leave the messy details for you to work out. A few hints will be provided in the exercises.

At this point you are probably thinking: "Hey, I can find the smallest element in an array in linear time. We did that in Chapter 1. What's the big deal?" You are right, of course. Finding the smallest element quickly is no problem. But now the problem statement is more general so we need a more general algorithm. Not only must this new algorithm be able to find the smallest element quickly, it must also find quickly other elements such as the largest element, and the median. And, you need a single algorithm to do all of this. Can you think of one algorithm that can find the kth smallest element, for any k, that works quickly? In fact, can you think of an algorithm that just finds the median, quickly? These are pretty hard questions.

As we already noticed, it is easy to find the first smallest and the nth smallest (the largest) element in linear time. Unfortunately, the approaches one tends to use for these problems does not readily extend to the problem of finding the median. There is, however, a simple algorithm that solves the general problem of finding the kth smallest element that is pretty fast. It looks like Figure 5.10.

Actually, this is not a bad algorithm. If we use a sorting algorithm like heapsort this becomes a worst case $O(n \ log \ n)$ algorithm. If, on the other hand, we use quick sort the worst case complexity will suffer, but we will

```
function select(a : arraytype; k, size : integer) : integer;
{ Function returns the kth smallest element }
{ in an array of size elements              }
begin
     sort(a, 1, size); { sort the array }
     select := a[k]
end;
```

Figure 5.10. A Simple Pascal Function to Find the kth Smallest Element

have a pretty fast algorithm for practical purposes. Surprisingly, though, we can improve on both of these algorithms. There is another practical algorithm that runs faster than the quicksort-based algorithm above. In fact, it is always faster. No matter what the data, it will take less time than the quicksort-based algorithm. Perhaps even more surprising, there is a better worst case algorithm than the heapsort-based algorithm. Believe it or not, there is a linear algorithm for finding the kth smallest element. This algorithm is a monument to the power of recursion. It is a subtle algorithm that calls itself twice (remember Section 2.4), appears to almost randomly rearrange data, and at first glance looks anything but linear. An understanding of the practical algorithm will help us understand this spectacular linear algorithm, so let us begin by studying the practical algorithm.

2.1. A Practical Algorithm to Find the Median

It is certainly true that if we quicksort an array with n elements and then choose the middle element (the $((n + 1) \ div \ 2)^{th}$ one), we are finding the median quite efficiently. But can you see an inefficiency in this algorithm? Think about how quicksort works. First partition, then sort the two partitions. What unnecessary work is being done here? If the first partition contains more than half of the elements, the median must be in that first partition, so there is no need to sort the second partition. Similarly, if the second partition contains more than half of the elements, there is no need to sort the first partition. This is reminiscent of binary search. We can ignore the half of the array that we know doesn't have the element we are looking for. This idea makes for a much faster algorithm. (How much faster?)

In general, if we are trying to find the kth smallest element in an array, we first partition the array, and then depending on whether or not the first partition contains k or more elements, we either recursively find the kth smallest element in the first partition or we find the $(k - j)^{th}$ element in the second partition where j is the number of elements in the first partition. The algorithm can be seen clearly in the pseudocode in Figure 5.11.

A few details need to be discussed before we present the Pascal version. The pseudocode skips a fair amount of arithmetic that needs to be done. For example, exactly where is the "appropriate element between a[pivot + 1] and a[right]?" How can we tell "if there are k or more elements between a[left] and a[pivot − 1]?" Rather than bore you with all the arithmetic details, suffice it to say that it is handy to have around a variable that is the actual index into the array corresponding to the location of the kth smallest element. This is called *index* in the Pascal code below. Given that, the rest of the arithmetic becomes fairly easy.

We will borrow the partition procedure that was used in quicksort. There

---

if left = right (only one element), k must be 1 so
    return a[left]
else we have more than one element so
    partition a, returning a pivot, which points to the "middle",
    an element between left and right
    if the kth element is the pivot element then
        return a[pivot]
    else if there are k or more elements between a[left] and a[pivot] then
        return the kth smallest element between a[left] and a[pivot − 1]
    else the element we seek is in the right partition so
        return the appropriate element between a[pivot + 1] and a[right]

Figure 5.11. A Practical Way of Finding the kth Smallest Element in a[left] ... a[right]

is no reason to change it in any substantial way, but a technical change needs to be made. The original partition procedure had the array that is being partitioned as one of the parameters, called *a*. But, since I will be using this procedure internal to the select function, and since the array is available to the select function, I will not bother passing it into partition every time. I will simply use the array *a* as a local global variable, that is, it is local to the select function but global to the partition procedure. This will make select run a tad faster, make it use a bit less memory, but most importantly, it should make the workings of select more clear.

Finally, we don't want the select function to change the array; we only want it to return the selected element. But, the algorithm as described in the pseudocode in Figure 5.11 requires *a* to change to work properly. To solve this dilemma, we will make use of a driver function that takes the array as a value parameter, and then uses this array globally in the recursive select function (see Figure 5.12).

Let's informally calculate the complexity of this algorithm. The better the pivot element, that is, the closer it is to the middle, the better this algorithm works. Unfortunately, in the worst cast the pivot element is always at one end of the array or the other. For example, suppose each recursive call alternates between finding the largest element and the smallest element in the array as the pivot element. This means that the array only gets one smaller at each recursive call and it also means that the median won't be found until the array only has one element. Further, since the recursive procedure always partitions the array and since partitioning is a linear time algorithm, we conclude that the recurrence relation for the time complexity is $T(n) = T(n - 1) + n$. Hence, this algorithm is $O(n^2)$. In practice, however, this usually doesn't happen. It usually turns out that the pivot ends up pretty close to the middle and so the algorithm usually performs

```pascal
function select(a : ArrayType; left, right, kth : integer) : integer;
{ Function returns the kth smallest element in the array }
{ between indices left and right                         }

procedure partition(left, right : integer; var pivot : integer);
{Modifies the global array a so that a[left], ... , a[pivot-1] are}
{all < a[pivot] and a[pivot+1], ... , a[right] > a[pivot] — also  }
             { returns the location of the pivot element }
             { through the parameter pivot                }
var temp : integer;
begin
   if left = right then { easiest case — nothing to }
       pivot := right  {                 partition  }
   else begin
       partition(left + 1, right, pivot);    { partition all but 1st }
       if a[left] > a[pivot] then begin { if first element is not }
           temp := a[pivot]; { in the correct partition then     }
           a[pivot] := a[left]; { move it there by shifting a few}
           a[left] := a[pivot - 1]; {elements around, including the}
           a[pivot - 1] := temp; { pivot element which must get }
           pivot := pivot - 1  { shifted to the left to make room }
           end                 { for the first element, a[left]  }
       end
end;

function recselect(left, right, kth : integer) : integer;
{ The recursive select to find the kth smallest element in a }
var pivot, index : integer;
begin
   index := left + kth - 1; { were a sorted the kth smallest}
                            { element in a would be a[index]}
   if right = left then
       recselect := a[index]
   else begin
       partition(left, right, pivot);
       if index = pivot then
           recselect := a[pivot]
       else if index < pivot then
           recselect := recselect(left, pivot - 1, kth)
       else
           recselect := recselect(pivot + 1, right, index - pivot)
       end
end;

begin
   select := recselect(left, right, kth)
end;
```

very well. This is analogous to quicksort. Both algorithms have quadratic worst case complexities, yet both of them are quite fast in practice. Also, as was true with quicksort, the algorithm can be modified to be even more practical. Just how is discussed in the exercises.

Wouldn't it be nice if we could somehow guarantee that the pivot were always in the center? Of course, this is asking too much. But, as you will see in the next section, it is possible to be sure that the pivot is always close enough to the center so that we can get a faster algorithm.

2.2. A Linear Algorithm to Find the Median

To improve upon select from the last section we must somehow find a way to put the pivot element close to the center without taking too much time. Of course it is unreasonable to expect to be able to put the pivot element exactly in the middle, for then the pivot would be the median and we'd be done. But how close to the middle is close enough? And how much time can we afford to spend trying to find a pivot element near the middle? We can't spend too much time placing the pivot near the middle because this will ultimately hurt the complexity too much. However, if we don't get close enough to the middle then the complexity will remain $O(n^2)$. We have to strike a very careful balance.

Let's begin by looking at an example that is not good enough. Suppose that in constant time we can guarantee the pivot will be at least some fixed number of elements away from the edge. Recall that the worst case corresponded to the situation where the partitioning put one element in one partition and the rest of the elements in the other. In this case we are assuming we can do better than one, that is, the smaller partition will have at least c elements, for some constant c. In the worst case, then, the median will always land in the larger partition containing $n - c$ elements so the recurrence relation is $T(n) = k + an + T(n - c)$, where k is the amount of time needed to assure that each partition has at least c elements, an is the time needed to do the actual partitioning, and $T(n - c)$ corresponds to the recursive call to find the median on the larger partition. A little bit of effort shows that $T(n) = O(n^2)$, so we haven't sped up the algorithm yet.

More optimistically, let's suppose that in linear time we can find a pivot element that will guarantee the smaller partition will have at least cn elements, and where $0 < c < 0.5$ and, in fact, could be very close to 0. This, of course, means that the larger partition will have $(1 - c)n$ elements. Using the same reasoning as above we can conclude that the recurrence relation for such an algorithm (if it exists) is $T(n) = kn + an + T((1 - c)n)$, where kn is the time needed to find the pivot element, an is the time needed to partition, and $T((1 - c)n)$ is the time taken by the recursive call on the larger partition. We can simplify this a bit by renaming a few of the constants: let $b = k + a$ and let $d = 1 - c$. The recurrence relation, then, looks like $T(n) = bn + T(dn)$. This recurrence relation can be solved by repeated substitutions as we have done many times in the past, but for this one it is much simpler to use the guessing technique. If we guess that $T(n) = kn$, for some constant k, substituting this into the recurrence relation gives us that $k = \dfrac{b}{c}$ and, thus, such a hypothetical algorithm for finding the median would be linear. Unfortunately, this approach was a little too optimistic. It turns out to be unreasonable to expect to find an algorithm that yields a recurrence relation of this form. This idea does suggest the correct approach, though.

We said that if we could find a pivot element in linear time that would guarantee each partition to have at least some fraction of the original array (cn), we would have a linear algorithm for selecting the kth smallest element, or for finding the median in particular. One way to find such a pivot would be to take a sampling of the entire array and to then find its median. We could then use this pivot to partition the array and then make a recursive call on the appropriate partition to find the kth smallest. The sample would have to be small enough so that finding its median won't dominate the complexity, but the sample must also be chosen cleverly enough so that its median really will give a good partition. Of course, all of this must be done very carefully because in the above description you may have noticed something that we usually try to avoid. There are two recursive calls. There is one recursive call to find the pivot element and there is a second for actually finding the kth smallest element. Recall that this was one of our rules of thumb for recognizing slow algorithms. Hence, the only hope for making this work and making it work quickly is to be sure that both recursive calls are made on sufficiently small arrays.

Here is the trick for choosing a good sample. Divide the array into groups of size 5. In other words a[1], . . . , a[5] is the first group, a[6], . . . , a[10] is the second group, etc. The last group may have less than 5 elements in it. Now sort each group. After sorting this will means that a[1], . . . a[5] are sorted, a[6], . . . a[10] are sorted, etc. The sample we will use to find the median (which will become the pivot element during the partitioning phase) will be the middle element of each of these sorted groups. That is, we will find the median of a[3], a[8], a[13], ... If we then use this element, the median of the middle elements of the sorted groups, as pivot to partition the array, how few elements can end up in the smaller partition? For argument sake, let's suppose the partition with the least number of elements is the partition with the small elements in it. The median is larger than exactly half of the sample elements. But each of these sample elements is larger than 2 other elements, the first two elements in their groups. Thus, each sample element that is less than the median actually contributes 3 elements smaller than the median: itself and the two smaller elements in the same group. Since there are $\frac{n}{5}$ sample elements and since the median is larger than half of them this means the median is larger than at least $\frac{3n}{10}$ elements. Hence, the the larger partition can have no more than $\frac{7n}{10}$ elements.

For the sake of example let's assume we have already sorted the 5-element groups and that we have found the median of the center elements of all of these groups, as described above. To help you visualize the counting I described above let's further suppose we have rearranged the groups so that the group with the median is in the middle, groups with smaller middle elements are to the left, and groups with larger middle elements are to the right (we would never really do this in the algorithm). The array might look something like this where the elements have been separated into 5-element groups, the sample elements (the middle ones) are represented by capital letters with the median being called M. The s's (upper and lower case) represent elements that must be smaller than M, the l's represent elements that must be larger than M, and the x's are elements for which we know nothing.

ssSxx ssSxx ssSxx ssSxx ssSxx ssMll xxLll xxLll xxLll xxLll xxLll

Notice how about three-tenth's of the array elements are labeled either s or S. Study this example and be sure you see how it corresponds to the counting that was done in the previous paragraph. Don't forget that each group is a sorted collection of 5 elements.

We are now in a position to look at the entire algorithm for finding the kth smallest element in linear time. Note the similarities between this one (Figure 5.13) and the practical one presented earlier.

Numerous details still remain to be explained before we can convert this to Pascal, but we better calculate the complexity before we go through the trouble. We wouldn't want to waste our time converting an inefficient algorithm into Pascal. To be able to write the recurrence relation we need to figure out how long each step in the outermost *else* takes. The first step requires sorting all the 5-element groups. Sorting a 5-element group requires a constant amount of time, so sorting all $\frac{n}{5}$ of them requires a constant times $\frac{n}{5}$ or a linear amount or time. Jumping ahead to the partition step, we know we can partition in linear time, so the sorting step and the partitioning step together take linear time. For the sake of generality, we will simply say that these two steps combined take a total of *an* steps. Then there is the recursive call that finds the median of the middle elements. Since it is called on a collection of elements that is one fifth the entire array, it

if left = right (only one element), k must be 1 so
   return a[left]
else we have more than one element so
   sort the first 5 elements, then the next 5, then the next 5, etc.

   recursively, find the median of the middle elements of these
   sorted groups of size 5

   partition a, using this median as the pivot element, returning an
   integer, middle, pointing to the last element in the smaller partition

   if there are k or more elements between a[left] and a[middle] then
      return the kth smallest element between a[left] and a[middle]

   else the element we seek is in the right partition so

      return the appropriate element between a[middle + 1] and a[right]

Figure 5.13. A Linear Algorithm for Finding the kth Smallest Element in a[left] . . . a[right]

requires time $T(\frac{n}{5})$. Finally, there is the second recursive call made on one of the two partitions. From an earlier discussion we know that this partition can be no bigger than $\frac{7n}{10}$, so the worst case time required by this step is $T(\frac{7n}{10})$. We conclude that the recurrence relation for this algorithm is $T(n) = an + T(\frac{n}{5}) + T(\frac{7n}{10})$. Trying to solve this recurrence using repeated substitutions can be discouraging. Go ahead and try it. No clear pattern quickly emerges. However, we can try our old trick of guessing. Since we were hoping that this would produce a linear algorithm why don't we guess that $T(n) = bn$ and see if it works?

$$T(n) = an + T(\frac{n}{5}) + T(\frac{7n}{10}) \qquad \text{the recurrence relation}$$

$$bn = an + \frac{bn}{5} + \frac{b7n}{10} \qquad \text{guessing that } T(n) = bn$$

$$= n\frac{10a + 2b + 7b}{10} \qquad \text{algebra}$$

$$b = \frac{10a + 9b}{10} \qquad \text{more algebra}$$

$$b = 10a \qquad \text{a little more algebra}$$

So, sure enough, it works; $b = 10a$ and so the algorithm as described is linear. Notice how delicately this all fit together. If either recursive call were made on a slightly larger array the resulting complexity would no longer be linear. Nevertheless, a triumph for recursion!

Now that we have a linear algorithm, it remains to express it in Pascal. First of all, how should we sort the 5-element groups? We have a number of sorting algorithms available, so how do we choose? Since, in each case we are sorting only 5 elements we want to avoid the high-powered sorts like quicksort because they are not the best for small arrays. Think about why this is so. In particular, think about the role of the constants in the complexity function, the constants that we usually ignore. When the value of n is small how significant can these constants be? This is discussed in more detail in the exercises. The point is, we should choose either a sort like insertion sort, or we might even design a special purpose sort that works especially fast for 5 element arrays. I will leave the final decision up to you.

Next, how do we conveniently find the median of the middle elements? I have chosen to move these elements to the beginning of the array so that they will be contiguous. This makes it simple to apply the recursive call. Remember, all that we are really after is the median of the middle elements so that we can use it as a pivot for the partitioning step. Once we have it, the other middle elements and the ordering on the 5-element groups is no longer needed.

Finally, something you may have noticed long ago, and I have intentionally been avoiding, is the fact that the partitioning algorithm we developed for quicksort cannot be used here. The quicksort partitioning algorithm found the pivot element and returned its location in the partitioned array. We now require a partitioning algorithm that is given the pivot element and must then partition the array based on this value. For the sake of generality, we will assume this element need not even be an element of the array. Since the partitioning function must somehow report how the array has been partitioned, let's have it return the index of the rightmost element in the partition containing the smaller elements. This implies that the next element in the array is the leftmost element in the partition containing the larger elements. You should be able to work out the remaining details. However, for completeness I will include it with the Pascal presentation (Figure 5.14) of the linear algorithm to find the kth smallest element in an array.

3. SETS AND COLLECTIONS OF THINGS

A *set,* usually considered the most basic of mathematical objects, is simply a collection of items. These items can be, among other things, integers, characters, strings, basketballs, other sets, or even combinations of different kinds of things. For our purposes we will restrict our attention to sets of integers and sets of characters. Most definitions of sets insist that sets may not contain duplicates. For example {3, 2, 3} strictly speaking is not a

```
function select(a : ArrayType; left, right, kth : integer) : integer;
{ Function returns the kth smallest element in the array }
{ between indices left and right, in linear time }

  function partition(left, right : integer; pivot : integer) : integer;
          { roturno a pointcr to the last (rightmost) element in the }
          { partition with the smaller elements                       }
var i, temp, lastsmall : integer;
begin
    if left > right then { easiest case — nothing to partition }
        partition := right { no elements in the smaller partition }
    else begin
        lastsmall := partition(left + 1, right, pivot);
                                        { partition all but first }
        if (a[left] = pivot) and (left = lastsmall) then
          { do nothing — consider a[left] the only small element; }
          { any other time it will be considered one of the large }
          { elements                                              }
        else if a[left] >= pivot then begin
          swap(a[left], a[lastsmall]); { move large element to rt }
          lastsmall := lastsmall − 1 { adjust pointer }
          end;
        partition := lastsmall
        end;
end;

function recselect(left, right, kth : integer) : integer;
{ The recursive select to find the kth smallest element in a }
var index, groupct, groupmidct, medianfmids, middle : integer;
begin
    index := left + kth − 1;
    if right = left then { only one element--k must be 1 }
      recselect := a[index]
    else begin
      groupct := left;
      groupmidct := left;
      while (groupct + 4) <= right do begin
                                    { 5-element gps remain }
          sort(a, groupct, groupct + 4; { sort group }
                              (continued on next page)
```

Figure 5.14. A Pascal Implementation of the Linear Search Algorithm

```
          swap(a[groupct + 2], a[groupmidct]); { move middle }
          { element to front of array for later median finding }
          groupmidct := groupmidct + 1;
          groupct := groupct + 5 { go to next 5-element group }
          end;
      groupmidct := groupmidct - 1;
                              { middle elements of sorted }
          { 5-element groups are now a[left] .. a[groupmidct] }
      medianofmids := recselect(left, groupmidct,
                              (groupmidct - left + 1) div 2);
      middle := partition(left, right, medianofmids);
      if index <= middle then
         recselect := recselect(left, middle, kth)
      else
         recselect := recselect(middle + 1, right,
                                            index - middle)
      end
end;

begin
    select := recselect(left, right, kth)
end;
```

Figure 5.14. (Continued)

set since it contains the element 3 twice. We will relax this restriction and sometimes allow sets to have one or more of the same element. Technically, such structures should be called *multisets,* but for simplicity, we will continue calling them sets. However, so as not to abuse the term *set* too often, I will frequently use the word *collection* instead of *set* when referring to a set that is known to contain a duplicate.

The general topic of sets poses many interesting problems which are frequently best solved recursively. We must be careful about how we implement sets, however. As is always the case, we should try to make the operations on the data type, sets in this case, as efficient as possible. For example, Pascal provides a built in type called *sets,* but there are some subtle traps we have to avoid if we are to use Pascal sets. For example, Pascal provides a set operation called *union* that takes two sets and produces a third set that contains all of the elements that are in both sets, that is, the union of the two sets. But what is the complexity of the union operation? Be careful not to jump to the conclusion that it is a constant-time operation just because it is a primitive operation in Pascal. As with all operations, its complexity depends upon the implementation of the data structure (in this case, sets), which might only be known to the compiler writer. Even though we can't know for sure what the complexity of the union operation is, we can make an educated guess and discover some other pitfalls with Pascal sets at the same time.

The discussion about how sets are probably implemented in Pascal begins with us recalling that Pascal only allows sets to be built from enumerated types. This, of course, is a big restriction since the definition of sets puts no restriction on elements at all. Pascal does this because the most common way of implementing sets is to use a bit string to represent a set. This is done by associating the first element of the bit string with the first element of the enumerated type, the second element of the bit string with the second element of the enumerated type, etc. Then, every 1 in the bit string means the corresponding element is in the set while every 0 in the bit string means the corresponding element from the enumerated type is not in the set. But how long can a bit string be? Most Pascal implementations choose some small multiple of the underlying machine's word length in order to make the operations as efficient as possible. Hence, you will typically find that sets can have no more than, say, 64 or 128 elements. The union operation is then performed by doing a bit-wise *and* operation on the bit strings to produce the new set. Certainly this is a constant-time operation, but only because sets can be no bigger than some fixed constant. If sets were allowed to be arbitrarily large then the union operation could require an *and* operation for every element in the two sets and so it is really a linear-time operation. So, rather than worry about particular implementations of sets, their size limits, element restrictions, etc., and since we will not need most of the operations provided to us by Pascal sets, we will implement sets according the conveniences of our application.

3.1. Permutations

The first problem about sets we will tackle is the problem of outputting all permutations of a set of elements. The permutations of a set are all the different ways of arranging the elements of the set. For example, given a three-element set like {a, b, c}, its permutations are *abc*, *acb*, *bac*, *bca*, *cab*, and *cba*. You might want to spend some time trying to find an algorithm for this problem before you read on. It is not as simple as it sounds, especially if you try to do it iteratively.

The fact that we must find all the different arrangements of the elements gives us a clue to a recursive algorithm. Looking at the previous example with the set {a, b, c}, this tells us that we must find all permutations that begin with the letter *a*, all that begin with the letter *b*, and all that begin with the letter *c*. In other words, for each possible letter in the first position, we must find all permutations of the remaining positions. This, by golly, is the heart of a fine recursive algorithm. It remains to describe the easiest case.

Notice how the problem is made easier. We fix an element and then find all permutations of the remaining elements. Since there are less elements remaining than what we started with (in fact, there is exactly one less), we have made the problem easier. The easiest case, then, is when there are no elements remaining to find the permutations of. What needs to be done at an easiest case? Remembering that we are suppose to output the permutations and since there are no more permutations left to consider at an easiest case, then it must be time to output. This completely describes the algorithm. Let's first look at it in pseudocode (Figure 5.15).

Clearly, the only difficulty in implementing this in Pascal is finding a reasonable implementation for sets. Since the only operation we are performing on the sets is to order them, an array seems to be the most natural way to go. We can simply put the set elements in an array, starting at Position 1 and ending at Position n, where n is the number of elements in the set. The recursive procedure that outputs the permutations will then take three arguments: the array and two indices corresponding to the part of the array where permutations still need to be generated. We will call these indices *left* and *right* though it should be clear that *right* will always be the same, namely, the number of elements in the array. We can then perform the step "output all permutations with this element first" by moving this element in the array (between *left* and *right*) into position $a[left]$ followed by an appropriate recursive call.

Since Pascal insists arrays be declared before they are used, we must decide in advance what the set is composed of so that we can declare the array accordingly. To be consistent with the example we have been using, let's assume that we are interested in permutations of sets of characters and so we will declare the array as an array of characters. This means that if the main program has an array of characters called *letters,* for example, with values between indices 1 and n, and the name of the procedure we are writing is called *permute,* then to output all permutations of the characters in the array the procedure would be called as follows: *permute(letters, 1, n)*. Figure 5.16 shows the Pascal procedure.

What is the complexity of this procedure? Roughly speaking all of the work done is in the recursive calls, so if there are n elements we are trying to permute and if all n must be placed in the first position, each followed by

---

    if no elements left in the set then
            output this permutation
    else
            for each element left in the set
                output all permutations with this element first

---

Figure 5.15.   Outputting the Permutations of a Set

```
procedure permute(a : ArrayType; left, right : integer);
{ Assumes a's index starts at 1. Generates all permutations  }
{ of a between left and right with the goal of outputting     }
{ permutations of a starting at 1.                            }
var i : integer;
    temp : char;
begin
    if left > right then begin   { nothing left to permute }
        for i := 1 to right do  { output this permutation }
            write(a[i]);
        writeln
        end
    else begin { generate all permutations in this part of array }
        permute(a, left + 1, right); { generate permutations using }
                                     { current element in a[left] }
        for i := left + 1 to right do begin
                                        { generate permutations }
            temp := a[left];            { using all the other   }
            a[left] := a[i];           { elements in a[left]    }
            a[i] := temp;
            permute(a, left + 1, right)
            end
        end
end;
```

Figure 5.16. Pascal Procedure to Output Permutations of Characters

a recursive call to an array with one less element we get a recurrence relation that looks like: $T(n) = n \, T(n - 1)$. You should recognize this recurrence from the first chapter. It is, of course, just the recursive definition of factorial, so the complexity of outputting the permutations of n elements is $n!$. (One could get a little more precise with the recurrence relation. This subject is left for the exercises.) At first this may sound like an abysmally bad complexity but we must consider how many permutations there are over n elements. If fact, there are exactly $n!$, so we can hardly expect to come up with a faster algorithm.

The algorithm of Figure 5.15 (and corresponding program of Figure 5.16) uses one assumption that we would like to remove. It assumes that no element appears more than once. For example, using the above algorithm we conclude that the permutations of the collection $\{a, a, b\}$ are *aab, aba, aab, aba, baa,* and *baa.* This is not the answer we really want since the two occurrences of *aab,* for example, are indistinguishable. We prefer not to have any duplicates. So, for the collection {*a, a, b*} we prefer the permutations be listed simply as *aab, aba,* and *baa.* Let's try to find a way to modify the previous algorithm so that it will work correctly with duplicates.

Looking at the program in Figure 5.16, we see a loop that "generates permutations using all the other elements in *a[left].*" But what happens if a certain element has already been used? We don't want to put it in *a[left]* again, because we will generate the exact same permutations a second time. Now we only want to put elements in *a[left]* that haven't already been used. By adding a simple loop to check that elements are only used once (notice the use of a sentinel), we get the following Pascal procedure (see Figure 5.17).

Like before, the complexity of this algorithm depends on the number of permutations actually output. The details are left for the exercises

3.2. An Interesting Puzzle

The following puzzle, though quite simple to state, can lead us down many long and interesting roads. In this section we will take a little peak at just a few of these and suggest a few longer journeys in the exercises. The puzzle can most easily be stated by the following example: Given the integers {22, 30, 11, 10, 32, 9, 12, 9, 11, 21, 32, 1}, is it possible to find some subcollection of these integers that add up to 94? Is there a subcollection that adds up to 79? How about 100? Before you go on, try to solve these three problems so that you can get a feel for just how difficult they really are. Try to find 94 first. It is the easiest of the three. Were you able to get it? One way is by summing the three elements 30, 32, and 32. Another solution is 11, 9, 21, 9, 11, 32, 1. In fact, there are 91 other ways to get 94, so you should not have found it too hard to find one of them. The other two problems are harder because one of them only has one solution and the other cannot be done. I will not tell you which is which. When you are done reading this section you will know how to write programs to solve these puzzles for yourself. In the meantime, keep trying to do it by hand.

The general form of the puzzle looks like the following: Given a collection of integers and a goal integer, is it possible to find a subcollection of that collection that sums to the goal and if so, what is that subcollection? We need an algorithm for this problem. The basic idea is deceptively simple. Let's look at the example collection above with a goal of 94. Looking at the first element (22) we ask if it can be used as part of a solution. If it can, then we are done because the problem was to find a solution (or conclude there is none). But if there is no solution using the 22 then we must ask if there is a solution without using it. If the answer to this question is "yes," as before, this means we have solved the problem by finding a solution. But,

```
procedure permute(a : ArrayType; left, right : integer);
var i, j : integer;
          temp : char;
          duplicate : boolean;
begin
     if left − right then begin { nothing left to permute }
          for i := 1 to right do { output this permutation }
               write(a[i]);
          writeln
          end
     else begin { generate all permutations in this part of array }
          permute(a, left + 1, right); { generate permutations using }
                                       { current element in a[left] }
          for i := left + 1 to right do begin { look at remaining}
               j := left;                       { elements         }
               while a[j] < > a[i] do
                                    { has this one been used before? }
                    j := j + 1;
               if i = j then begin   { if not ...               }
                    temp := a[left];  { switch it with           }
                    a[left] := a[i];  { the current element }
                    a[i] := temp;     { in a[left] and ...      }
                    permute(a, left + 1, right)
                                    { generate permutations using }
                                    { this new element in a[left]   }
                    end
               end
          end
end;
```

Figure 5.17. Pascal Procedure to Output Permutations Where Characters May be Duplicated

if the answer is again "no" then there is no solution to the problem since a solution will either use 22 or not; there is no other choice. This outlines the algorithm. It remains to decide how to ask the two questions suggested above: "Is there a solution with 22?" and "Is there a solution without 22?" These we do recursively. To find if there is a solution using the integer 22, we remove 22 from the collection and then (recursively) solve another easier problem using the collection without the element 22 and with a goal of 94 − 22 = 72. This problem is easier because the size of the collection of integers has become one smaller. Similarly, to find if there is a solution without using the 22, we simply remove 22 from the collection and solve the again easier problem using this smaller collection and the same goal, 94. Given this example, it is easy to generalize this for arbitrary problems. I will leave it to you to figure out the easiest case. I will give you one hint, though. There are actually three easiest cases.

The Pascal implementation of this algorithm is not difficult, so let's forge ahead. As we did in the last section, it is simplest to represent the collection of integers as an array. We then choose the last element in the array to be the selected element that will be tested as part of a solution and then, if necessary, as not being part of a solution. The recursive call is made to the array, excluding the last element. It is presented in Figure 5.18.

I believe everybody will agree that this is a lovely algorithm. It is short, clear, solves a difficult problem, and works correctly. There is just one flaw. Knowing that a solution exists is one thing. Knowing *what* the solution is is quite another. This algorithm gives no hint as to what subcollection of integers actually sum to the goal. We need to study Figure 5.18 and find a way to modify the function so that we can learn what the solution is when a solution does indeed exist.

There are certainly many ways to do this. We will do it by committing what most consider a serious breach of programming etiquette. We will modify the function of Figure 5.18 so that it will still return a boolean value, but, if a solution is found, it will also output the integers that sum to the goal. For good reason, most people consider it bad programming style to have a function both return a value and do output. I hope I will be forgiven once you see how elegant the new function is.

The question we must now ask ourselves is: where in the function can we

```
function CanDo(goal : integer; a : ArrayType; n : integer)
                                                    : boolean;
begin
     if goal = 0 then { easiest case: solution requires no   }
        CanDo := true { elements from the collection          }
     else if goal < 0 then { easiest case: no solution can be <0}
        CanDo := false
     else if n = 0 then  { easiest case: no elements in the   }
        CanDo := false { collection to add up to the goal    }
     else if Cando(goal - a[n], a, n - 1) then { a[n] is part of }
        CanDo := true                          { a solution      }
     else                          { no solution using a[n] so  }
        CanDo := CanDo(goal, a, n-1) { if there is a solution it }
                                     { it doesn't use a[n]       }
end;
```

Figure 5.18. Pascal Function to Solve the Puzzle

do some output in order to output a solution when it is found? Looking back at Figure 5.18 we suspect it will have to be someplace in the vicinity of statements like *CanDo* := *true*, since it is at these locations that the function realizes it has found a solution. There are two such statements. Where should we do the output and what should we output?

The first occurrence of a *CanDo* := *true* occurs at the first easiest case. Thinking back to Chapter 3 we know at this point that all of the integers forming the solution exist somewhere on the stack. The problem is getting them off. Since there is no way for us to access Pascal's stack, we would have to use our own stack and keep track of each *a*[*n*] as it is subtracted from the goal. This seems like a lot of trouble. This *is* a lot of trouble. There must be an easier way.

Let's look at the second occurrence of *CanDo* := *true*. Recalling our earlier arguments, this statement is part of an *if* statement that checks if *a*[*n*] can be used in a solution. If the recursive call in the *if* returns a *true* then *a*[*n*] can be used in a solution and, therefore, should be output. The recursive call will output all of the other integers that were used to achieve the smaller goal, the goal without *a*[*n*]. So, by just adding a single output statement here we can accomplish our goal. Let me show you the new function (Figure 5.19) so that you can be convinced it is as easy as I claim.

What might not be clear at this point is to how to actually use this function. If, say, it is used in the main program, you must remember that if a solution is found, it will both output it and return *true*. If no solution

```
function CanDo(goal : integer; a : ArrayType; n : integer)
                                                      : boolean;
begin
    if goal = 0 then    { easiest case: solution requires no }
        CanDo := true    { elements from the collection      }
    else if goal < 0 then { easiest case: no soution can be <0 }
        CanDo := false
    else if n = 0 then    { easiest case: no elements in the }
        CanDo := false { collection to add up to the goal }
    else if Cando(goal - a[n], a, n - 1) then begin { a[n] part }
        CanDo := true;                             { of solution }
        write(a[n])                                { so output it }
        end
    else                          { no solution using a[n] so }
        CanDo := CanDo(goal, a, n-1) { if there is a solution it }
                                     { it doesn't use a[n]    }
end;
```

Figure 5.19.   Pascal Function to Output a Solution to the Puzzle

is found it will simply return *false*. With this in mind, Figure 5.20 is a sample of how *CanDo* of Figure 5.19 might be used. You might consider using this as the bulk of a driver procedure so that the subroutine the user uses does not have the unfortunate property of both being a function and outputting information.

Certainly the functions of Figures 5.18 and 5.19 have the same complexity. In the worst case they both call themselves twice on a problem that has just one integer less, so the recurrence relation is $T(n) = 2 * T(n - 1)$. You may remember this recurrence from chapter 2. Even if you don't it is easy to solve and we come to the unfortunate conclusion that both algorithms have exponential time complexity. (See Problem 2.8 if you've forgotten what this means.) This is bad news. The first thing we are supposed to do when we find an exponential algorithm is throw it away and try to find a better one. Unfortunately, in this case many people have tried and nobody has been able to find an algorithm for this problem that is not exponential. In fact, this is one of the longest standing and most heavily studied open problems in computer science. Can we prove that the best algorithm for this problem is exponential or is there really a better algorithm lurking out there that everybody has missed so far? Computer science anxiously awaits an answer.

3.3. Other Subset Problems

Given the experience gained in the last two sections you should find the algorithms discussed in this section quite straightforward. For the most part you will find that, like in the last two sections, most algorithms that deal with subsets have the general form: recursively try doing the smaller problem using the current element to make the problem smaller, then try doing the original problem without the current element. Once you have this general form in mind problems dealing with subsets becomes quite easy.

3.3.1. All subsets of a given size. Let's consider a problem that combines ideas from both of the last two sections. Given a set with *n*-elements list all the subsets with exactly *k*-elements. For example, given the four-element set {*a, b, c, d*}, the subsets with exactly three elements are:

```
if CanDo(goal, nums, n) then
      writeln(' ... is a solution.')
else
      writeln('No solution possible.');
```

Figure 5.20. An IF Statement Using the CanDo Function

$\{a, b, c\}$, $\{a, b, d\}$, $\{a, c, d\}$, and $\{b, c, d\}$. The algorithm follows the general form mentioned above perfectly. To list all k-element subsets of an n-element set, first list all k-element subsets with the nth element (this is done by listing the $k - 1$ element subsets of the set without the nth element and then, somehow, adding it back to all of the subsets listed) then list all k-element subsets of the set without the nth element. We need to be a little careful about this last step. The last step implies that the recursive call is to a smaller set, a set with only $n - 1$ elements. What happens if $n - 1 < k$? Certainly there cannot be a subset that is larger than the set itself. Thus, there is no need to make the recursive call if $n - 1 < k$. What would happen if we did? Would it make the algorithm wrong or just slow it down? The answer depends, in part, on the way you actually implement the algorithm. This subject is dealt with a bit more in the exercises.

There is one remaining nasty detail to be attended to. How do we "somehow" add the nth element back to the subsets after they have been recursively listed without it? There are many possible approaches, some of which are suggested in the exercises. The one I like is to try to be clever about the way the subsets are output. I will try to indent the various elements of the subsets so that the level of indenting indicates which subsets the element belongs to. For example, when listing the 3-element subsets of $\{a, b, c, d\}$ the algorithm says we must list all the 2-element subsets without "d" and then add it back in. It is difficult to actually print the "d" more than once, so I suggest printing the "d" once and then indenting all the 2-element subsets of $\{a, b, c\}$. This scheme is, or course, applied recursively. For example, the 3-element subsets of $\{a, b, c, d\}$ would be output as:

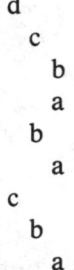

corresponding to the subsets $\{d, c, b\}$, $\{d, c, a\}$, $\{d, b, a\}$, and $\{c, b, a\}$. Naturally, these are the same subsets listed earlier only in a different order and with the elements within the subsets also arranged differently. (In fact, everything is just backwards.) Notice how the 2-element subsets of $\{a, b, c\}$ are output. It should help you to understand what is going on.

Now that we have decided how to output, it is not hard to implement. We must have four parameters: (a) k, the size of the subset, which I will call *size*, (b) something to tell us how much to indent the current element when output, (c) the array containing the elements of the set, and (d) n, the size of the set. Figure 5.21 shows the Pascal procedure to do it.

We can get a rough idea of the complexity of this procedure by making a few simple observations. The number of different k-element subsets of an n-element set is $\dfrac{n!}{(n - k)!k!}$ so the complexity must be at least this large. Also, since output is done every time the procedure is called (except for the easiest case) and since at most k things need to be output for each subset of size k, the complexity is no worse than $\dfrac{n!}{(n - k)!k!} \, k = \dfrac{n!}{(n - k)!(k - 1)!}$. You will be asked to tighten up these observations a bit more in the exercises.

3.3.2. Partitionings of a set. The problem this time again has to do with finding subsets but now we are interested in finding all ways of getting a disjoint collection of subsets whose union is the original set. Intuitively, given a handful of objects, what are the different ways to distribute these objects in piles. For example, given the set {*a, b, c*} we may build three separate piles (*a; b; c*), put them all in one big pile (*abc*) or put two in one pile and one in another in three different ways ((1.) *ab*; *c*, (2.) *a*; *bc*, (3.) *ac*; *b*). This shows all five possible ways of distributing the elements. Yet another way to view this problem is that we are trying to find all possible

```
procedure subsets(size, indent : integer; a : ArrayType;
                                               n : integer );
var i : integer;
begin
    if size = 0 then
        { No more elements to add to subset }
    else begin
        for i := 1 to indent do
            write(' ');    { indent and then ...                  }
        writeln(a[n]:3);   { output the current element           }
        subsets(size-1, indent+1, a, n-1); { recursively output}
                  { all subsets without a[n] and one smaller }
        if size <= n-1 then { the subsets we are listing are  }
                            { not larger than the set itself}
            subsets(size, indent, a, n - 1) { output all subsets}
        end                                 { without a[n]      }
end;
```

Figure 5.21. Pascal Procedure to Output Fixed Sized Subsets of a Set

ways of dividing up, or partitioning, a set of elements. The problem is easy to understand, but can you find an algorithm for solving it? You might find it helpful to first try and list all 15 ways of partitioning a set of 4 elements.

Let's discuss one algorithm that I think is quite simple to understand and fairly easy to implement, too. Let's imagine we are already somewhere in the middle of running the algorithm and we have to decide what to do next. For the sake of discussion and the coming procedure let's also assume that we are dealing with a set of characters. Suppose we have *numlets* characters in the set and we have already placed *place* − 1 of them in a total of *numsets* subsets. We now have to place the next element. In order to get all possible partitionings we must put it in all of the existing *numsets* subsets, one-by-one, and it must also be put into a subset of its own. After each such placement we recursively place the remaining elements. That's it! Of course the easiest case corresponds to the situation where all elements have been placed, that is, *place* > *numlets*. In such a case, the subsets should be output because the partitioning is complete. Figure 5.22 looks at this algorithm in pseudocode.

You should compare this algorithm with the one for outputting all permutations of a set, Figure 5.16, and notice the similarities. Despite first appearances, they have a great deal in common.

As always, there are a few implementation details to worry about. Since we are interested in subsets of characters, a clever way to do this would be to have an array, let's call it *setnum,* declared as:

```
type ArrayType = array['a'..'t'] of integer;
```

so that the index of the array refers to the set element and the value of the array at a given index refers to the subset that element has been placed in. With this implementation we must always assume that the set is comprised of consecutive characters beginning with 'a', but this does not seem like too big of a restriction. When it becomes time to output the subsets, we simply

---

if no elements left in the set to be placed (*place* > *numlets*) then
    output this partitioning
else
    for each partition formed so far (*numsets* of them)
        put current element in the partition
        place the remaining elements
    put current element in a new partition
    place the remaining elements

Figure 5.22. Listing All Partitionings of a Set

scan *setnum* looking for elements belonging to each set. It seems to me most natural to have *setnum* global to the procedure but it would be just as reasonable to make it a *var* parameter. So, assuming *setnum* is a global variable of type *ArrayType,* we are in a position to understand the procedure for listing all partitionings of a set (Figure 5.23).

This is the last, and I think prettiest, example having to do with sets. We managed to find an implementation for sets that made the procedure easy to write and easy to understand. Be careful not to let the different implementations we have used for sets cloud the fact that there are many similarities among all of these algorithms. They all have this notion about sometimes putting an element in a subset and sometimes not. In fact, in the exercises I encourage you to try some other implementations for these same algorithms. There is no reason to think that the ones in this chapter are the best in any sense of the word. You may very well find other ways to do these things that are more clear, or more efficient, or both.

```
procedure partitionings(place, numlets : char; numsets : integer);
var letter : char;
    i : integer;
begin
    if place > numlets then begin     { all letters are placed }
        for i := 1 to numsets do begin { output each subset }
            for letter := 'a' to place do     { in other words, }
                if setnum[letter] = i then {     output this     }
                    write(letter);            {     partitioning  }
            write('; ')
            end;
        writeln
        end
    else begin
        for i := 1 to numsets do begin { put the next letter in }
            setnum[place] := i;         { each of the existing }
                                        { subsets              }
            partitionings(succ(place), numlets, numsets) { place }
            end;                        { the rest of the letters }
        numsets := numsets + 1;   { put the next letter   }
        setnum[place] := numsets;  { in a new subset       }
        partitionings(succ(place),numlets, numsets) { place the }
        end                         { rest of the letters }
end;
```

Figure 5.23.   Pascal Procedure to List All Partitionings of a Set

4. TIC-TAC-TOE

No book on recursion would be complete without some mention of game playing programming. By game playing I am referring to games of skill (e.g., chess, checkers, tic-tac-toe) where players alternate turns and the outcome of the game depends solely on the choice of moves made by the players. We will not be discussing computer games like Pac-Man and Mario Brothers. Though most would argue that these games require considerable skill to play well, the outcome depends on other factors beyond just the choice of moves. For example, *when* an action is taken is critically important in such games.

Game playing programming is a topic on which volumes can and have been written, so I will have to settle for just giving you a taste of the subject. A fundamental algorithm used by most game playing programs happens to be recursive and this algorithm will be the main topic of this section. I have chosen to program the game tic-tac-toe because it is a game that most people already know how to play, it is easy to program, it clearly demonstrates the recursive nature of game playing programs, and it can readily be expanded to suggest some of the difficulties involved in developing such programs.

Let's look at a sample position from a game of tic-tac-toe. It is Os turn to play. We want to study the line of reasoning O must go through in order for him to choose the best move. We will number the locations on a tic-tac-toe board so that it will be easy to reference moves. Here is the numbering scheme and the sample position.

1	2	3
4	5	6
7	8	9

	O	X
X	O	
	X	

O has a choice of four different moves. If he chooses Move 1, we will assume that X chooses his best move, which is Move 9. This move both prevents O from winning by playing 9 himself and threatens wins at 6 and 7. Now if O plays 6 X wins by playing 7 and if O plays 7 X wins by playing 6. Conclusion: If O plays 1 he loses. If O chooses Move 6, X will choose his best move, 7, and X will again win because of the double threat of 1 and 9. If O chooses 7, the first move X can make (if fact, any move he makes) will force the game into a draw. Finally, if O chooses 9, the best move for X is 1 (blocking the win), then O must block Xs win by playing 7, and the only move left for X is 6 and the game is drawn. Recapping, Moves 1 and 6 lose for O while Moves 7 and 9 draw for O, so O chooses Move 7 or 9.

Do you see the recursion in this line of thinking? For O to find his best move he must try all moves available to him and for each of these moves (recursively) find Xs best move. O then selects the move which is the worst for X, therefore, best for O. What is the easiest case? When there are no more moves. In the case of tic-tac-toe, this can happen either when a player has gotten three in a row, or when all 9 spots have been filled.

When implementing this algorithm it is usual to write a function that takes the move being considered as an argument and returns the value of that move, where the value is a -1 if the move is a losing (bad move), a 0 if the move causes the game to end in a draw, and a 1 if the move wins for the player making the move. To make the function applicable to both X and O moves, a common trick is to negate the values that are returned from the recursive calls. This has the effect of giving bad moves for the opponent larger values, which means the best move is the maximum of these negated values, whether it is an X move or a O move. This algorithm is often called the *nega-max algorithm* (Figure 5.24) because the best move is selected by negating (nega) the values returned from the recursive calls and finding their maximum (max).

We are almost ready to see an implementation. You probably already have a pretty good idea what the recursive function looks like. I called it *findvalue* in my Pascal program. It may not be clear exactly how to use *findvalue,* however. I found it best to write a procedure, *computermove,* that looks a lot like *findvalue* only in finding the best move it not only keeps track of the best value (like *findvalue* does) but also keeps track of the move itself, so that the move can actually be made once the best move is determined (Figure 5.25). Implementation details can be easily deduced by studying the code. I will not bother showing you the functions *threeinarow* and *empties.* They are both boolean functions that determine if a move makes three in a row and if there are any moves left, respectively.

If you try using these two subroutines you will notice one problem. When the computer calculates the first move it can take quite a long time. In the exercises you are asked to calculate the complexity where you will discover just how bad things really are. What this means is that if another game is even slightly more complicated (that is, offers some more choices) these procedures will take far too long to calculate a move. But this should be intuitively obvious. The procedure *findvalue* has exactly two easiest cases, corresponding to the two ways a game can end. In other words *findvalue* considers making recursive calls until the game is decided. For a more complicated game this is many too many calls. Let's look at another, slightly more complicated, version of tic-tac-toe.

A popular way to make tic-tac-toe more interesting when I was a child was to play it in three dimensions. We called it 3D-tic-tac-toe. In this game, instead of using a two-dimensional 3×3 array, we used a three-

```
function findvalue(a : grid; xo: char; row, col : integer)
                                                    : integer;
{ An implementation of the nega-max algorithm.              }
{ parameters: a represents the current game status, is of type  }
{          grid = array[1..3, 1..3] of char and takes       }
{          values either 'x', 'o', or ' '                   }
{        xo either 'x' or 'o' depending on whose move it is   }
{        row and col the location of the move being made     }
var value, bestval, newrow, newcol : integer;
begin
    a[row, col] := xo; { make the move }
    if xo = 'x' then { if 'x' just moved, 'o' should }
        xo := 'o'     { move next, and visa versa  }
    else
        xo := 'x';
    if threeinarow(a, row, col) then { the previous player won }
        findvalue := -1
    else if not empties(a) then { no more moves left - }
        findvalue := 0          { the game is a draw      }
    else begin { find the best next move }
        bestval := -2;
        for newrow := 1 to 3 do                  { for all    }
            for newcol := 1 to 3 do              { possible  }
                if a[newrow, newcol] = ' ' then begin {next moves }
                    value := -findvalue(a, xo, newrow, newcol);
                    if value > bestval then { choose the best }
                        bestval := value { available move }
                end;
        findvalue := bestval
    end
end;
```

Figure 5.24. A Pascal Function for the Nega-Max Algorithm

dimensional 4 × 4 × 4 array. A player won by getting four in a row in any straight line in three dimensions. For example, if the array is named *a* and *X* was able to mark positions $a[1,1,4]$, $a[2,2,3]$, $a[3,3,2]$, and $a[4,4,1]$ then *X* would win. (Perhaps if you draw it out it will become a bit more clear.) With 3D-tic-tac-toe *findvalue*, as seen in Figure 5.24, for all practical purposes, would never stop because there are now so many different choices at each move and so many moves to consider. Another easiest case needs to be introduced so that *findvalue* can return a value before the game is

```
procedure computermove(var a : grid; xo : char; var result
                                              : resulttype);
{ Finds the best move in a tic-tac-toe game and makes the move   }
{ on the board, a. Returns the effect of the move in result      }
{ which is of type resulttype = (win, draw, stillplaying);       }
var value, row, col, bestval, bestrow, bestcol : integer;
begin
     bestval := -2;
     for row := 1 to 3 do                  { for all          }
          for col := 1 to 3 do             { possible         }
               if a[row, col] = ' ' then begin { next moves   }
                    value := -findvalue(a, xo, row, col);
                    if value > bestval then begin { find the   }
                         bestrow := row;          { best move }
                         bestcol := col;
                         bestval := value
                         end
                    end;
     a[bestrow, bestcol] := xo; { make the best move on the board }
     if threeinarow(a, bestrow, bestcol) then { inform the calling}
          result := win                    { program if the   }
     else if not empties(a) then           { game is over ... }
          result := draw
     else begin                            { or not. If not,  }
          result := stillplaying;          { output the current }
          if bestval = 1 then              { status of the game }
               writeln('I can''t lose now!')
          else if bestval = -1 then
               writeln('Looks like you might win....')
          else
               writeln('It''s an even game so far.')
          end
end;
```

Figure 5.25.   A Pascal Procedure to Find the Best Move in a Tic-Tac-Toe Game

decided. Intuitively, you already know what to do. When you play a game like this your reasoning usually goes something like: If I play here and she plays here and I play here, things look good so I'll make that move. Notice the two ways this differs from the way *findvalue* currently works. First, you only "looked ahead" three moves, not to the end of the game. You realize you can't deal with every contingency all the way to the end of the game so you content yourself to look ahead a few moves and then stop. How many moves you look ahead is usually called the *depth* of the *lookahead*. In terms of implementation in *findvalue*, this means a new argument needs to be introduced, which I called *depth,* that tells *findvalue* how much lookahead it should do. A recursive call to *findvalue* should decrement *depth* and if *depth* is zero this is an easiest case because this says we are not to look ahead at all.

The second way this intuitive algorithm differs from the old *findvalue* is the part that says "things look good." After looking ahead a few moves, how do you decide if things are going well for you or badly. You must somehow evaluate the position the game is in and make a decision. This is often the hardest part of writing a good game playing program. Technically, it is typically written as a function that returns values in some range so that the higher the value the better the move is. This function is usually called the *evaluation function* and I implemented it by calling it *evaluate*. For 3D-tic-tac-toe my evaluation function simply said that things were going well for me if most of my moves were in the center of the board unless, of course, I managed to get four in a row, in which case the evaluation function would return the largest possible value. This is a rather naive evaluation function, but it is a start and manages to generate moves that aren't too bad. You are encouraged to try to improve on the evaluation function and produce a better playing game.

Much more can be said about game playing programming, but I hope you at least now have a feel for the recursive nature of looking ahead in a game. The next time you play tic-tac-toe or chess notice if you are doing the lookahead iteratively or recursively. I think it is best to stop here and submit to you my three subroutines, *evaluate, findvalue,* and *computermove* for 3D-tic-tac-toe (Figure 5.26, 5.27, and 5.28). I believe that if you study these subroutines the above discussion will become clear.

5. SUMMARY

This chapter is somewhat less focused than the other chapters of the book, but it was intentionally written that way. The point is to show you the variety of forms recursive algorithms can take. As a problem-solving tool you can see that recursion is ubiquitous. Where the previous chapter suggested specific areas where recursion is likely to appear, this chapter suggests that recursion can appear almost anywhere, and to great advantage. When solving problems you should be willing and eager to give recursion a try. Most of the algorithms of this chapter never would have seen the light of day had recursion not been available. Who is to say what great recursive algorithms remain to be written?

```
function evaluate(a : grid; xo : char) : integer;
{ Evaluation function that returns higher values if moves     }
{ are concentrated towards the center. Notice that this       }
{ function only considers friendly entries. It probably       }
{ should also consider the placement of enemy marks.          }
var lev, row, col, value : integer;
begin
    value := 0;
    for lev := 1 to 4 do
        for row := 1 to 4 do
            for col := 1 to 4 do
                if a[lev, row, col] = xo then
                    value := value + (lev - 2)*(lev - 3) + (row - 2)*(row - 3)
                                    + (col - 2)*(col - 3);
    evaluate := value
end;
```

Figure 5.26. A Crude Evaluation Function for 3D-Tic-Tac-Toe

Looking back over this chapter you should appreciate just how far we've come. The book began with but the simplest of algorithms and has taken us to some very deep and sophisticated ones, like the linear algorithm for finding the median of Figure 5.13. Having come this far together you should now be in a position to proceed on your own. More advanced texts on algorithms usually contain many recursive algorithms. Algorithms you will be writing for other classes, work, or just for fun will often be recursive. Go forth with your knowledge of recursion and use it to probe the mysteries of modern algorithms and to develop more of your own.

6. EXERCISES

1. Write a procedure that takes an array where the first and second halves of the array are both sorted and turns it into a sorted array. You may not, however, use any other arrays in your procedure. What is the complexity of your procedure? If you were to use this merging procedure to write a mergesort program, what would the complexity of your program be?

2. Write a procedure that is similar to *mergesort* except instead of dividing the array in half, divide it into thirds, recursively sort each third and then merge the three pieces. What is the complexity of this algorithm?

3. Another modification of *mergesort* is to still divide the array into two pieces, but instead of putting half of the elements in each piece, put one

```
function findvalue(a : grid; xo: char;
                        lev, row, col, depth : integer) : integer;
var value, bestval, newlev, newrow, newcol : integer;
begin
    a[lev, row, col] := xo;   { make the move }
    if xo = 'x' then       { now consider }
        xo := 'o'          { enemy moves }
    else
        xo := 'x';
    if fourinarow(a, lev, row, col) then { the previous player won }
        findvalue := -999
    else if not empties(a) then { no more moves left -    }
        findvalue := 0          { the game is a draw       }
    else if depth = 0 then       { looked far enough ahead - }
        findvalue := -evaluate(a, xo) { evaluate the position }
    else begin
        bestval := -1000; { find the best move from here }
        for newlev := 1 to 4 do          { for all    }
            for newrow := 1 to 4 do       { possible   }
                for newcol := 1 to 4 do  { moves      }
                    if a[newlev, newrow, newcol] ='' then begin
                        value := -findvalue(a, xo, newlev,
                                    newrow, newcol, depth - 1);
                        if value > bestval then { keep the }
                            bestval := value  { best move }
                    end;
        findvalue := bestval
        end;
end;
```

Figure 5.27. A Pascal Function for Nega-Max With a Lookahead Depth Limit

third in the first piece and two thirds in the second piece. What is the complexity of this algorithm? What if the first piece has $n - 1$ elements and the second has 1 element?

4. The partitioning algorithm used in quicksort first made a recursive call and then dealt with the first element in the array. Design a partitioning algorithm that first deals with the last element of the array and then recursively partitions a smaller array. You may find it necessary to have another parameter that explicitly announces what the pivot element is since you will need to know what it is before you make any recursive calls. Be sure your algorithm is linear.

```
procedure computermove(var a : grid; xo : char;
                                        var result : resulttype);
{Finds the best move in a 3d-tic-tac-toe game and makes the move}
{ on the board, a. Returns the effect of the move in result   }
{ which is of type resulttype = (win, draw, stillplaying);      }
var value, lev, row, col, bestval, bestlev, bestrow, bestcol
                                        : integer;
begin
    bestval := − 1000;
        for lev := 1 to 4 do        { for all        }
        for row := 1 to 4 do        { possible       }
            for col := 1 to 4 do  { next moves }
            if a[lev, row, col] = ' ' then begin
                value := − findvalue(a, xo, lev, row, col, 1);
                if value > bestval then begin { find the   }
                    bestlev := lev;              { best one }
                    bestrow := row;
                    bestcol := col;
                    bestval := value
                    end
                end;
    writeln('Score: ', bestval);
    a[bestlev, bestrow, bestcol] := xo; { make the best move }
    if fourinarow(a, bestlev, bestrow, bestcol) then { inform   }
        result := win                              { the      }
    else if not empties(a) then                    { calling  }
        result := draw                             { program }
    else                                           { if the   }
        result := stillplaying                     { game is }
end;                                               { over     }
```

Figure 5.28.   A Pascal Procedure to Find the Best Move in a 3D-Tic-Tac-Toe Game

5. Quicksort has the somewhat irritating property that the worst case corresponds to the situation when the array is already sorted. One usually wants, or at least expects, a sorting algorithm to perform well in such cases. The problem comes because of the way *partition* works. Recall that the worst case for partition occurs with a sorted array in which case one of the two partitions ends up with no elements at all. Write another partitioning algorithm that partitions the array more evenly if the array is already sorted. If you think about it, what this really amounts to is finding a better

pivot. It is usually best to choose as pivot some element that is already in the array. Explain why this is so. As in the last problem, you might find it useful to provide another parameter to your procedure to send in the pivot element. A good place to get some hints on this problem is to see how partitioning was done for the fast median finding algorithm. Describe the worst case for your partitioning algorithm. If you use your new partitioning algorithm to implement a fancier quicksort, describe the worst case for the new quicksort. Be careful. This may not be as easy as it seems.

6. Despite how much we love our recursive algorithms and appreciate their beauty and simplicity, they can occasionally be a bit inefficient, not in the big-oh sense, but in the real sense of nanoseconds. For example, if we were to just sort 4 elements, say, insertion sort would surely run faster than quicksort because quicksort requires so much overhead to partition, save variables on a stack during recursive calls, etc. Write a more efficient quicksort that treats as easiest case not just a one element array but any array with less than 10 elements in it. Any array with less than 10 elements should then be sorted with a simple sort like insertion or selection sort. Notice that we are actually discussing a lot of different algorithms here, depending on exactly where the cutoff is for the easiest case (I suggested 10, but why not 11 or 12, or 9?) and which sorting algorithm we use for the easiest case. Try to find the most efficient variant of quicksort empirically. For a few more hints on how you might do this, look at the next problem.

7. One way to make an even faster sorting algorithm in the spirit of those suggested in the last problem is to again choose some number (probably around 10) for the size of the easiest case but have the algorithm do nothing in such cases. When this algorithm completes you will have an array that is nearly sorted except for clumps the size of or smaller than your cutoff value. Now, run insertion sort **once** on this array to create a sorted array. This has the advantage of greatly reducing the number of calls to insertion sort and so should improve the speed of your sort.

8. Section 2.6 showed how one might figure out the complexity of an algorithm empirically by running it with lots of different data. If this method is used on two algorithms with the same complexity it can be used to choose the better of the two by simply picking the one that executes fewer steps. Using the ideas of Section 2.6 compare selection sort and insertion sort to see which is better. "Better" is, of course, an imprecise word here. You should check to see which is better with random data, which is better when the data is already sorted, which is better when the data is in reversed order, etc. In the same spirit, compare mergesort, heapsort, quicksort, and the two best sorts from problems 4 and 5 and see which is best with sorted data, random data, etc. Find out which sort is best and which is worst among *mergesort,* the sorts from Problems 2 and 3.

9. How many leaves are there in a heap with n elements?

10. Show that the number of nodes in the two children of a heap with n elements can never differ by more than $\dfrac{n + 1}{3}$, in other words show that at most two thirds of the elements can be in the left child of a heap. This means that a better recurrence relation for the complexity of *sift* is $T(n) = T(\frac{2}{3}n)$ $+ 1$. So, what is the complexity of *sift* after all?

11. The heapsort algorithm presented in this chapter was actually iterative. Rewrite the procedure so that the exchange and sift part is done recursively. Be careful not to build a heap each time. This only has to be done once. One way to go about this is to write the procedure something like this:

```
procedure heapsort(var a : arraytype; size : integer);
begin
      buildheap(a, 1, size);
      recursivesort(a, 1, size)
end;
```

In this case, the recursive part of the sorting, where the exchanging and the sifting takes place, will be done in *recursivesort*. Suppose you did rebuild the heap every time. In other words, suppose you wrote your recursive procedure for heapsort something like the following:

```
procedure heapsort(var a : arraytype; size : integer);
var i : integer;
begin
      if size = 1 then
            { one element array already sorted }
      else begin
            buildheap(a, 1, size);
            swap(a[1], a[size]);
                  { move large element to bottom of heap }
            sift(a, 1, size − 1); { and then rebuild the heap }
            heapsort(a, 1, size − 1)
            end
end;
```

What would the complexity of your sort be in this case?

12. Looking back at the algorithms presented for finding the median of an array it should be easy for you to verify that they work just fine even if the array contains some duplicates. Why, then, did we make it a point to

assume there were no duplicates in the array? Hint: Look back through the complexity analyses. You may find some places there where we assumed no duplicates. What needs to be done to make sure the algorithms still have the promised asymptotic complexities, given the presence of duplicates? Hint of the hint: If the pivot element occurs more than once during a partition, count the total occurrences and adjust the next recursive call accordingly.

13. All of the median finding algorithms presented contained an inefficiency. Not only do they run unnecessarily slow, but they also use too much stack space (recall Chapter 3). Using Problem 6 as a hint, remove the inefficiency and compare running times between the two versions. Your improved version should be able to find the median of much larger arrays than you were able to before. Did you improve the big-oh complexity?

14. We argued that select, the practical algorithm for finding the median of an array of integers, had quadratic-time complexity. Given the program as presented in Figure 5.12, find a 5-element array such that recselect is called five times and, thus, actually exhibits the worst case behavior. If you have trouble finding such an array resort to trial and error. After all, there are really only 120 different possibilities. Once you've found a worst case array, try to generalize it. That is, find an arrangement of the numbers 1, . . . , n in an array so that recselect would require n calls to find the median.

15. Find an exact solution to the recurrence $T(n) = k + an + T(n - c)$, the recurrence relation for an algorithm that we had hoped would be an improvement over the $O(n^2)$ median algorithm.

16. Find an exact solution to the recurrence relation $T(n) = bn + T(dn)$ by using repeated substitutions. Hint: if $0 < d < 1$, what can be said about $1 + d + d^2 + d^3 + \ldots$?

17. The recurrence relation for the linear median algorithm was $T(n) = an + T(\frac{n}{5}) + T(\frac{7n}{10})$. What would be the complexity of the algorithm if the larger partition could be as large as $\frac{8n}{10} = \frac{4n}{5}$ instead of $\frac{7n}{10}$? Would it still be linear? How does one go about solving such a recurrence?

18. The linear algorithm for finding the median suggests many other similar algorithms. What, after all, is so sacred about groups of size 5? Why not groups of size 7, 9, or even 3? Why not even sized groups like 6 or 8? Solve the recurrence relation for each of these different algorithms, pick 3 of the better ones and then modify the select function in the chapter to work with these different sized groups. Empirically find the complexity of these algorithms and compare your results with those you obtained from the recurrences. When the group is size 3, is the complexity still linear? What

seems better, even- or odd-sized groups? Why? What is the smallest even-sized group that gives a linear algorithm?

19. In this chapter we briefly discussed how the bit string representation of sets produces a linear-time union operation. For example, if the word size of our computer is 32, and if we have two sets, each having about n elements, to calculate the union we would have to do an *and* operation for each machine word used to represent the two sets. Since, in this case, each word keeps track of 32 elements, the number of *and* 's that are necessary is about $\frac{n}{32}$, so union is a linear in the number of elements in the set. But might it be even worse than this? Explain why the obvious bit string implementation of a set of integers provides a union operation that depends more on the difference between the largest and smallest elements in the sets rather than the number of elements. For example, explain how the union of two one-element sets could actually take a very long time. How might you improve the implementation to handle this problem? What effect does your new implementation have on other operations like *intersection* and *in*? Perhaps you can do better by giving up on bit strings entirely.

20. We said that the complexity of the procedure to output permutations (Figure 5.15) was $n!$ because its recurrence relation was $T(n) = n\,T(n-1)$. In fact, there is really some other work being done in the procedure besides the recursive calls. For example, two elements are being exchanged before each recursive call is made. Justify the following as a better recurrence relation: $T(n) = n\,T(n-1) + n$. Solve this recurrence relation. How much worse is this one? How does it compare to $n!$? How does it compare to $(n+1)!$? Can one, therefore, expect to improve on this procedure?

21. To calculate the complexity of the procedure that outputs permutations where duplicates may appear in the character set (Figure 5.17) you must first be able to figure out how many distinct permutations there are because, after all, that is the minimal amount of work such a procedure must do. Develop a formula that does just this. Some hints: (a) Given a set with n elements where exactly one element is repeated once the number of distinct permutations is $\frac{n}{2}$; (b) given a set with n elements where exactly two elements occur twice the number of permutations is $\frac{n}{4} = \frac{n}{2! \times 2!}$; (c) given a set with n elements where one element occurs three times the number of permutations is $\frac{n}{6} = \frac{n}{3!}$. (Aside: Given a set with j a's and k b's, how many different distinct permutations are there? How does this compare with the number of ways of choosing k elements from a set of $j +$

k elements? Explain the similarity.) Now compute the complexity of the procedure in Figure 5.17 and see how it compares with the formula you obtained for counting the permutations.

22. Consider the following Pascal function for solving the puzzle presented in this chapter. This function is very similar to Figure 5.18 in that it only reports if there is a solution or not. It does not output the solution. The only difference between this one and Figure 5.18 is the order of the easiest cases. This particular ordering makes the algorithm wrong. Explain why it is wrong and give a small, specific example on which it works improperly. Of the six different arrangements of the easiest cases, which will work and which will fail?

```
function CanDo(goal : integer; a : ArrayType; n : integer)
                                                 : boolean;
begin
    if n = 0 then
        CanDo := false
    else if goal < 0 then
        CanDo := false
    else if goal = 0 then
        CanDo := true
    else if Cando(goal − a[n], a, n − 1) then
        CanDo := true
    else
        CanDo := CanDo(goal, a, n − 1)
end;
```

23. Sometimes when we are given an array of integers and a goal, we would like to know all of the solutions. The function of Figure 5.19 only outputs one solution. How can that function be changed so that it will output all solutions? Hint: Only one substantive change needs to be made. If a solution was found using *a*[*n*] the function did not bother checking to see if a solution is also possible without using *a*[*n*]. You must add something to take this situation into account. Intuitively, then, the function finds all solutions with *a*[*n*] and all solutions without *a*[*n*].

There is one other smaller but bothersome problem you will have to deal with: How to output all of the solutions. You could go back to the idea suggested in this chapter about maintaining a stack, but that's still a lot of trouble. Instead, consider outputting the solutions in "outline form." For example, with the data {1, 2, 1, 2, 3, 4, 3, 4} and a goal of 6 the output might look like the following example:

```
    2
      1
    1
    2
  4
    3
        1
        1
    2
         2
    1
        1
    2
  3
    2
        1
    1
    2
  4
        1
        1
    2
         2
    1
        1
    2
  3
          1
        2
    1
  2
```

To help you read this, the first three solutions this output is describing are: 4, 2; 4, 1, 1; 4, 2. Notice that in the solution with 4, 2 appears twice because 2 appears twice in the collection of integers. In fact, these two solutions appear again later because there is a second 4 in the collection as well.

To generate this output you will probably find it helpful to add another parameter to the function so that when an integer is output this new parameter will tell how much to indent it. You might also be tempted to write this as a procedure rather than function. You will probably find this to be a bad idea, however, because without that boolean return value it will be difficult to know when to output.

24. Using the indenting scheme suggested in the text, display all of the 4-element subsets of the set {*a, e, i, r, s, t*}.

25. How many characters are actually printed by the procedure in Figure 5.21 in terms of *size* and *n*? Try counting the number of characters in the first column, then the second, etc. What does this suggest about the complexity of the procedure?

26. Given the procedure in Figure 5.21 for finding all *k*-element subsets of an *n*-element set, consider the *if* statement that checks to see if the size of the subsets to be generated is indeed no larger than the set itself. Can it be removed without changing the behavior of the procedure? If the answer is *yes*, then what effect will removing it have on the complexity? If the answer is *no*, what effect will the change have on the procedure?

27. Modify the implementation of the algorithm to find all partitions of a set of elements so that it will allow any collection of characters as the set, not just consecutive characters starting at 'a'. Most of the implementation is seen in Figure 5.23, but pay attention to *ArrayType* which is described a bit before the figure. This, after all, is the major data structure used since it is the type of *setnum*.

28. Write a function that will count the number of partitions of a set without outputting anything.

29. What is the complexity of the *findvalue* function of Figure 5.24? Assuming *computermove* can find the first move of a tic-tac-toe game in one second (it takes *much* longer on my computer!), how long will it take to calculate the first move of a 3D-tic-tac-toe game?

30. Change the evaluation function of Figure 5.26 so that the opponent's position is also taken into account. Try to think of a function that will perform better than mine. Run a version with your evaluation function against one with mine to see which is really better.

An Annotated Bibliography

Blum, M., Floyd, R. W., Pratt, V. R., Rivest, R. L., & Tarjan, R. E. (1973). Time bounds for selection. *Journal of Computer and System Science, 7,* 448–461.
> The original article demonstrating a linear algorithm to find the median. The algorithm we present is essentially this algorithm.

Euclid, Elements, Book 7.
> Propositions 1 and 2 explain the Euclidean algorithm to find the greatest common divisor of two integers. Considered by many to be the first nontrivial algorithm ever written.

Floyd, R. W. (1964). Algorithm 245 (Treesort). *Communications of the Association of Computing Machinery, 7,* 701.
> Although Williams was the first to publish the heapsort algorithm, it is here that the linear algorithm for building a heap is presented.

Helman, P., Veroff, R. (1988). Walls and Mirrors Modula-2, Intermediate Problem Solving and Data Structures. Menlo Park, CA: Benjamin/Cummings.
> A typical Computer Science 2 textbook with an atypical presentation of recursion. Their presentation is early, much more thorough and, contains more good examples than most others. Yet even with their outstanding presentation they felt the need to hedge with sentences such as: "There is no reason to incur the overhead of recursion when its use does not gain anything for us." I would much prefer if authors would put recursion on an equal footing with other programming constructs. I would like to see more sentences like: "There is no reason *not* to use recursion unless you have reason to suspect that the recursive calls will nest so deeply that you might run out of memory. Making this decision is similar to decisions you must make concerning arrays versus dynamic types, local versus global variables, etc."

Floyd, R. W., Rivest, R. L. (1975). Algorithm 489 (Select). *Communications of the Association of Computing Machinery, 18,* 173.
> This is an enhancement of the practical algorithm for finding the median. Although Hoare was the first to present this idea, these authors go one step further in that they suggest various sampling techniques to find the pivot element. We chose not to do this in our presentation in an effort to keep the algorithm presentation simple and clear.

189

Hoare, C. A. R. (1961). Algorithm 63 (Partition) and Algorithm 65 (Find). *Communications of the Association of Computing Machinery, 4,* 321.

  This is the practical algorithm for finding the median (in fact, for selecting any element) in an array. This presentation is essentially the one we present.

Hoare, C. A. R. (1962). Quicksort. *Computer Journal, 5,* 10–15.

  Hoare claims to have had this idea many years before he published this algorithm but he had no easy way to present it because no progamming languages supported recursion at the time.

Knuth, D. E. (1973). *The Art of Computer Programming, Volume 1, Fundamental Algorithms.* (2nd ed.). Reading, MA: Addison-Wesley.

  Contains a good description of the power and usefulness of stacks. The presentation is somewhat dated, though, in that low-level implementation details are emphasized over the abstract data type description.

Knuth, D. E. (1973). *The Art of Computer Programming, Volume 3, Sorting and Searching.* Reading, MA: Addison-Wesley.

  "The Bible" on sorting algorithms. Every sorting algorithm we present appears in this volume, along with complexity analysis, examples, and many interesting exercises.

Nilsson, N. J. (1971). *Problem-Solving Methods in Artificial Intelligence.* New York: McGraw-Hill.

  One of many books in artificial intelligence that discusses game trees, evaluation functions, etc.

Sleator, D. D., Tarjan, R. E. (1985). Self adjusting binary search trees. *Journal of the Association of Computing Machinery, 32,* 652–686.

  The complete presentation of splay trees. Here they prove the "amortized complexity" of the operations is $O(log\ n)$ per operation. The amortized complexity is the time per operation averaged over a worst case sequence of operations. This means that during this sequence of operations some may take $O(n)$ time, but the speed of other operations will bring the average down. Amortized complexity analysis is beyond the scope of this text.

Tarjan, R. E. (1983). *Data Structures and Network Algorithms.* Philadelphia, PA: Society for Industrial and Applied Mathematics.

  A very readable presentation of splay trees and other data structures that provide the basis for numerous efficient algorithms.

Williams, J. W. J. (1964). Algorithm 232 (Heapsort). *Communications of the Association of Computing Machinery, 7,* 347–348.

  The original presentation of heapsort.

Subject Index